This book heralds a new generation of know  in schools. As such it is an indispensable tioners and scholars who seek fresh perspect goes beyond seemingly endless publications used, or not used, to inform us about how to use it well.

Professor Emeritus Brian Caldwell, *University of Melbourne, Australia*

We know, all too well, that research-informed practice can make a substantive difference to teaching and learning. But we often forget that research has to be used *well* if these differences are to materialise. And that is the beauty of this book. Based on the ground breaking, five-year, Monash Q Project, Mark Rickinson and colleagues do an amazing job of unearthing what it means to use research effectively and in doing so, signpost to educators how best to achieve effective research-informed practices within their schools, for the benefit of all.

Professor Chris Brown, *University of Warwick, England*

In an era where many countries still struggle to make good use of research evidence to guide education policy and practice, the Monash Q Project breathes new life into knowledge mobilisation. This book offers fresh insights into leveraging research evidence effectively, driving systemic change, and ultimately empowering schools and education systems to enhance quality and effectiveness. A must-read for educators, policymakers, researchers and knowledge brokers alike.

Dr Nóra Révai, *Organisation for Economic Cooperation and Development, France*

Better evidence-based decision making and implementation of evidence-based practice are key clarion calls in education policy internationally. But what does it mean to use research well in education? Mark Rickinson and his colleagues interrogate this simple question with clarity, comprehensiveness and depth. They bring fresh conceptual and practical insights on quality use of research evidence that are of profound importance to the field.

Laureate Professor Jenny Gore, *University of Newcastle, Australia*

The movement to support better use of research evidence has been crying out for substantial studies exploring what it means to use evidence well in practice. The Monash Q Project was therefore a timely deep dive into evidence use in education. Focusing on the interesting question of not just promoting evidence use but quality evidence use, this wide ranging study makes an important contribution not just to education but other areas of practice. This book is a key text for anyone who wants to see better quality use of evidence in future practice. I have been recommending this study to everyone and now I can signpost this important text.

Professor Annette Boaz, *London School of Hygiene and Tropical Medicine, England*

This book is a great contribution to the 'science of using science', by conceptualizing the quality use of research evidence and analyzing it in practice. Rickinson and his team provide practitioners and policymakers with a powerful tool to self-assess the actual use of research, and whether conditions for quality use are met.

Rien Rouw, *Ministry of Education, Culture and Science, the Netherlands*

Understanding the Quality Use of Research Evidence in Education

This book focuses on the question of how to understand quality use of research evidence in education, or what it means to use research evidence *well*.

Internationally there are widespread efforts to increase the use of research evidence within educational policy and practice. Such efforts raise important questions about how we understand not just the quality of evidence, but also the quality of its use. To date, there has been wide-ranging debate about the former, but very little dialogue about the latter. Based on a five-year study with schools and school systems in Australia, this book sheds new light on:

- why clarity about quality of use is critical to educational improvement;
- how quality use of research evidence can be framed in education;
- what using research well involves and looks like in practice;
- what quality research use means for individuals, organisations and systems; and
- what aspects of using research well still need to be better understood.

This book will be an invaluable resource for professionals within and beyond education who want to better understand what using research evidence well means and involves and how it can be supported.

Mark Rickinson is an Associate Professor in the Faculty of Education at Monash University in Australia. He currently leads the Monash Q Project, a five-year partnership with the Paul Ramsay Foundation to improve the use of research in Australian schools.

Lucas Walsh is a Professor of Education Policy and Practice, Youth Studies, in the Faculty of Education at Monash University. He is currently a Chief Investigator on the Monash Q Project and Director of the Monash Centre for Youth Policy and Education Practice.

Joanne Gleeson is a Senior Research Fellow with the Monash Q Project in the Faculty of Education at Monash University. Her research is focused on educational evidence use and improving adolescents' career identity, employability and education-work transitions.

Blake Cutler is a PhD Candidate and Research Assistant with the Monash Q Project in the Faculty of Education at Monash University. Their doctoral study explores how educators' social justice efforts to support queer young people are shaped and influenced by research use.

Connie Cirkony is a Lecturer in Science Education at the University of Tasmania and was a Research Fellow with the Monash Q Project. Her research is focused on science, STEM and sustainability education as well as evidence-informed policy and practice.

Mandy Salisbury is a PhD Candidate in the Faculty of Education at Monash University and was a Research Assistant with the Monash Q Project. Her doctoral study is focused on Early Childhood educators' use of evidence.

Understanding the Quality Use of Research Evidence in Education

What It Means to Use Research Well

Mark Rickinson, Lucas Walsh,
Joanne Gleeson, Blake Cutler,
Connie Cirkony and
Mandy Salisbury

Routledge
Taylor & Francis Group

LONDON AND NEW YORK

Designed cover image: © Getty Images

First published 2024
by Routledge
4 Park Square, Milton Park, Abingdon, Oxon OX14 4RN

and by Routledge
605 Third Avenue, New York, NY 10158

Routledge is an imprint of the Taylor & Francis Group, an informa business

British Library Cataloguing-in-Publication Data
A catalogue record for this book is available from the British Library

ISBN: 978-1-032-40617-6 (hbk)
ISBN: 978-1-032-40616-9 (pbk)
ISBN: 978-1-003-35396-6 (ebk)

DOI: 10.4324/9781003353966

Typeset in Optima
by MPS Limited, Dehradun

This book is dedicated to the teachers and school leaders who made this work possible and whose insights are its backbone.

Contents

Figures

Tables

Vignettes

Acknowledgements

The authors would like to acknowledge:

- the Wurundjeri and Bunurong Peoples of the Kulin Nation as the traditional owners and custodians of the lands on which this work was undertaken;
- the many Australian teachers, school leaders and system leaders who took part in this work despite the many other demands on their time;
- colleagues at the Paul Ramsay Foundation (John Bush, Maria Simonelli, Clare Hodgson, Galina Laurie and the wider team) for believing in and supporting this project and working with us to bring it to life;
- Q Project team members (Phoebe Marshall, Komal Daredia, Genevieve Hall, Adriana Capponi, Hang Khong and Darlene McGown) for their communications, project management, graphic design and professional learning expertise;
- Q Project research partners (Mark Boulet, Bernice Plant and Liam Smith, BehaviourWorks Australia; Kim Sullivan, Erin Newell, May Doan and Jennifer Hodges, Orima Research; Joe Connell, Laura Bird, Lambrini Kakogiannis and Ayushi Pillai, dandolopartners; Benita Tan, Catherine Boekel and Charles Coulton, Whereto Research; Prashanna Kathiresan, Online Research Unit) for their ongoing collaboration and commitment;
- Q Project Steering Committee members (Tom Bentley, Royal Melbourne Institute of Technology; Pitsa Binnion, McKinnon Secondary College; Brett Moore, Ashwood High School; John Bush, Paul Ramsay Foundation; Matt Deeble, Social Ventures Australia; Danielle Toon, Evidence for Learning; Shani Prendergast, Australian Education Research Organisation; Jean Scott, Edgeworth Heights Public School; Amanda Berry and Neil Selwyn,

Monash University; Liam Smith and Mark Boulet, BehaviourWorks Australia) for their advice, ideas and support;

- Q Project Jurisdiction Group members (Martin Westwell, Rachel Crees, David Ensor, Michael Mauch, Sarah Mavrikis and Anne and Paul Wilson, South Australia Department of Education; Angela Ferguson, Deb Kember, Mark McDonell, Elizabeth Bullock and Sandra Nissen, Queensland Department of Education; Barbara Watterston and Chris Newcombe, Australian Council for Educational Leaders; Narelle Struth, Melbourne Archdiocese of Catholic Schools; Robert Stevens, Shantha Liyanage and Rah Kirsten, New South Wales Department of Education; Karen Taylor, Brendan Rigby, Neil Twist, Ashley Duggan, Mohita Roman, Tom Cain, Katie Morris and Zoran Endekov, Victoria Department of Education and Training; Clinton Milroy, Xian-Zhi Soon, Amanda Stevenson, Susan-Marie Harding and Anneke Meehl, Australian Institute for Teaching and School Leadership; Julie People, Australian Education Research Organisation; Neil Barker, Louise Stewart and Stephanie Condon, Bastow Institute of Educational Leadership; Maria Oddo and Geoff Rose, Victoria Academy of Teaching and Leadership) for their collaboration and support;
- Q Project Stakeholder Reference Group members (Debra Gibson, Doveton College; Graham Broadbent, Education Consultant; Debby Chaves, Beaumaris Secondary College; Esme Capp, Princes Hill Primary School; Nigel Holloway, Hamlyn Banks Primary School; Maria Karvouni, Auburn High School; Maria Gindidis, Monash University; Simon Sherlock, Hallam Senior College; Frank Vetere, Footscray High School; Gordon Duff, National Disability Research Partnership; Deborah Harman, Balwyn High School; Bronwyn Ryrie Jones, Educational Consultant; Meg Brydon, Melbourne Girls Grammar; Syke Ramsay, Barrack Heights Public School; Troy Verey, Marsden Road Public School; Carrie Wallis and Natalie Manser, Wantirna College; Penny De Waele, Dalby State School) for their continued involvement and support;
- Q Project School Advisory Group members (Amelia Apogremiotis, Brisbane Boys' College; Cathy Crouch, Aurora College; Ted Noon, Ashcroft High School; Eleanor Wilkinson, Heatley State School; Megan Ganter, Pembroke Primary School; Maria Alberto, Penola Catholic College and Steven Kolber, Brunswick Secondary College) for their expert advice and feedback;
- Q Project national and international collaborators (Sue Cridge, Erin Corbyn and Nick Johns, SVA The Connection; Jenny Gore, Jess Harris,

Drew Miller and Brooke Rosser, University of Newcastle; Coralee Pratt and Brian Caldwell, Australian Council for Educational Leaders Victoria; Tiffany Roos and Rachel Perry, The Association of Independent Schools of NSW; Ollie Lovell, Brighton Grammar School; Simon Kent, Senior Adviser to Commonwealth Minister for Skills and Training; Stephen Fraser, Victoria Department of Education and Training; Jenny Donovan, Belinda Parker, Zid Mancenido and Sally Larsen, Australian Education Research Organisation; Liz Farley-Ripple, University of Delaware; Julie Nelson, National Foundation for Educational Research; Jonathan Sharples, Education Endowment Foundation; Annette Boaz and Kathryn Oliver, London School of Hygiene and Tropical Medicine; Nóra Révai and team, OECD Centre for Educational Research and Innovation; Tracey Burns, National Center on Education and the Economy; Jim Rogers, Education Development Trust; Anne Edwards and Alis Oancea, University of Oxford; Michael Clark, London School of Economics and Political Science; Carrie Conaway, Harvard University; Jon Eaton, Kingsbridge Community College; Vivian Tseng, Foundation for Child Development; Kim DuMont, William T Grant Foundation) for their expertise and support;

- the copy editor (Peter Symons) for his careful work with this manuscript; and
- the Faculty of Education and Monash University for their encouragement and support for this project.

1 Introduction

Chapter overview

This chapter introduces the issue of quality use of research in education and outlines the focus, scope, significance, evidence base, audiences and structure of the book as a whole. With reference to discussions and developments happening within and beyond education, it explains that:

- improved research use requires high-quality research and high-quality use, but quality of use is not well understood relative to quality of research;
- understanding what it means to use research well in education is important because there is significant investment in improving research use in schools and systems;
- understanding quality use of research is also important because the concept of evidence-based practice is contested and the practice of using research is complex;
- the ideas and insights in this book come out of a five-year empirical study focused specifically on quality use of research in Australian schools;
- the chapters introduce and illustrate different ways of understanding quality use – as a gap, as an aspiration, as a capacity, as a culture, as a practice and as a system; and

DOI: 10.4324/9781003353966-1

- this book is written for professionals who want to understand what using research well means and involves and how it can be supported.

The issue of quality use

This book is responding to a need that became apparent to us several years ago. Back in 2015, two of us (Mark Rickinson and Lucas Walsh) were investigating the use of evidence in education policy making. Working with a state education department, we were trying to better understand the challenges and complexities surrounding the use of evidence within education policy development (Rickinson et al., 2016; 2017; 2019). The work involved in-depth interviews with department policy makers, observation of policy development processes and analysis of relevant internal documents. The aim was to build up a detailed picture of the department's current evidence use practices and, more importantly, to identify pointers for future capacity building and improvement. It was in relation to the pointers for future improvement that we ran into a difficulty.

In order to highlight priorities for future improvement, we needed to identify areas of strength and weakness in the department's current use of evidence. This meant moving from our initial questions about how evidence was being used, towards new questions about how *well* evidence was being used. We therefore went looking for other work that might be able to help us with this task. We were hoping that there might be studies that had looked at how well evidence was being used in other policy areas or practice fields, or conceptual writing that had discussed the idea of using evidence well. To our surprise, though, we found very little work of this kind within the literature on evidence use, and certainly no well-established definitions, conceptual frameworks or empirical studies of using evidence well. In the short-term, this situation proved an inconvenience for the policy study we were trying to complete, but in the medium-term highlighted an important shortcoming in the evidence use field – that is, the need to better understand the "quality and qualities of evidence use" (Rickinson et al., 2017, p. 187).

This book is the story of our efforts since that time to respond to this need. It is about the use of research evidence in education, and in particular the idea of *quality use* or using research evidence *well*. This idea of quality use is about moving from a focus on *whether* we use research to a focus on *how well* we use research. It is about recognising that improved use of research requires not only *high-quality research*, but also *high-quality use*. But what is high-quality use? How can quality of research use be understood? And what does it mean to use research well in education?

Writing in the field of policy, Parkhurst (2017, p. 170) argues that "to improve the use of evidence in policy requires an explicit engagement with the question of what constitutes *better use* from a political perspective" [original emphasis]. Using Parkhurst's language, then, this book is an attempt to engage with the question of what constitutes better use of research evidence from an educational perspective. As mentioned above, this is a topic that has been discussed surprisingly little within and beyond education.

Sheldrick and colleagues (2022), for example, report that "while many studies look at the extent to which research is used in a given situation (i.e., the quantity of research use), studies that account for *how well* or *how poorly* research is used in such situations (i.e., the quality of research use) remain far less common" (para. 2; original emphasis). Along similar lines, we have noted that "there is a well-developed literature around under-standing and appraising the quality of different kinds of evidence, but little in the way of an equivalent for understanding and appraising the quality of different kinds of use" (Rickinson et al., 2022, p. 134).

Responding to these gaps in current understanding, this book comes out of a five-year Australian study, the Monash Q Project, that has focused specifically on 'quality use of research evidence' within schools and school systems (see Rickinson, Walsh, et al., 2020; Walsh et al., 2022). It is written for researchers, policy makers, practitioners and research brokers who want to improve the use of research within education. It is designed as a resource for those who have some experience of undertaking, supporting and/or investigating research use, but want a deeper understanding of quality use. With a strong emphasis on practitioners' perspectives and experiences, it aims to shed new light on:

- why clarity about quality of use is critical to educational improvement;
- how quality use of research evidence can be framed in education;

- what using research well involves and looks like in practice;
- what quality research use means for individuals, organisations and systems; and
- what aspects of using research well still need to be better understood.

The book's focus on quality use of research in education, though, needs to be seen within the context of wider developments in education policy, educational research and educational practice. As explained in the next three sections, the task of better understanding quality use of research comes in response to growing international policy expectations for schools and systems to use research as part of improvement, long-standing researcher concerns about evidence-based practice as a goal and recurring challenges facing practitioners seeking to use research in practice.

Evidence use developments in education policy

Internationally there are widespread efforts to improve the use of research evidence across many sectors, including health, social care, international development and environment and sustainability (Boaz et al., 2019). There is now "a diverse landscape of initiatives to promote evidence use" (Boaz & Nutley, 2019, p. 261), ranging from efforts to improve research generation and dissemination, through to activities to build practitioners' capacity to use research, foster collaborations between researchers and research users and develop system-wide approaches to evidence use. Education has been no exception to such trends, having seen "a global push to bolster the connections between research and practice" (Malin et al., 2020, p. 1).

One reflection of this global push has been increasing calls for research-engaged schools, evidence-based teaching and evidence-informed policy and practice within national policy agendas. Examples include the development of an evidence-informed teaching profession in Singapore (Gopinathan, 2012), a research-rich self-improving system in the UK (British Educational Research Association [BERA], 2014), evidence-based school development in Germany (Dormann et al., 2016) and a research-rich teaching profession in Australia (White et al., 2018). Further cases can be seen in two recent publications – one charting evidence-informed educational practice developments across more than 20 countries and systems

(Brown & Malin, 2022) and the other analysing educational research mobilisation efforts in more than 30 Organisation for Economic Cooperation and Development (OECD) nations (OECD, 2022).

Connected to these developments has been the establishment of new organisations with a specific remit to support the synthesis, communication and application of research in education. A recent study of OECD countries found that "official brokerage agencies with a specific mandated function to support the use of research were active in 16 systems" (Hill, 2022, p. 81). Examples of brokerage agencies include the Education Endowment Foundation (EEF) in the UK, the What Works Clearinghouse in the US, the Best Evidence Synthesis Programme in New Zealand, the Danish Clearinghouse for Educational Research, the Australian Educational Research Organisation and the Knowledge Centre for Education in Norway.

Another focus has been on the development of collaborative networks to connect practitioners, researchers and other actors. Recent years have seen the creation of the Research Schools Network in England (Dixon et al., 2020), Research Learning Networks in England (Brown, 2018), Research-Practice Partnerships in the US (Coburn & Penuel, 2016) and the Knowledge Network for Applied Education Research in Canada (Nelson & Campbell, 2019). Recent data from OECD countries, however, suggests that school networks to support research use are not particularly widespread, being "not active in a large number of systems" (Hill, 2022, p. 82).

These kinds of initiatives, which are all focused on improving research use in some way, can be seen to raise important questions about what it means to use research evidence well. This book, then, is a response to growing global aspirations for teachers, school leaders and system leaders to use research evidence to inform their work. Such aspirations, however, have not been universally embraced by all within the education field and it is important to consider how this book also comes in response to critiques of the educational evidence movement.

Evidence use critiques in educational research

There are lines of debate about evidence agendas in education that provide important insights for this book's consideration of quality use. These debates have arisen within both the educational research field (e.g., Biesta, 2007;

Hammersley, 2004) and the evidence use field (e.g., Boaz et al., 2019; Penuel et al., 2015). They can be seen to raise critical conceptual questions about the ways in which evidence-based practice can misunderstand education as a practice, mischaracterise the contribution of research and pre-suppose a particular relationship between research and practice.

In relation to misunderstanding education as a practice, there has been long-standing debate about whether evidence-based approaches from health are applicable to education (e.g., Biesta, 2007; Hammersley, 2004; Lingard, 2013; Thomas & Pring, 2004). A key concern has been the assumptions about professional practice that are implicit within evidence-based approaches. Biesta (2007, p. 10), for example, argued that:

> the model of professional action implied in evidence-based practice – that is, the idea of education as a treatment or intervention that is a causal means to bring about particular, preestablished ends – is not appropriate for the field of education.

For Biesta, this model of professional action is inappropriate because it fails to acknowledge education as a "moral practice rather than a technical one" where educators need to make judgements about "not simply what is possible (a factual judgement) but also what is educationally desirable (a value judgement)" (2007, p. 10).

A second focus of debate has been around the contribution that research can (and cannot) provide to practice or policy. A common criticism of evidence-based approaches is that they overinflate the value of research-based knowledge. Hammersley (2004, p. 138), for example, argues that "research usually cannot supply what the notion of evidence-based practice demands of it – specific and highly reliable answers to questions about what works and what does not". This is because research knowledge "is always fallible" and "usually takes the form of generalisations, and interpreting the implications of these for dealing with particular cases is rarely straightforward" (p. 136). Biesta (2007) makes a similar point in arguing that "research cannot supply us with rules for action but only with hypotheses for intelligent problem solving" (p. 20).

Thirdly, critics of evidence-based practice have highlighted how it pre-supposes a particular relationship between research and practice. Some have talked about how efforts to translate educational research for educational practitioners have implied a particular instrumental form of research use:

Translation implies that what decision makers should prize most about research is that it can generate trustworthy evidence that they can use instrumentally to make decisions [which overlooks how practitioners also] value research that helps them gain new insights into problems and that facilitates the search for new kinds of solutions to persistent problems.

(Penuel et al., 2015, p. 186)

Others have made a similar point about the research-practice relationship being conceived in purely technical terms which negates other important possibilities:

The provision of instrumental knowledge is not the only way in which educational research can inform and be beneficial for educational practice […] research can also play a valuable role in helping educational practitioners to acquire a different understanding of their practice.

(Biesta, 2007, p. 19)

Taken together, these various critiques highlight the conceptual complexity that is inherent to educational research use. In relation to our specific focus of quality use, they make clear the need for, and the challenges that will be involved in, deliberation about what it means for research to be used well. What is important, though, is that conceptual issues are not the only source of complexity. We also need to discuss potential practical challenges.

Evidence use challenges in educational practice

A common finding from studies of educators in different countries is that, despite often having positive attitudes towards research, their use of research in practice is quite limited. Levin et al.'s (2011, p. 10) survey of 188 school leaders in Canada, for example, found that "respondents reported strong interest in research" but "when it came to measures of actual practice, such as time spent on research-related reading, events or networks, two-thirds to three-quarters reported quite low levels of involvement". Along similar lines, a study of 1670 teachers in England reported that although the majority showed a positive disposition towards research, they were "much more likely to draw ideas and support from their own experiences, or the experiences of other teachers/schools, when deciding on approaches to support pupil progress" (Walker et al., 2019, p. 4). This same pattern has been seen in other studies of educators in Australia (Prendergast & Rickinson, 2019), Canada (Lysenko et al., 2014) and England (Proctor, 2015).

These findings raise questions about how and why using research in practice can present challenges for practitioners. As Cain (2019, p. 206) argues, "engaging with research is hugely challenging" and it is important to understand the kinds of obstacles that can hamper the process. One way to think about potential barriers is in terms of the contexts, the processes and the users involved in educational research use.

In relation to contexts, there are specific challenges connected to the nature of the school environment. The busy-ness of schools and classrooms can mean that "the whole idea of reading research and formulating ideas about it" can get lost (Cain, 2019, p. 207). Finding time is critical for any initiative within schools, but it is particularly important for research use given the time needed "to read, debate, plan, trial and evaluate ideas from research" (Cain, 2019, p. 207). This can be highly problematic within a wider context of increasing teacher workloads (e.g., Heffernan et al., 2022). The wider policy context of schools and schooling can also affect research use. In the English school system, for example, Harley (2020, p. 71) argues that asking teachers to engage with educational research is "asking them to go against the grain of the current educational climate". As Gore (2020, p. 204) makes clear, "implementing research-informed practice requires school executives to grant agency and time for teachers to positively engage in research".

In relation to processes, there are characteristics of using research that can also present difficulties. Cain (2019, p. 211) writes, for example, about how "using research can carry risks" because it can challenge existing practices and involve new approaches that may not work. It can also be challenging in a personal sense because "engagement with research calls for teachers to reflect on who they are in the classroom" (Harley, 2020, p. 71). In these ways, meaningful research use can be prevented or constrained by a "fear of failure" (Harley, 2020, p. 71) or a desire to "play it safe" (Cain, 2019, p. 211). The process of using research can also be challenging in terms of what it demands of educators. For example, being able to "intentionally combine tacit and explicit knowledge from evidence and research to come to new insights" (Earl, 2015, pp. 148–9).

In relation to users, there is a number of ways in which educators themselves can present challenges for research use. One example is the fact that educators vary in how confident and well-equipped they feel to be able to access and make sense of educational research. As Harley (2020, p. 73) points out, "There are colleagues who have returned to university at some point [...] but for many their teacher training has been the last time they engaged with academic literature". Educators can also vary considerably in their attitudes towards research and its use in practice. Drawing on work by Nicholson-Goodman and Garman (2007), for example, Cain (2019, p. 208) highlights "overcoming scepticism" about research as one obstacle to research use that needs navigating in education. Educators can also hold varied views on the role of research use within teaching. Harley (2020, p. 72) describes how leaders can have staff who "feel that research engagement is not part of their role".

These various challenges highlight the demanding nature of applying research in practice and the kinds of complexities that can be involved. They show how using research in education is far from straightforward and, in turn, why understanding what using research well means matters in a practical as well as a conceptual sense.

This section and the two that preceded it, then, have laid out the backdrop for this book in terms of relevant developments and debates in policy, research and practice. These developments and debates provide an indication as to why understanding quality use of research in education is important. In short, the idea of using research well and, more importantly, developing ways to better understand what that means and involves is critical because:

- there has been significant investment internationally in developing policy to increase and improve the use of research evidence by schools and school systems, which highlights *the need to engage with the question of not just whether research is used but how well research is used*;
- the promotion of evidence-based practice in education has been criticised for over-simplifying the relationship between research and practice and overlooking important qualities of the educational process, which flags *the need for careful deliberation about what using research well means for educators and education*; and
- the use of research in educational practice has been shown to be complex work that demands a lot of educators and their schools, which

emphasises *the need for practical guidance and support about what is involved in using research well.*

Evidence base of the book

This book comes out of a five-year study, the Monash Q Project, that has focused specifically on the issue of quality use of research evidence. A partnership between Monash University and the Paul Ramsay Foundation, the Q Project has involved close collaboration with teachers, school leaders, policy makers, researchers, research brokers and other key education stakeholders across Australia. The project's overarching goal has been to understand and improve high-quality use of research evidence in Australian schools. It has involved four main strands, the first two of which were focused more on understanding quality use and the second two of which were focused more on improving quality use.

- Strand 1: Conceptualisation of quality use (2019–2020) – synthesising insights relating to high-quality evidence use in health, social care, policy and education in order to develop a quality use of research evidence framework for educators.
- Strand 2: School-based investigation of quality use (2020–2022) – examining the research use perspectives and practices of educators across several Australian states to generate empirical insights into high-quality research use in varied schools.
- Strand 3: Development of improvement interventions (2021–2023) – co-designing and trialling with groups of educators, interventions to support high-quality research use in practice.
- Strand 4: Engagement and communication campaign (2019–2023) – bringing together key players within Australian education to spark strategic dialogue and drive system-level change around research use in education.

This book presents findings and insights from Strand 1, Strand 2 and the early part of Strand 3, which were concerned with what quality use means conceptually and what quality use and its development involves in practice empirically. As shown in Figure 1.1, conceptualising and investigating quality use involved different data collection and analysis processes, and

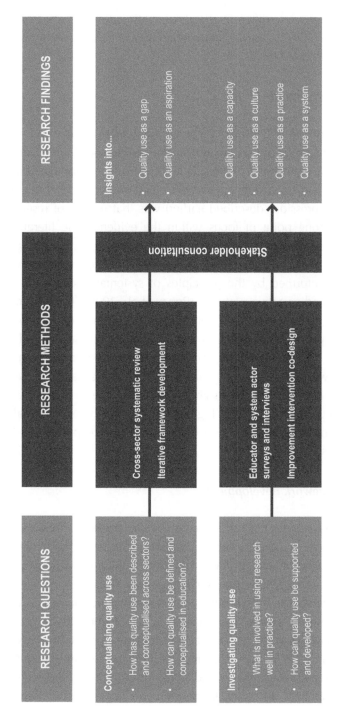

Figure 1.1 Q Project research questions, methods and findings

generated insights into different aspects of quality use. The nature of each of the main data collection processes within Figure 1.1 will now be expanded upon in a little more detail.

Cross-sector systematic review

The early phase of the Q Project involved a systematic review and narrative synthesis of 112 relevant publications from health, social care, policy and education. The review and synthesis sought to explore if and how quality of research use had been defined and described within each of the sectors. Our initial impression (described earlier) was that quality of research use was not a strong point of focus within the evidence use literature, but we wanted to investigate this in more detail by looking systematically at the literature in four sectors. As explained more fully in Appendix 1, the review process was informed by the principles of systematic reviewing (Gough et al., 2017) and narrative synthesis (Popay et al., 2006). The 112 included publications (30 from health, 29 from social care, 31 from education and 22 from policy) provided the basis for four narrative syntheses that addressed how quality of research use had been defined, described and con-ceptualised within each sector. Taken together, these narrative syntheses enabled the identification of insights into *quality use as a gap* which, as discussed in Chapter 2, is about highlighting the lack of explicit quality use definitions and descriptions but also some notable exceptions and helpful implicit ideas.

Iterative framework development

The narrative syntheses then underwent two main stages of analysis to inform the development of a quality use of research evidence framework for educa-tion. As explained in more detail in Appendix 1, the first stage involved the-matic analyses to identify cross-cutting insights related to quality use of research evidence across the health, social care and policy narratives. We then compared these cross-sector themes with an early framework on quality use (Rickinson, Sharples, et al., 2020), that was developed prior to the cross-sector review. This process led to the creation of an expanded and revised frame-work. In the second stage, the revised framework was then compared with the education narratives in order to develop education-specific descriptions for each of the components of the final Quality Use of Research Evidence (QURE) Framework (Rickinson, Cirkony, et al., 2020). Throughout this process, our evolving ideas and iterations were shared with project partners and stakeholders, whose feedback informed the development and refinement of the framework. As a whole, this framework development process generated conceptual insights into *quality use as an aspiration* which, as discussed in Chapter 3, is about articulating what is involved and what enables high-quality use of research in education.

Educator and system actor surveys and interviews

Building on the systematic review and framework development processes outlined above, the Q Project's work then turned to empirical investigation of quality use in schools. The focus here was on probing into educators' and, to a lesser extent, system actors' perspectives on quality use in practice through surveys and interviews. The aim was to explore educators' and system actors' views on what is involved in using research well in practice and how it can be supported and developed within schools and systems. As described in more detail in Appendix 1, three surveys were undertaken with a total of 1,725 educators and 158 system actors:

- Survey 1 (May to September 2020) – 492 educators from four Australian states responded to questions about how they use research and what using research well means and involves;
- Survey 2 (May to July 2021) – 819 educators and 158 system actors from all Australian states and territories responded to questions about how they share and use research and how this can be supported; and
- Survey 3 (August to September 2021) – 414 educators from four Australian states responded to questions about their own research use practices and what supports improved research use within schools.

As follow-up to Survey 1, interviews were undertaken from August to October 2020 with 29 educators from 27 schools who had taken part in that survey. The interviews were semi-structured, exploratory conversations over 45–60 minutes that sought to develop deeper insights into educators' views and experiences of using research well. The analysis of the quantitative and qualitative data from the surveys, coupled with the qualitative interview data, generated empirical insights into quality use as a professional *capacity* (Chapter 4), an organisational *culture* (Chapter 5), a school-based *practice* (Chapter 6) and a *system* phenomenon (Chapter 7).

Co-design of improvement interventions

Following the conceptual (systematic review and framework development) and empirical (surveys and interviews) data collection and analysis processes outlined above, the focus shifted to developing ways to improve research use in schools. A key activity was undertaking two series of co-design workshops with 49 teachers, school leaders and other education stakeholders from five different jurisdictions (Cirkony et al., 2022). As explained in more detail in Appendix 1, the first series of workshops focused on developing a research use professional learning programme, while the second series focused on identifying system-wide enablers to support research use in schools. Content and thematic analysis of data collected before, during and after the co-design workshops, particularly the second workshop series which focused on system-level enablers, provided insights into quality use *as a system* (Chapter 7).

Stakeholder consultation

Stakeholder consultation was an important feature of all of the research processes described above. The design and conduct of the systematic review and narrative synthesis, for example, was informed by advice and feedback from experts in systematic reviewing, information scientists and evidence use academics and practitioners from all four sectors. During the development of the framework, our evolving ideas about quality use of research were shared with project partners and stakeholders via meetings, workshops and conferences. Other stakeholders, including researchers, policy makers, evidence brokers and educators, were invited to consider and provide feedback on successive versions of the framework. For the empirical data collection, all of the surveys were piloted with several groups of educators to test and refine survey items and later versions were shared with researchers, policy makers and research brokers for feedback (see Rickinson et al., 2021). Similarly, interview questions were checked and piloted with educators and other stakeholders.

Overall, then, the ideas and insights shared within this book are based on conceptual enquiry (cross-sector systematic review and iterative framework development) and empirical investigation (educator and system actor surveys and interviews) into using research well in practice, both of which were supported by ongoing stakeholder consultation.

Terminology within the book

The *evidence agenda* (Burns & Schuller, 2007, p. 15) within and beyond education has brought with it a wide range of terms and phrases that can be used by different authors in varying ways. It is therefore important to explain the meaning of the key terms that are used within this book.

We recognise that educational practice can be informed by many different types of evidence, such as research-based evidence, practice-based evidence and data-based evidence (Nelson & Campbell, 2019). The discussion in this book, though, focuses on educators' use of a specific type of evidence, namely *research evidence*. By *research evidence*, we mean evidence generated through systematic studies undertaken by universities or research organisations and reported in books, reports, articles, research summaries, training courses or events (Nelson et al., 2017).

We are also aware that educators' research engagement can involve both engagement in (doing) research and/or engagement with (using) research (Bell et al., 2010; Prendergast & Rickinson, 2019). This book focuses on one of these forms of research engagement, namely *using research* (or *research use*). By *using research*, we mean the process of actively engaging with and drawing on research evidence to inform, change and improve decision making and practice (Coldwell et al., 2017). In certain parts of the book, however, we also refer to *using evidence* (or *evidence use*) when we are discussing the use of evidence generally as opposed to the use of research evidence specifically.

While we draw on work undertaken across varied sectors, this book's main focus is on the use of research within education. There is therefore a lot of discussion about *educators, schools, systems and system actors*. We use the term *educators* to refer to teachers, leaders and other staff working within schools such as support staff, librarians and so on. Alongside collective references to educators generally, we also, where relevant, refer to more specific groups such as senior leaders, middle leaders or teachers. By *schools*, we are referring to educational organisations of varied kinds across the primary and secondary age ranges. By *systems*, we are referring to educational jurisdictions, such as state-based education departments, which oversee or administer schools in a specific area. *System actors*, then, refers to organisations and individuals that play a role within an education system such as policy organisations, brokerage organisations, research organisations, professional learning organisations and professional associations.

Another key term we use frequently in this book, of course, is that of *quality use of research* (also referred to as *quality use*). Building up a rich picture of what this concept means and involves within education is the core purpose of this book. In essence, though, we define it as "thoughtful engagement with and implementation of appropriate research evidence" (Rickinson, Walsh, et al., 2020, p. 5) – the meaning and significance of which is discussed in Chapter 3.

Finally, we draw on and refer to the notions of *evidence-informed* and *research-informed practice*, as distinct from evidence-*based* and research-*based* practice. With the former, the use of evidence and/or research informs, rather than replaces, educators' professional judgement and expertise. Evidence-informed and research-informed practice is therefore about "integrating professional expertise with the best external evidence from research to improve the quality of practice" (Sharples, 2013, p. 7).

Audiences for this book

This book is written as a resource for professionals within and beyond education who want to better understand what using research evidence well means and involves and how it can be supported. This might include:

- education system leaders who are looking to strengthen research-informed approaches in their own work and the work of schools and need a clearer sense of what to pay attention to in order to support effective use of research-informed approaches;
- school leaders who are working to foster a more research-engaged culture within their school and would like to know more about what is involved in using research well as an organisation;
- school research leaders or professional learning leaders who are responsible for building the capacity of their colleagues to be more research-informed and want to be clearer in their own minds about what using research well really means;

- educators who want to improve their practice by using research and are looking for insights into the kinds of processes and capacities that one needs to think about to become better at using research;
- research brokers who are looking to support the mobilisation of research evidence and research-informed practices across groups of schools and want clarity about what effective use involves and requires;
- school improvement partners and professional learning providers who seek to foster engagement with and use of research-informed practices in different schools and want their work to promote quality use as well as quality evidence; and
- researchers and evaluators who want to generate insights into the development and impacts of research-informed practice within schools and systems and need ways of investigating not only the quantity, but also the quality, of research use.

We hope that within and across the different chapters of this book there will be ideas and insights that will be of interest and use to all of the above groups. To support this aspiration, all of the main chapters contain short vignettes to illustrate either what quality use concepts look like in practice (the "Looks like in practice" vignettes) or how quality use concepts can be helpful (the "How is it helpful?" vignettes). Based on anonymised, real-life examples from educators, system leaders and others involved in the Q Project, these vignettes give quality use a shape and form by showing what it looks like in different kinds of practical settings or showing how it can be helpful for different kinds of purposes. Through these vignettes, readers will meet a range of different characters whose work intersects with using research well in many different ways. Throughout the book, there is also a strong emphasis on foregrounding the perspectives and experiences of teachers, school leaders and system leaders in relation to using research well in practice. Readers will hear from individuals in different kinds of schools and systems talking about their research use practices and understandings.

Structure of the book

In this chapter, we have outlined the focus and scope of this book, considered its significance in relation to developments in policy, research and practice, and explained the research that underpins it, the terminology that it employs and the varied audiences it seeks to address. Building on this introduction to quality use of research as an issue, subsequent chapters then take the reader through different ways of understanding quality use – as a *gap*, as an *aspiration*, as a *capacity*, as a *culture*, as a *practice* and as a *system* – before drawing together what these collectively tell us about quality use and what issues and questions remain for future work on this topic. Like the parts of a folding fan that are being slowly opened, the successive chapters of the book can be thought of as an unfolding picture of quality use of research in education (Figure 1.2). By exploring different key questions, each of the chapters contributes to an overall understanding of quality use of research. Each chapter looks at the issue of quality use of research from a different perspective and so, like the parts of a fan, bring new colours and detail to the unfolding picture. The picture that emerges, though, is far from complete – there are more parts of the fan that are yet to be opened, just as there are further aspects of quality use of research that are yet to be understood.

Chapter 2 explores *quality use as a gap*. It examines questions such as: How has quality of use been described and conceptualised within education and other sectors? Drawing on the systematic review and narrative synthesis described above, it shows how quality of use has been little discussed within health, social care, policy and education. From the perspective of trying to better understand quality use, this chapter highlights what is missing from the current literature, but also what can be drawn upon in terms of the small number of publications that have touched on quality of use and certain implicit ideas across the sectors that can be related to quality use.

Chapter 3 considers *quality use as an aspiration*. It explores how quality use of research can be defined and conceptualised in education by asking questions such as: What does it mean to use research well in education? Drawing on the themes from the literature discussed in the preceding chapter, it presents a framework that defines and elaborates high-quality use of research in terms of: two core components (*thoughtful engagement and implementation* and *appropriate research evidence*), three individual enabling components (*skillsets, mindsets, relationships*), three organisational enabling components (*leadership, culture* and *infrastructure*) and system-level influences.

In Chapter 4, the discussion shifts from the conceptual to the empirical by examining *quality use as a capacity*. Drawing on educators' survey

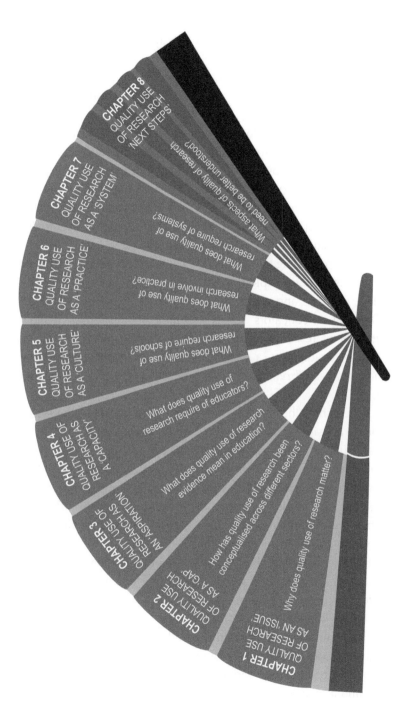

Figure 1.2 Quality use of research – an unfolding picture

and interview responses about using research well in practice, it explores questions such as: What does quality use of research require of educators? It makes clear that using research well is complex and demanding work, that involves particular types of knowledge and skills (*skillsets*), values and dispositions (*mindsets*) and relational capacities (*relationships*).

Chapter 5 moves from the individual educator level to the organisational level by considering *quality use as a culture*. Drawing on educators' survey and interview responses about using research well in practice, it explores questions such as: What does quality use of research require of schools as organisations? It shows how using research well needs supportive values and ethos (*culture*), supportive role modelling and promotion (*leadership*) and supportive structures and processes (*infrastructure*).

Building on the preceding two chapters, Chapter 6 focuses on *quality use as a practice*. This involves exploring questions such as: How do educators conceptualise, envision and enact using research well in their day-to-day practice? Drawing on educators' survey and interview responses, it shows how quality use of research is an *individual practice* that is driven by curiosity and professionalism, a *shared practice* that is collective and embedded and an *invested practice* that is purposeful and time- and effort-dependent.

Chapter 7 then shifts the discussion from the school level to the system level in order to consider *quality use as a system*. It explores questions such as: How can quality use of research be understood from a system perspective and what role can system-level actors and organisations play in quality research use in schools? Drawing on educators' and system actors' survey, interview and co-design responses, it examines system *influences*, system *support* and system *practices*, and argues that the system dimensions of quality use are currently under-developed.

Chapter 8, the concluding chapter, draws together the key messages of the book in terms of: what they reveal about using research well (an unfolding picture, a detailed picture and a connected picture); what they suggest for future improvement efforts (productive uses to emulate, productive spaces to nurture and productive paradoxes to consider) and what they highlight as future research possibilities (further work on quality use as a capacity, a culture, a practice and a system and new work on quality use as a journey and a measure).

References

Bell, M., Cordingley, P., Isham, C., & Davis, R. (2010). *Report of professional practitioner use of research review: Practitioner engagement in and/or with research*. Centre for the Use of Research and Evidence in Education; General Teaching Council for England; Learning and Skills Improvement Service; National Teacher Research Panel. http://www.curee.co.uk/node/2303

Biesta, G. (2007). Why "what works" won't work: Evidence-based practice and the democratic deficit in educational research. *Educational Theory, 57*(1), 1–22. 10.1111/j.1741-5446.2006.00241.x

Boaz, A., & Nutley, S. (2019). Using evidence. In A. Boaz, A. Frances & S. M. Nutley. (Eds.), *What works now? Evidence informed policy and practice* (pp. 251–258). Policy Press.

Boaz, A., Davies, H. T. O., Fraser, A., & Nutley, S. M. (2019). *What works now? Evidence informed policy and practice*. Policy Press. https://policy. bristoluniversitypress.co.uk/what-works-now

British Educational Research Association. (2014). *Research and the teaching profession: Building the capacity for a self-improving education system. Final report of the BERA-RSA inquiry into the role of research in teacher education*. British Educational Research Association; The Royal Society for the Encouragement of the Arts, Manufacturing and Commerce. https://www.thersa.org/reports/research-and-the-teaching-profession-building-the-capacity-for-a-self-improving-education-system

Brown, C. (2018). Research learning networks: A case study in using networks to increase knowledge mobilization at scale. In C. Brown (Ed.), *Networks for learning* (1st ed.) (pp. 38–55). Routledge. 10.4324/9781315276649-4

Brown, C., & Malin, J. R. (2022). *The Emerald handbook of evidence-informed practice in education: Learning from international contexts*. Emerald Publishing Limited.

Burns, T., & Schuller, T. (2007). The evidence agenda. In Organisation for Economic Cooperation and Development (Ed.), *Evidence in education* (pp. 15–32). Organisation for Economic Cooperation and Development Publishing. 10.1787/9789264033672-2-en

Cain, T. (2019). Research extends 'teaching mindsets'. In T. Cain (Ed.), *Becoming a Research-Informed School: Why? What? How?* (pp. 33–48). Routledge. 10.4324/9781315143033-3

Cirkony, C., Rickinson, M., Walsh, L., Gleeson, J., Salisbury, M., Cutler, B., & Boulet, M. (2022). *Improving quality use of research evidence in practice: Insights from cross-sector co-design*. Monash University. 10.26180/19380677.v3

Coburn, C. E., & Penuel, W. R. (2016). Research–practice partnerships in education: Outcomes, dynamics, and open questions. *Educational Researcher, 45*(1), 48–54. 10.3102/0013189X16631750

Coldwell, M., Greany, T., Higgins, S., Brown, C., Maxwell, B., Stiell, B., Stoll, L., Willis, B., & Burns, H. (2017). *Evidence-informed teaching: An evaluation of progress in England: Research report*. Department for Education. https://www.gov.uk/government/publications/evidence-informed-teaching-evaluation-of-progress-in-england

Dixon, M., Brookes, J., & Siddle, J. (2020). Hearts and minds. The research schools' network: From evidence to engagement. In S. Gorard (Ed.), *Getting evidence into education: Evaluating the routes to policy and practice* (pp. 53–68). Routledge. 10.4324/9780429290343

Dormann, C., Binnewies, C., Koch, A. R., Ackeren, I., Clausen, M., Preisendörfer, P., Schmidt, U., & Zlatkin-Troitschanskaia, O. (2016). Transferring best evidence into practice: Assessment of evidence-based school management. *Journal for Educational Research Online*, *8*(3), 14–38. https://www.pedocs.de/volltexte/2017/12803/pdf/JERO_2016_3_pdf

Earl, L. (2015). Reflections on the challenges of leading research and evidence use in schools. In C. Brown, (Ed.), *Leading the use of research and evidence in schools* (pp. 148–149). Institute of Education Press.

Gopinathan, S. (2012). Fourth way in action? The evolution of Singapore's education system. *Educational Research for Policy and Practice*, *11*, 65–70. 10.1007/s10671-011-9117-6

Gore, J. (2020). Why isn't this empowering? The discursive positioning of teachers in efforts to improve teaching. In A. Brown & E. Wisby (Eds.), *Knowledge, policy and practice in education and the struggle for social justice: Essays inspired by the work of Geoff Whitty* (pp. 199–216). UCL Press. https://www.jstor.org/stable/j.ctv13xpshq

Gough. D., Oliver, S., & Thomas, J. (2017). *An introduction to systematic reviews* (2nd ed.). Sage.

Hammersley, M. (2004). Some questions about evidence-based practice in education. In G. Thomas & R. Pring (Eds.), *Evidence-based practice in education* (pp. 133–149). Open University Press.

Harley, C. (2020). Overcoming teachers' reservations and barriers to engaging with educational research. In C. Brown, J. Flood, & G. Handscomb (Eds.), *The research-informed teaching revolution: A handbook for the 21st century teacher* (pp. 69–77). John Catt Educational Limited.

Heffernan, A., Bright, D., Kim, M., Longmuir, F., & Magyar, B. (2022). 'I cannot sustain the workload and the emotional toll': Reasons behind Australian teachers' intentions to leave the profession. *Australian Journal of Education*, *66*(2), 196–209. 10.1177/00049441221086654

Hill, J. (2022). Who is facilitating research use in education systems? In Organisation for Economic Cooperation and Development (Ed.), *Who cares about using education research in policy and practice? Strengthening research engagement* (pp. 74–101). OECD Publishing. 10.1787/f872248c-en

Levin, B., Cooper, A., Arjomand, S., & Thompson, K. (2011). Can simple interventions increase research use in secondary schools? *Canadian Journal of Educational Administration and Policy*, 1–29. https://cdm.ucalgary.ca/index.php/cjeap/article/view/42823

Lingard, B. (2013). The impact of research on education policy in an era of evidence-based policy. *Critical Studies in Education*, *(54)*2, 113–131. 10.1080/17508487.2013.781515

Lysenko, L. V., Abrami, P. C., Bernard, R. M., Dagenais, C., & Janosz, M. (2014). Educational research in educational practice: Predictors of use. *Canadian Journal of Education*, 37(2), 1–26. https://www.jstor.org/stable/10.2307/canajeducrevucan.37.2.06

Malin, J. R., Brown, C., Ion, G., van Ackeren, I., Bremm, N., Luzmore, R., Flood, J., & Rind, G. M. (2020). World-wide barriers and enablers to achieving evidence-informed practice in education: What can be learnt from Spain, England, the United States, and Germany? *Humanities & Social Sciences Communications*, 7(1), 1–14. 10.1057/s41599-020-00587-8

Nelson, J., & Campbell, C. (2019). Using evidence in education. In A. Boaz, A. Frances & S. M. Nutley. (Eds.), *What works now? Evidence-informed policy and practice* (pp. 131–145). Policy Press.

Nelson, J., Mehta, P., Sharples, J., & Davey, C. (2017). *Measuring teachers' research engagement: Findings from a pilot study*. Education Endowment Foundation. https://educationendowmentfoundation.org.uk/projects-and-evaluation ... research-engagement

Nicholson-Goodman, J., & Garman, N. B. (2007). Mapping practitioner perceptions of 'It's research based': Scientific discourse, speech acts and the use and abuse of research, *International Journal of Leadership in Education*, 10(3), 283–299. 10.1080/13603120701257297

Organisation for Economic Cooperation and Development (2022). *Who cares about using education research in policy and practice? Strengthening research engagement*. Organisation for Economic Cooperation and Development Publishing. 10.1787/d7ff793d-en

Parkhurst, J. (2017). *The politics of evidence: From evidence-based policy to the good governance of evidence*. Routledge.

Penuel, W. R., Allen, A., Coburn, C. E., & Farrell, C. (2015). Conceptualizing research–practice partnerships as joint work at boundaries. *Journal of Education for Students Placed at Risk*, 20(1-2), 182–197. 10.1080/10824669.2014.988334

Popay, J., Roberts, H., Sowden, A., Petticrew, M., Arai, L., Rodgers, M., Britten, N., Roen, K., & Duffy, S. (2006). Guidance on the conduct of narrative synthesis in systematic reviews. *A product from the ESRC methods programme*. Institute for Health Research; Child Health Research and Policy Unit; Centre for Reviews and Dissemination; MRC Social and Public Health Sciences Unit; Peninsula Medical School. https://citeseerx.ist.psu.edu/ ... /ed8b23836338f6fdea0cc55e161b0fc5805f9e27

Prendergast, S., & Rickinson, M. (2019). Understanding school engagement in and with research. *The Australian Educational Researcher*, 46, 17–39. 10.1007/s13384-018-0292-9

Procter, R. (2015). Teachers and school research practices: The gaps between the values and practices of teachers. *Journal of Education for Teaching*, (41)5, 464–477. 10.1080/02607476.2015.1105535

Rickinson, M., Cirkony, C., Walsh, L., Gleeson, J., & Salisbury, M. (2020). *Towards quality use of research evidence in education: Discussion paper*. Monash University. 10.26180/14071571.v2

Rickinson, M., Cirkony, C., Walsh, L., Gleeson, J., Cutler, B., & Salisbury, M. (2022). A framework for understanding the quality of evidence use in education. *Educational Research, 64*(2), 133–158. 10.1080/00131881.2022.2054452

Rickinson, M., De Bruin, K., Walsh, L., & Hall, M. (2016). *The use of evidence in education policy: A pilot study in Victoria.* Department of Education and Training.

Rickinson, M., De Bruin, K., Walsh, L., & Hall, M. (2017). What can evidence-use in practice learn from evidence-use in policy? *Educational Research, 59*(2), 173–189. 10.1080/00131881.2017.1304306

Rickinson, M., Gleeson, J., Walsh, L., Cutler, B., Cirkony, C., & Salisbury, M. (2021). *Research and evidence use in Australian schools: Survey, analysis and key findings.* Monash University. 10.26180/14445663

Rickinson, M., Sharples, J., & Lovell, O. (2020). Towards a better understanding of quality of evidence use. In S. Gorard (Ed.), *Getting evidence into education: Evaluating the routes to policy and practice* (pp. 219–233). Routledge.

Rickinson, M., Walsh, L., Cirkony, C., Salisbury, M., & Gleeson, J. (2020). *Quality use of research evidence framework.* Monash University. 10.26180/14071508.v2

Rickinson, M., Walsh, L., De Bruin, K., & Hall, M. (2019). Understanding evidence use within education policy: A policy narrative perspective. *Evidence & Policy, 15*(2), 235–252. 10.1332/174426418X15172393826277

Sharples, J. (2013). *Evidence for the frontline: A report for the Alliance for Useful Evidence.* Alliance for Useful Evidence. https://apo.org.au/sites/default/files/resource-files/2013-06/apo-nid34800.pdf

Sheldrick, C., Mackie, T., Supplee, L., Cruden, G., Farley-Ripple, L., Firestone, B. G., Purtle, J., & Wilson-Ahlstrom, A. (2022). *An invitation: Help us to conceptualize what "quality" research evidence use means.* William T. Grant Foundation. https://sites.google.com/view/wtg-ure-meeting-march-2021/materials-and-pre-readings?authuser=0

Thomas, G., & Pring, R. (Eds.) (2004). *Evidence-based practice in education.* McGraw-Hill Education.

Walker, M., Nelson, J., & Bradshaw, S. (2019). *Teachers' engagement with research: What do we know? A research briefing.* Education Endowment Foundation. https://educationendowmentfoundation.org.uk/projects-and-evaluation/eef-evaluation-reports-and-research-papers/methodological-research-and-innovations/teachers-engagement-with-research

Walsh, L., Gleeson, J., Cutler, B., Rickinson, M., Cirkony, C., & Salisbury, M. (2022). *What, why, when and how: Australian educators' use of research in schools.* Monash University. 10.26180/17192990.v1

White, S., Nuttall, J., Down, B., Shore, S., Woods, A., Mills, M., & Bussey, K. (2018). *Strengthening a research-rich teaching profession for Australia.* Australian Teacher Education Association; Australian Association for Research in Education; Australian Council of Deans of Education. https://www.aare.edu.au/assets/documents/Strengthening-a-research-rich-teaching-profession-FOR-RESEARCH-PAGE-v2.pdf

2 | Quality use of research as a gap

Chapter overview

This chapter discusses what has (and what has not) been written about quality use of research within the health, social care, policy and education sectors. Based on a cross-sector systematic review and narrative synthesis of relevant literature, it shows that:

- there is a general lack of explicit definitions or descriptions of quality of use across all four sectors;
- quality use of research can be seen "as a gap" not only in education but also in health, social care and policy;
- there are some important exceptions in terms of a small number of publications that have discussed aspects of quality of use in an explicit way;
- these publications are helpful in raising questions about the manner in which evidence is used and suggesting vocabulary with which to capture higher-quality use;
- there are also themes cutting across the four sectors that can be seen to have implicit or indirect links to the issue of quality of use; and
- these themes are helpful in highlighting the importance of practitioner expertise in using evidence and the systems complexity of evidence use improvement; and

DOI: 10.4324/9781003353966-2

- all of the above ideas have implications for our task of conceptualising quality use of research in education.

Introduction

In Chapter 1, we introduced the idea that improved research use requires not only high-quality research but also high-quality use. We also expressed concern that while there has been a lot written about the quality of evidence, there seems to have been far less discussion about the quality of use. With this distinction in mind, this chapter examines what has (and has not) been written about quality of use within four different sectors (health, social care, policy and education). The aim is to shed light on whether and in what ways quality of use has been discussed and described within these sectors, to inform how we might define and conceptualise quality use of research evidence in education.

Drawing on a systematic review and narrative synthesis of relevant publications from across the four sectors, this chapter highlights a general lack of explicit definitions or descriptions of quality of use within health, social care, policy and education. In this way, it provides insights into "quality use as a gap" by showing what is missing within the current literature. However, it also identifies what is present in terms of certain publications that have discussed aspects of quality of use and certain cross-sector ideas that have implications for conceptualising quality of use.

Following this introduction, the remainder of this chapter is divided into five sections. It begins by discussing what is involved in understanding quality use as a gap and how this perspective can contribute to, and underline the importance of, conceptualising quality of use. There are then three sections that describe and explain the general lack of explicit definitions and descriptions of quality use across all of the sectors, the small amount of work within each sector that has touched on aspects of quality of use and certain themes from across the sectors that have implicit connections to quality of use. We then conclude by summarising the key arguments of the chapter and outlining their implications for making sense of what it means to use research well within education.

Understanding quality use as a gap

Understanding quality use as a gap involves asking questions such as: How has quality of use been described and discussed within and across different sectors? What work has been undertaken that relates either explicitly or implicitly to the issue of quality use? And how might such work inform the process of conceptualising quality use of research in education? These are literature-based questions about the nature of the academic and professional publications within specific sectors and what might be gleaned from such work in relation to quality use of research in education.

Within the Q Project, these questions were addressed through a systematic review and narrative synthesis of relevant evidence use publications from health, social care, policy and education. The cross-sector scope of the review process was motivated by arguments within the evidence use field about the value of learning from different policy areas and disciplines (Davies et al., 2019). The review process was informed by the principles of systematic reviewing (Gough et al., 2017) and involved a transparent method with clearly defined search strategy, quality appraisal and synthesis processes (see Appendix 1 for details).

To identify relevant papers, we needed to develop a screening strategy to determine what topics associated with "quality of evidence use" were to be included and excluded. While it was a relatively easy task to determine what we were *not* looking for (e.g., quality of the evidence, use of data, dissemination of research), it was more challenging to describe what we *were* looking for, given the emergent nature of quality use as a research area. To address this, we developed two sets of keyword search terms – one set made up of terms related to "evidence and research use" and another set with terms related to "quality of use" (see Appendix 1 for details). The keywords for "quality of use" were developed using terms related to notions of quality (e.g., wise, professional, deep), capability (e.g., expertise, ability, aptitude, expert) and effectiveness (e.g., intelligent, effective, best practice). The search strategy yielded 10,813 research and professional publications from four databases relevant to each of the sectors. Following data extraction and appraisal, we included 112 papers from health (30), social care (29), education (31) and policy (22). These papers provided the basis for the development of four narrative syntheses, which elaborated how quality use had, and had not been, discussed within each of the sectors.

This chapter's next three sections share insights generated from the thematic analysis of these four narrative syntheses. It shows how there was:

- little in the way of well-developed definitions or descriptions of quality of evidence use across all sectors;
- some important exceptions to this general pattern in the form of specific studies that have discussed aspects of quality of use; and
- certain themes across the sectors that could be seen to have implications for conceptualising quality of use.

General lack of explicit definitions and descriptions

The notion of evidence use was well represented, with each of the sectors providing a distinct view of its practice. The health synthesis used terms such as "evidence-based practice", "evidence-based decision making", "knowledge translation", "knowledge to action", "research use" and "implementation" (Adams & Titler, 2013). Most papers proposed frameworks and models, encompassing all stages of the evidence use cycle (e.g., decision making, implementation, evaluation). Others elaborated on the nature and characteristics of evidence users and systems.

The social care synthesis drew on similar terms, such as "evidence-informed practice" (Austin et al., 2012; Graaf & Ratliff, 2018), "knowledge sharing and exchange" (Austin et al., 2012; Morton & Seditas, 2018), "evidence-based practice" (Cunningham & Duffee, 2009) and "evidence-based interventions" (Gambrill, 2018). The literature largely addressed the need to balance evidence use with both practitioner expertise and the needs of individual care cases. Discussions related to decision making, implementation and education frameworks, along with the success factors and barriers to evidence use in practice.

Evidence use in the education sector was largely referred to as "evidence-based practice" or "evidence-informed practice", with tensions associated with the perceived agency of the practitioner, similar to that in the health sector (Brown & Rogers, 2015; Greany & Maxwell, 2017). The literature focused on frameworks for processes and measurements of evidence use. Some publications also focused on the nature of evidence use, along with enablers and barriers to it.

Evidence use in policy making was referred to as "research utilisation" (Nutley et al., 2007), "evidence-informed" versus "evidence-based" policy making (Hawkins & Parkhurst, 2016; Moore, 2006), "knowledge-based policy" or "knowledge application" (Nutley et al., 2010), "knowledge co-production" (Boaz & Nutley, 2019), "knowledge translation and uptake" (Hawkins & Parkhurst, 2016) and "knowledge transfer, exchange and mobilisation" (Boaz & Nutley, 2019). The included papers focused on evidence use in general, an evidence use governance framework, an evidence assessment framework and associated case studies and standards of evidence and evidence use.

Despite each of the sectors providing rich descriptions of evidence use, a clear finding of the systematic review process was to confirm a shortage of explicit work on quality of use. Across all sectors, there were very few publications that discussed quality of use specifically and there was a lack of clear definitions and descriptions of quality use either as a concept or as a practice. There were many examples of investigations into the quantity of research use (e.g., Cooper and Levin, 2013; Penuel et al., 2016), but not into the *quality* of research use. There were many frameworks and models outlining the components of research use (e.g., Levin, 2004; Nutley et al., 2007), evidence-based practice (e.g., Cunningham & Duffee, 2009; Nutley et al., 2003) and implementation (e.g., Kitson et al., 1998; Sharples et al., 2019), but no parallel frameworks or models outlining the components of quality use. There was lots of work on standards and qualities of different kinds of evidence (e.g., Breckon, 2016; Puttick, 2018), but very little equivalent on standards and qualities of different kinds of use. There was work on the skills, knowledge and dispositions needed to use data well (e.g., Mandinach & Gummer, 2016), but almost no parallel work on what is required to use research well. There were some studies of practitioners' or policy makers' perspectives on evidence and its use (e.g., Cain, 2015; Lomas & Brown, 2009), but none that probed their views about what it means to use evidence well.

Overall, then, across the four sectors, there was no strong indication of quality research use having been a sustained focus of theoretical discussion or empirical investigation. There were no signs of major programmes of research having been undertaken on the issue of quality of use. However, there was a small number of individual studies in different sectors that had discussed issues connected to quality research use. As clear exceptions to

29

the general shortage of work on quality of use, these studies are an important part of the picture of quality use as a gap.

Some important exceptions focused on quality of use

As well as highlighting how quality of use was absent from much of the literature, the review process also found certain publications where quality of use was very much in focus.

One example came within the health literature in the form of an influential article articulating what "evidence-based medicine" is and is not (Sackett et al., 1996). Sackett, the lead author of this article, was a pioneer in the development of evidence-based medicine from the 1980s onwards (Claridge & Fabian, 2005; Thoma & Eaves, 2015). In this article, Sackett and colleagues (1996, p. 71) defined evidence-based medicine as "the conscientious, explicit, and judicious use of current best evidence in making decisions about the care of individual patients". They explained that it is a practice that involves "integrating individual clinical expertise with the best available external clinical evidence from systematic research" (Sackett et al., 1996, p. 71). They stressed how the combination of professional expertise and external evidence is critical as: "Without clinical expertise, practice risks becoming tyrannised by evidence [... and ...] Without current best evidence, practice risks becoming rapidly out of date, to the detriment of patients" (Sackett et al., 1996, p. 72).

From the perspective of wanting to understand quality use of research evidence, this article was helpful in drawing attention to the manner in which evidence is used. The inclusion of adjectives such as "conscientious, explicit, and judicious" within their definition introduced the idea of evidence-based medicine needing to encompass certain qualities. In other words, it suggested that it is not enough for clinicians to use evidence, rather the evidence needs to be used conscientiously, explicitly and judiciously. Sackett et al.'s article was also helpful in highlighting the role that professional expertise plays in using evidence – a point which is picked up as a cross-sector theme in the next section.

A second example of a publication that raised issues connected to quality of use came from education, albeit about the use of educational data as opposed to educational research. Earl and Timperley's (2009, p. 3) edited volume about *Professional Learning Conversations* included discussions about what is required for "productive" evidence-informed conversations in schools. They emphasised that using evidence is "hard because [it] requires more than just adding evidence to the conversation; it involves a way of thinking and challenging ideas towards new knowledge" (Earl & Timperley, 2009, p. 2). For evidence-informed conversations to be productive, then, they suggested that three qualities were required: having an "inquiry habit of mind", considering a broad range of "relevant evidence" and engaging in "learning conversations [based on relationships of respect and challenge]" (Earl & Timperley, 2009, p. 3).

Like the previous example from health, Earl and Timperley's work has relevance for conceptualising quality use because it emphasised the manner in which evidence is used. This work was also helpful in starting to unpack what is involved and needed to use data "productively". They made clear, for example, that it is not just about the evidence (e.g., "using relevant data", p. 6), but also mindsets (e.g., "an inquiry habit of mind", p. 3) and social processes (e.g., "relationships of respect and challenge", p. 9).

Another example from education was Farley-Ripple et al.'s (2018, p. 238) conceptual exploration of what they call "depth" of use as a key part of the process of strengthening connections between research and practice. Their framework comprises six dimensions that they argued are important for research being used "meaningfully and systematically" (Farley-Ripple et el., 2018, p. 238). These dimensions draw attention to the:

i evidence (Is the evidence single dimensional or is it comprised of multiple dimensions/forms?);
ii search (Is the search limited to existing/a few sources or multiple sources?);
iii interpretation (Is the interpretation unreflective or critical?);
iv participation (Is the participation by one or a few individuals or groups with diverse perspectives?);
v frequency (Is the frequency sporadic/one-off or regular/iterative?); and
vi decision stage (Is evidence used only in problem identification or across all stages?).

Along similar lines to Earl and Timperley's (2009) work, Farley-Ripple et al.'s (2018) ideas were helpful for conceptualising quality research use because they opened up what is involved in using evidence "deeply". They suggested that effective (or "deep") use of evidence requires not just particular kinds of inputs (e.g., evidence, search), but also particular kinds of approaches and processes (e.g., interpretation, participation, frequency, decision stage).

Looking to the policy sector, there were two further publications that connected to the issue of quality research use. The first example was Rutter and Gold's (2015, p. 5) work on developing an "evidence transparency framework" with which "to rate government departments on their use of evidence [in order] to show who used evidence well and who less well". With a focus on policy documents, their framework provided a way to assess the extent to which different sections of a new policy document make clear what evidence has been used and what role it has played. Within the framework, distinctions are drawn based around whether evidence is mentioned, whether the use of evidence is explained, how specifically the evidence is used, how effectively the evidence is cited and whether the quality of the evidence is assessed with any uncertainties acknowledged.

For the task of conceptualising quality of use, this work provided a specific example of an attempt to articulate what using evidence "well" and "less well" looked like in a particular professional context. It was also important from the perspective that Rutter and Gold (2015, p. 4) had to "pull the problem apart and [...] start with thinking about what "good" [use of evidence] might look like" (Rutter & Gold, 2015, p. 4), as there were no existing frameworks for quality use in policy that could be easily applied or adapted.

The other policy example was Parkhurst's (2017) *The Politics of Evidence*. Parkhurst argued that the notion of "evidence-based policy" needs to be replaced by a new goal of "the good governance of evidence" (Parkhurst, 2017, p. 9; see also Hawkins & Parkhurst, 2016). This proposed shift has implications not only for the evidence that is used ("what constitutes good evidence to inform policy"), but also the *way* in which it is used ("what constitutes the good use of evidence within a policy process") (Parkhurst, 2017, p. 8). Good governance of evidence, then, is about "the use of rigorous, systematic and technically valid pieces of evidence within decision-making processes that are representative of, and accountable to, populations served" (Parkhurst, 2017, p. iii). As such, it involves eight key principles or elements:

i   systematic and rigorous evidence;
ii evidence of high quality;
iii appropriate evidence for policy concern;

iv stewardship in terms of public mandate in designing the advisory system;

v public representation in decision making authority;

vi transparency in evidence use;

vii public deliberation in evidence-informed processes; and

viii contestability in terms of evidence open to challenge or appeal (Parkhurst, 2017, p. 163).

In relation to our interest in conceptualising quality research use, Parkhurst's work was significant in asking fundamental questions about not only the nature of evidence, but also the nature of its use. His arguments and frameworks made very clear the central role that values, such as transparency, democratic accountability and contestability, play in thinking about quality of evidence use. His work also underlined the need to understand quality of use in a highly contextualised way. He spoke, for example, about "good use of evidence from a policy perspective" (Parkhurst, 2017, p. 10) where the "from a policy perspective" qualifier arguably highlights the need to ground discussions about quality evidence use in the specifics of the practice under consideration.

Taken together, these five pieces of work were distinctive in addressing quality of use in an explicit way. While their contexts and foci varied considerably, they were similar in a number of important ways. They asked questions about the manner in which evidence is used. They suggested vocabulary that might help to better capture higher-quality use. They probed into the different aspects of using evidence and what is required to do that well or better. They flagged the context-specific nature of quality of use, the role of professional expertise and the centrality of values. As will become clear in subsequent chapters of this book, particularly in Chapter 3, these ideas have played an important role in the development of our understanding and framing of quality use of research in education.

Cross-sector themes with implications for quality of use

As well as the publications discussed above that focused directly on quality of use, there were also lines of thinking cutting across the four sectors that could be seen to have implicit or indirect links to the issue of quality of use

(Rickinson et al., 2021). Two themes that were particularly helpful were cross-sector ideas about the role of practitioner expertise in using evidence and the system complexity of evidence use improvement.

The importance of practitioner expertise

All four sectors and, in particular, the practice-based sectors of health, social care and education, emphasised the importance of practitioner expertise in using evidence in context. In health, for example, Sackett et al.'s (1996, p. 72) articulation of evidence-based medicine made clear that "external clinical evidence can inform, but can never replace, individual clinical expertise and it is this expertise that decides whether the external evidence applies to the individual patient at all" (Sackett et al., 1996, p. 72). This recognition for the role of professional expertise and judgement was reflected in many other models and frameworks within the health literature (e.g., Greenhalgh et al., 2004; Satterfield et al., 2009; Ward et al., 2009). In social care, there were also many evidence use frameworks that highlighted the importance of practitioner expertise, contextual factors and client needs (e.g., Anderson, 2011; Morton & Seditas, 2018; Rosen, 2003). Indeed, there was concern that the social care profession had overemphasised rational practice and ignored or minimised contextual factors such as client data, client values and views, clinical judgement and skills, and collaboration (Keenan & Grady, 2014).

In education, the connection between research and data use was strongly linked with practical or tacit knowledge (e.g., British Educational Research Association [BERA], 2014; Earl, 2015; Farley-Ripple et al., 2018; Greany & Maxwell, 2017). For example, Nelson and Campbell (2019) highlighted the need for practice-based evidence (e.g., professional judgement), research-based evidence (e.g., research studies) and data-based evidence (e.g., pupil performance) to be used in combination. In policy, the role of judgement and expertise was related to the political nature of policy-related decision making (Boaz & Nutley, 2019; Nutley et al., 2010). There was a need to balance the policy situation and issue (Parkhurst, 2017) with the needs and aims of different stakeholders (Hawkins & Parkhurst, 2016) and the types and applicability of different kinds of evidence (Breckon, 2016; Gluckman, 2011).

Other aspects of practitioner expertise that were highlighted across the sectors were specific capabilities needed for evidence use. In the health sector, several publications focused on individual capacities for evidence use (e.g., Baker-Erickzen et al., 2015; Craik & Rappolt, 2006; Mallidou et al., 2018). Mallidou et al. (2018), for example, identified 19 core competencies related to the knowledge, skills and attitudes needed to build capacity for research use in practice. Similar ideas were evident in the social care sector, with a number of publications highlighting the importance of practitioner reflection and critical thinking (Anastas, 2014; Austin et al., 2012; McCracken & Marsh, 2008), curiosity and interest (Austin et al., 2012; Gambrill, 2018), problem solving abilities (Ghanem et al., 2018), clinical-judgement skills (Austin & Leahy, 2015), research-mindedness (Austin et al., 2012; Karvinen-Niinikoski, 2005; McLaughlin, 2011), evaluation and decision making skills (Gambrill, 2018) and effective search- and critical-appraisal skills (Gambrill, 2018). Along similar lines, the education sector literature highlighted the importance of mindsets (e.g., Earl, 2015; Stoll et al., 2018a; Tripney et al., 2018), critical-thinking skills (e.g., Brown & Rogers, 2015; Earl & Timperley, 2009; Sharples, 2013; Spencer et al., 2012) and collaboration (e.g., Earl, 2015; Earl & Timperley, 2009; Greany & Maxwell, 2017).

Ways to develop, improve and evaluate expertise and capability were also highlighted in the literature. As part of building capacity, the education literature illustrated various tools to improve and evaluate individual and school-wide evidence use. These included individual measures of evidence use expertise, from novice through to expert (e.g., Brown & Rogers, 2015). Other measures focused on the continuous self-monitoring of individual and school engagement in research use (e.g., Stoll et al., 2018a, b). The notion of continuously improving school systems that relied on ongoing evidence-informed reflective practices (e.g., Brown, 2015; Brown & Greany, 2018; Coldwell et al., 2017), as well as intentional links to whole-school improvement initiatives (e.g., Creaby et al., 2017; Sharples et al., 2019), were also emphasised. The health sector focused on building organisational capacity to support research use as well (Brennan et al., 2017; Dobrow et al., 2006; Leeman et al., 2017). For example, Brennan et al. (2017) developed a tool to assess the specific individual and system-wide factors that influence an individual policy makers' research use (e.g., individual confidence, organisational tools, policy).

Overall, these discussions made clear the challenging nature of using evidence in practical contexts and the critical role that practitioner expertise, judgement and capability play in the process. These points are reflective of a "shift to an evidence-informed as opposed to evidence-based discourse" (Boaz et al., 2019, p. 370), which is about professional practice being informed by (not based on) research evidence and research evidence complementing (rather than replacing) professional knowledge. Even though these ideas about practitioner expertise were not explicitly linked to quality of use within many of the publications cited above, they nonetheless have important implications for the process of conceptualising quality use. As will become clear in Chapter 3, the above lines of thinking about practitioner expertise were significant in the development of the core and enabling components of our Quality Use of Research Evidence (QURE) Framework.

Significance of systems complexity

A second important cross-sector theme concerned the multi-level stake-holders and processes associated with evidence use and improvement within larger systems. The policy literature, for example, highlighted unique stakeholder complexities that involved policy makers and the public (Boaz & Nutley, 2019; Nutley et al., 2010). These complexities were further ex-acerbated by timeframes, where evidence at one point in the cycle may not be appropriate at another point (Breckon, 2016). A key insight from this sector was that quality evidence use was thought to be determined by the processes through which decisions were made and implemented, rather than by the outcomes produced within a policy making environment (Hawkins & Parkhurst, 2016; Parkhurst, 2017).

Many of the health frameworks highlighted the interactions between the actors (such as health professionals and patients), the evidence and the context (e.g., Ellen et al., 2011; Kitson et al., 1998; Ward et al., 2009). A key idea within the health literature was how evidence use needs to be con-ceptualised as a dynamic process, challenging notions of deterministic and linear knowledge transfer processes (Adams & Titler, 2013; Chambers et al., 2013; Ward et al., 2009). For example, Chambers and colleagues (2013, p. 1) argued that implementation involves "continued learning and problem solving, ongoing adaptation of interventions with a primary focus on fit between interventions and multi-level contexts, and expectations for ongoing improvement".

Similar ideas were also expressed in the other practice-based sectors. The social care literature stressed how evidence use needs to be an inherent and continuously evolving practice across the system (Avby et al., 2014; Ghate & Hood, 2019). For example, Ghate and Hood (2019, p. 104) argued that evidence use in social care should be about "mobilis[ing] evidence *in practice* (in contrast to simply moving evidence *into practice*)" (emphasis original). This perspective suggests that evidence use does not sit outside or alongside social care practice as a separate thing to consider or integrate, but must be inherent and continuously evolving in all aspects of the profession.

In the education sector, Sharples (2013, p. 24) suggested that the coordination across a "wide range of stakeholders – researchers, practitioners, policy makers and intermediaries" was needed for an "effective evidence ecosystem". Others also emphasised how system-level interactions across stakeholders and organisations could support high-quality evidence use (BERA, 2014; Godfrey, 2019). In this sector, school leaders played a central role in establishing a research-rich culture in their schools through, for example, the provision of policy and resources (e.g., Dyssegaard et al., 2017; Godfrey, 2019; Nelson & Campbell, 2019). Collaboration was also integral by connecting colleagues within a school with other education stakeholders in the forms of networks and partnerships (e.g., Bryk et al., 2011; Farley-Ripple et al., 2018, Nelson & Campbell, 2019). Within systems, research use also needed to be prioritised at the policy level (Education Endowment Foundation [EEF], 2019; Farley-Ripple et al., 2018; Park, 2018).

Taken together, these discussions from the health, social care, policy and education sectors served to highlight the varying complexities involved in the improvement of evidence use. Such complexities, then, have potential implications for what is involved in the quality use of research evidence. As discussed in the next chapter, these ideas were important in shaping the enabling components and system-level influences of our QURE Framework.

Conclusion

This chapter has explored what has (and what has not) been written about quality of use within the evidence use literature in health, social care, policy and education. The aim was to understand if and how quality of use had been discussed and described within these four sectors, in order to inform how we might conceptualise quality use of research evidence in education.

Our systematic review and narrative synthesis of the cross-sector literature showed, firstly, that there is a general shortage of explicit work on quality use. While there were many different evidence use models and approaches within the literature, these had usually not explicitly addressed the issue of quality evidence use. Across all sectors, there was a lack of clear definitions and descriptions of quality use, either as a concept or as a practice. The ideas presented in this book are therefore responding to a gap in the evidence use literature, not just within education, but also in health, social care and policy.

In understanding quality use as a gap, this chapter has also made clear that, secondly, there was a small number of studies where quality of use had been in focus. These included discussions about what evidence-based medicine is (Sackett et al., 1996), what productive evidence-informed conversations involve (Earl & Timperley, 2009), what supports depth of evidence use (Farley-Ripple et al., 2018), how to rate evidence use in policy documents (Rutter & Gold, 2015) and what constitutes good use of evidence within policy processes (Parkhurst, 2017). From the perspective of conceptualising quality use of research in education, these studies are helpful in raising questions about the manner in which evidence is used, suggesting vocabulary that might help to capture higher-quality use, unpacking different aspects of using evidence better and emphasising the context-specific nature of quality use.

Thirdly, this chapter has explained how there were themes cutting across the different sectors that had implicit or indirect links to the issue of quality of use. The importance of practitioner expertise in using evidence in context was one such theme. This theme highlighted the challenging nature of using evidence in practical contexts and the critical role that practitioner expertise, judgement and capability play in the process. The other cross-sector theme concerned system complexity and the multi-level stakeholders and processes associated with evidence use improvement. This theme emphasised the need to focus on interactions across different system levels and activities that enable and support evidence use. While not explicitly linked to quality of use, both of these themes have implications for conceptualising quality use of research in education. As will become clear in Chapter 3, ideas about practitioner expertise and systems complexity were important in shaping the core and enabling components of our QURE Framework.

Overall, this chapter's exploration of quality use as a gap gives rise to two main considerations. One is the need for more significant and sustained research into the issue of quality research use. The concept of quality use as a gap can be helpful, then, as a stimulus for researchers, research funders and others to initiate, encourage and support future work on this topic. There are many different ways in which such a stimulus may play out but one example from the work of a specific philanthropic research funder can be seen in Vignette 1.

Vignette 1 ("How is it helpful?") – "Quality use of research as a gap" informing the strategy of a research funder

This vignette features a philanthropic foundation that invests in research to improve the lives of young people. For some years, this organisation's work has involved a strategic focus on strengthening the use of research by state and local decision makers in ways that benefit youth. In line with this focus, it has had a range of research grant schemes for studies related to different aspects of improving the use of research evidence.

Two recent developments in this organisation's approach, though, can be seen as connected and responsive to the idea of "quality use of research as a gap":

- **In 2022, the organisation published an essay reflecting on the research use field, which highlighted quality research use as a priority for future study**. In connection with "getting to impact", the essay argued that "to get to societal outcomes we need a clearer sense of what it means for research to be used well". Building on this argument, it made clear that "We welcome proposals that theorise what it means to use research well and that empirically study quality research use".
- **During the same year, the organisation established a special interest group on "conceptualising the quality of research use"**. This group sought to bring together participants from different disciplinary orientations and areas of content expertise "to consider potential characteristics that contribute to or indicate the quality of research use". In an early communication from the group, it was explained that "the time is ripe for the research use field to take stock of its theoretical foundations and address the question of how best to conceptualise and characterise what it means to use research evidence well".

This vignette provides an example of how the concept of quality of use and the idea of quality use being a gap within the research use literature has been relevant and helpful to a philanthropic research funder. In particular, it shows how quality use of research as a gap was influential on the direction of their funding strategy in terms of earmarking quality use as a priority for future study and convening a group of researchers to work on this issue as a cross-disciplinary challenge.

Another consideration stemming from this chapter is that, even though quality use is a gap, future efforts to conceptualise quality use of research should not be seen as starting from scratch. In other words, there are individual studies and cross-sector themes that are potentially relevant and helpful for conceptualising quality research use. The way in which this has played out in our own work will become clear in the next chapter's exploration of "quality use as an aspiration".

References

Adams, S., & Titler, M. (2013). Implementing evidence-based practice. In M. Foreman & M. Mateo (Eds.), *Research for advanced practice nurses: From evidence to practice* (pp. 321–350). Springer.

Anastas, J. W. (2014). When is research good evidence? Issues in reading research. *Journal of Clinical Social Work, 42*, 107–115. 10.1007/s10615-013-0452-3

Anderson, I. (2011). Evidence, policy and guidance for practice: A critical reflection on the case of social housing landlords and antisocial behaviour in Scotland. *Evidence & Policy, 7*(1), 41–58. 10.1332/174426411X552990

Avby, G., Nilsen, P., & Dahlgren, M. A. (2014). Ways of understanding evidence-based practice in social work: A qualitative study. *The British Journal of Social Work, 44*, 1366–1383. 10.1093/bjsw/bcs198

Austin, B. S., & Leahy, M. J. (2015). Construction and validation of the clinical judgement skill inventory: Clinical judgement skill competencies that measure counsellor debiasing techniques. *Rehabilitation Research, Policy, and Education, 29*(1), 27–46. 10.1891/2168-6653.29.1.27

Austin, M. J., Dal Santo, T. S., & Lee, C. (2012). Building organizational supports for research-minded practitioners. *Journal of Evidence-Based Social Work, 9*(1–2), 174–211. 10.1080/15433714.2012.636327

Baker-Ericzén, M., Jenkins, J., Park, M., & Garland, M. (2015). Clinical decision-making in community children's mental health: Using innovative methods to compare clinicians with and without training in evidence-based treatment. *Child & Youth Care Forum, 44*(1), 133–157. 10.1007/s10566-014-9274-x

Boaz, A., & Nutley, S. (2019). Using evidence. In A. Boaz, H. Davies, A. Fraser, & S. Nutley (Eds.), *What works now? Evidence-informed policy and practice* (pp. 251–277). Policy Press.

Boaz, A., Davies, H., Fraser, A., & Nutley, S. (2019). *What works now? Evidence-informed policy and practice.* Policy Press.

Breckon, J. (2016). *Using research evidence: A practice guide.* Alliance for Useful Evidence.

Brennan, S. E., McKenzie, J. E., Turner, T., Redman, S., Makkar, S., Williamson, A., Haynes, A., & Green, S. E. (2017). Development and validation of SEER (Seeking, Engaging with and Evaluating Research): A measure of policymakers' capacity to engage with and use research. *Health Research Policy and Systems, 15*(1), 1. 10.1186/s12961-016-0162-8

British Educational Research Association. (2014). *Research and the teaching profession: Building the capacity for a self-improving education system (Final Report).* https://www.thersa.org/globalassets/pdfs/bera-rsa-research-teaching-profession-full-report-for-web-2.pdf

Brown, C. (2015). Conclusion: Leading the use of research in schools. In C. D. Brown (Ed.). *Leading the use of research and evidence in schools* (pp. 153–160). Institute of Education Press.

Brown, C., & Greany, T. (2018) The evidence-informed school system in England: Where should school leaders be focusing their efforts? *Leadership and Policy in Schools, 17*(1), 115–137. 10.1080/15700763.2016.1270330

Brown, C., & Rogers, S. (2015). Knowledge creation as an approach to facilitating evidence informed practice: Examining ways to measure the success of using this method with early years practitioners in Camden (London). *Journal of Educational Change, 16*(1), 79–99. 10.1007/s10833-014-9238-9

Bryk, A. S., Gomez, L. M., Grunow, A., & Hallinan, M. T. (2011). Getting ideas into action: Building networked improvement communities in education. In M. Hallinan (Ed.), *Frontiers in sociology of education* (pp. 127–162). Springer. 10.1007/978-94-007-1576-9_7

Cain, T. (2015). Teachers' engagement with research texts: Beyond instrumental, conceptual or strategic use. *Journal of Education for Teaching, 41*(5), 478–492. 10.1080/02607476.2015.1105536

Chambers, D. A., Glasgow, R. E., & Stange, K. C. (2013). The dynamic sustainability framework: Addressing the paradox of sustainment amid ongoing change. *Implementation Science, 8*(1), 117. 10.1186/1748-5908-8-117

Claridge, J. A., & Fabian, T. C. (2005). History and development of evidence-based medicine. *World Journal of Surgery, 29*, 547–553. 10.1007/s00268-005-7910-1

Coldwell, M., Greany, T., Higgins, S., Brown, C., Maxwell, B., Stiell, B., Stoll, L., Willis, B., & Burns, H. (2017). *Evidence-informed teaching: An evaluation of progress in England. Research Report.* Department for Education. http://shura.shu.ac.uk/16140/

Cooper, A. & Levin, B. (2013). Research use by leaders in Canadian school districts. *International Journal of Education Policy and Leadership*, 8(7), 1–13. 10.22230/ijepl.2013v8n7a449

Craik, J., & Rappolt, S. (2006). Enhancing research utilization capacity through multifaceted professional development. *The American Journal of Occupational Therapy*, 60(2), 155–164. 10.5014/ajot.60.2.155

Creaby C., Dann, R., Morris, A., Theobald, K., Walker, M., & White, B. (2017). *Leading Research Engagement in Education: Guidance for organisational change*. Coalition for Evidence-Based Education. https://www.cebenetwork.org/sites/cebenetwork.org/files/CEBE%20-%20Leading%20Research%20Engagement%20in%20Education%20-%20Apr%202017.pdf

Cunningham, W. M. S., & Duffee, D. E. (2009). Styles of evidence-based practice in the child welfare system. *Journal of Evidence-Based Social Work*, 6(2), 176–197. 10.1080/15433710802686732

Davies, H., Boaz, A., Nutley, S., & Fraser, A. (2019) Conclusions: Lessons from the past, prospects for the future. In A. Boaz, H. Davies, A. Fraser, & S. Nutley (Eds.), *What works now? Evidence-informed policy and practice revisited* (pp. 359–382). Policy Press.

Dobrow, M. J., Goel, V., Lemieux-Charles, L., & Black, N. A. (2006). The impact of context on evidence utilization: A framework for expert groups developing health policy recommendations. *Social Science & Medicine*, 63(7), 1811–1824. 10.1016/j.socscimed.2006.04.020

Dyssegaard, C., Egelund, N., & Sommersel, H. (2017). *A systematic review of what enables or hinders the use of research-based knowledge in primary and lower secondary school*. Danish Clearinghouse for Educational Research. https://www.videnomlaesning.dk/media/2176/what-enables-or-hinders-the-use-of-research-based-knowledge-in-primary-and-lower-secondary-school-a-systematic-review-and-state-of-the-field-analysis.pdf

Earl, L. M. (2015). Reflections on the challenges of leading research and evidence use in schools. In C. D. Brown (Ed.), *Leading the use of research and evidence in schools* (pp. 146–152). Institute of Education Press.

Earl, L. M., & Timperley, T. (2009). Understanding how evidence and learning conversations work. In L. M. Earl & H. Timperley (Eds.), *Professional learning conversations* (pp. 1–12). Springer.

Education Endowment Foundation. (2019). *The EEF guide to becoming an evidence-informed school governor and trustee*. Education Endowment Foundation. https://educationendowmentfoundation.org.uk/public/files/Publications/EEF_Guide_for_School_Governors_and_Trustees_2019_-_print_version.pdf

Ellen, M., Lavis, J., Ouimet, M., Grimshaw, J., & Bédard, P. (2011). Determining research knowledge infrastructure for healthcare systems: A qualitative study. *Implementation Science*, 6(1), 60. 10.1186/1748-5908-6-60

Farley-Ripple, E., May, H., Karpyn, A., Tilley, K., & McDonough, K. (2018). Rethinking connections between research and practice in education: A conceptual framework. *Educational Researcher*, 47(4), 235–245. 10.3102/0013189X18761042

Gambrill, E. (2018). Contributions of the process of evidence-based practice to implementation: Educational opportunities. *Journal of Social Work Education, 54* (supp. 1), S113–S125. 10.1080/10437797.2018.1438941

Ghanem, C., Kollar, I., Fischer, F., Lawson, T. R., & Pankofer, S. (2018). How do social work novices and experts solve professional problems? A micro-analysis of epistemic activities and the use of evidence. *European Journal of Social Work, 21*(1), 3–19. 10.1080/13691457.2016.1255931

Ghate, D., & Hood, R. (2019). Using evidence in social care. In A. Boaz, H. Davies, A. Fraser, & S. Nutley (Eds.), *What works now? Evidence-informed policy and practice* (pp. 89–109). Policy Press.

Gluckman, P. (2011). *Towards better use of evidence in policy formation: A discussion paper*. Office of the Prime Minister's Science Advisory Committee.

Godfrey, D. (2019). Moving forward – How to create and sustain an evidence-informed school eco-system. In D. Godfrey & C. Brown (Eds.), *An ecosystem for research-engaged schools* (pp. 202–219). Routledge.

Gough, D., Oliver, S., & Thomas, J. (2017). *An introduction to systematic reviews*. Sage.

Graaf, G., & Ratliff, G. A. (2018). Preparing social workers for evidence-informed community-based practice: An integrative framework. *Journal of Social Work Education, 54* (supp. 1), S5–S19. 10.1080/10437797.2018.1434437

Greany, T., & Maxwell, B. (2017). Evidence-informed innovation in schools: Aligning collaborative research and development with high quality professional learning for teachers. *International Journal of Innovation in Education, 4*(2–3), 147–170. 10.1504/IJIIE.2017.088095

Greenhalgh, T., Robert, G., Macfarlane, F., Bate, P., & Kyriakidou, O. (2004). Diffusion of innovations in service organizations: Systematic review and recommendations. *Milbank Quarterly, 82*(4), 581–629. 10.1111/j.0887-378X.2004.00325.x

Hawkins, B., & Parkhurst, J. (2016). The 'good governance' of evidence in health policy. *Evidence & Policy, 12*(4), 575–592. 10.1332/174426415X14430058455412

Karvinen-Niinikoski, S. (2005). Research orientation and expertise in social work - Challenges for social work education. *European Journal of Social Work, 8*(3), 259–271, 10.1080/13691450500210756

Keenan, E. K., & Grady, M. D. (2014). From silos to scaffolding: Engaging and effective social work practice. *Clinical Social Work Journal, 42*, 193–204. 10.1007/s10615-014-0490-5

Kitson, A., Harvey, G., & Mccormack, B. (1998). Enabling the implementation of evidence based practice: A conceptual framework. *Quality in Health Care, 7*(3), 149–158.

Leeman, J., Calancie, L., Kegler, M., Escoffery, C., Herrmann, A., Thatcher, E., Hartman, M. A., & Fernandez, M. (2017). Developing theory to guide building practitioners' capacity to implement evidence-based interventions. *Health Education & Behavior, 44*(1), 59–69. 10.1177/1090198115610572

Levin, B. (2004). Making research matter more. *Education Policy Analysis Archives, 12*(56). 10.14507/epaa.v12n56.2004

Lomas, J., & Brown, A. D. (2009). Research and advice giving: A functional view of evidence-informed policy advice in a Canadian Ministry of Health. *The Milbank Quarterly, 87*(4), 903–926. 10.1111/j.1468-0009.2009.00583.x

Mallidou, A., Atherton, P., Chan, L., Frisch, N., Glegg, S., & Scarrow, G. (2018). Core knowledge translation competencies: A scoping review. *BMC Health Services Research, 18*(1), 1–15. 10.1186/s12913-018-3314-4

Mandinach, E. B., & Gummer, E. S. (2016). What does it mean for teachers to be data literate: Laying out the skills, knowledge, and dispositions. *Teaching and Teacher Education, 60*, 366–376. 10.1016/j.tate.2016.07.011

McCracken, S. G., & Marsh, J. C. (2008). Practitioner expertise in evidence-based practice decision making. *Research on Social Work Practice, 18*(4), 301–310. 10.1177/1049731507308143

McLaughlin, H. (2011). Promoting a research-minded culture in welfare organizations. *European Journal of Social Work, 14*(1), 109–121. 10.1080/13691457.2010.516631

Moore, P. (2006). *Iterative evidence synthesis programme: Hei Kete Raukura. Evidence based policy project report, August 2006*. Ministry of Education.

Morton, S., & Seditas, K. (2018). Evidence synthesis for knowledge exchange: Balancing responsiveness and quality in providing evidence for policy and practice. *Evidence & Policy, 14*(1), 155–167. 10.1332/174426416X14779388510327

Nelson, J., & Campbell, C. (2019). Using evidence in education. In A. Boaz, H. Davies, A. Fraser, & S. Nutley (Eds.), *What works now? Evidence-informed policy and practice* revisited (pp. 131–149). Policy Press.

Nutley, S., Morton, S., Jung, T., & Boaz, A. (2010). Evidence and policy in six European countries: Diverse approaches and common challenges. *Evidence & Policy, 6*(2), 131–144. 10.1332/174426410X502275

Nutley, S., Walter, I., & Davies, H. T. O. (2003). From knowing to doing: A framework for understanding the evidence-into-practice agenda. *Evaluation, 9*(2), 125–148. 10.1177/1356389003009002002

Nutley, S., Walter, I., & Davies, H. T. O. (2007). *Using evidence: How research can inform public services*. Policy Press.

Park, V. (2018). Leading data conversation moves: Toward data-informed leadership for equity and learning. *Educational Administration Quarterly, 54*(4), 617–647. 10.1177/0013161X18769050

Parkhurst, J. (2017). *The politics of evidence: From evidence-based policy to the good governance of evidence*. Routledge.

Penuel, W. R., Briggs, D. C., Davidson, K. L., Herlihy, C., Sherer, D., Hill, H. C., Farrell, C. C., & Allen, A-R. (2016). *Findings from a national survey of research use among school and district leaders*. National Center for Research in Policy and Practice. https://files.eric.ed.gov/fulltext/ED599966.pdf

Puttick, R. (2018). *Mapping the standards of evidence used in UK social policy*. Alliance for Useful Evidence. https://media.nesta.org.uk/documents/Mapping_Standards_of_Evidence_A4UE_final.pdf

Rickinson, M., Cirkony, C., Walsh, L., Gleeson, J., Salisbury, M., & Boaz, A. (2021). Insights from a cross-sector review on how to conceptualise the quality of use of research evidence. *Humanities and Social Sciences Communications, 8*, 141. 10.1057/s41599-021-00821-x

Rosen, A. (2003). Evidence-based social work practice: Challenges and promise. *Social Work Research, 27*(4), 197–208. 10.1093/swr/27.4.197

Rutter, J., & Gold, J. (2015). *Show your workings: Assessing how government uses evidence to make policy*. Institute for Government.

Sackett, D., Rosenberg, W., Gray, J., Haynes, R., & Richardson, W. (1996). Evidence based medicine: What it is and what it isn't. *BMJ, 312*(7023), 71–72. 10.1136/bmj.312.7023.71

Satterfield, J., Spring, B., Brownson, R., Mullen, E., Newhouse, R., Walker, B., & Whitlock, E. (2009). Toward a transdisciplinary model of evidence-based practice. *Milbank Quarterly, 87*(2), 368–390. 10.1111/j.1468-0009.2009.00561.x

Sharples, J. (2013). *Evidence for the frontline: A report for the Alliance for Useful Evidence*. https://apo.org.au/node/34800

Sharples, J., Albers, B., Fraser, S., & Kime, S. (2019). *Putting evidence to work: A school's guide to implementation: Guidance report*. https://educationendowmentfoundation.org.uk/education-evidence/guidance-reports/implementation

Spencer, T. D., Detrich, R., & Slocum, T. A. (2012). Evidence-based practice: A framework for making effective decisions. *Education and Treatment of Children, 35*(2), 127–151. 10.1353/etc.2012.0013

Stoll, L., Greany, T., Coldwell, M., Higgins, S., Brown, C., Maxwell, B., Stiell, B., Willis, B., & Burns, H. (2018a). *Evidence-informed teaching: Self-assessment tool for teachers*. Chartered College of Teachers. https://iris.ucl.ac.uk/iris/publication/1533174/1

Stoll, L., Greany, T., Coldwell, M., Higgins, S., Brown, C., Maxwell, B., Stiell, B., Willis, B., & Burns, H. (2018b). *Evidence-informed teaching: Self-assessment tool for schools*. Chartered College of Teachers.

Thoma, A., & Eaves III, F. F. (2015). A brief history of evidence-based medicine (EBM) and the contributions of Dr David Sackett. *Aesthetic Surgery Journal, 35*(8), NP261–NP263. 10.1093/asj/sjv130

Tripney, J., Gough, D., Sharples, J., Lester, S., & Bristow, D. (2018). *Promoting teacher engagement with research evidence*. Wales Centre for Public Policy. https://www.wcpp.org.uk/wp-content/uploads/2018/11/WCPP-Promoting-Teacher-Engagement-with-Research-Evidence-October-2018.pdf

Ward, V., House, A., & Hamer, S. (2009). Developing a framework for transferring knowledge into action: A thematic analysis of the literature. *Journal of Health Services Research & Policy, 14*(3), 156–164. 10.1258/jhsrp.2009.008120

Quality use of research as an aspiration

3

Chapter overview

This chapter presents a conceptual framework to define and elaborate what quality use of research evidence means in relation to education. Drawing on ideas from our cross-sector systematic review and narrative synthesis as well as stakeholder consultation, it argues that high-quality use of research:

- can be defined as "thoughtful engagement with and implementation of appropriate research evidence, supported by a blend of individual and organisational enabling components and system-level influences";
- depends on the research evidence being rigorous and fit for context (appropriate) and the engagement and implementation being critical and deliberative (thoughtful);
- requires educators with particular skillsets (skills and knowledge), mindsets (values and dispositions) and relationships (interpersonal connections and capabilities);
- needs supportive organisational leadership (vision and modelling), culture (ethos and values), infrastructure (time and resources) and system-level influences;

DOI: 10.4324/9781003353966-3

- invites reflection about current approaches to using research and supporting research use at the individual, organisational and system levels; and
- has implications for anyone who is interested in strengthening the role of research within school and system improvement.

Introduction

The preceding chapter highlighted a lack of explicit discussion about quality use of research within the fields of health, social care, policy and education. However, it also showed that there are a small number of individual studies and certain cross-sector themes that are potentially relevant and helpful for the task of conceptualising quality research use. Drawing on these ideas from our systematic review and narrative synthesis, this chapter explores how quality use of research can be conceptualised in education. It presents a way of defining what high-quality use of research means and how it can be framed in terms of its core and enabling components. In this way, it moves the focus from quality use of research as a gap to "quality use of research as an aspiration".

Conceptualising what constitutes quality use of research in education, as well as the different factors and forces that shape it, is neither simple nor straightforward. As will become clear in the following sections, we define quality use of research as "thoughtful engagement with and implementation of appropriate research evidence" (Rickinson et al., 2020b, p. 6). Then, through our Quality Use of Research Evidence (QURE) Framework, we argue that it is a process that requires "a blend of individual and organisational enabling components and system-level influences" (Rickinson et al., 2020b, p. 6).

The remainder of this chapter is organised into seven sections. We begin by considering what is involved in understanding quality use of research as an aspiration and how this perspective on quality use relates to others within the book. The next five sections then introduce the QURE Framework as a whole, before unpacking its core components, individual-level enabling components, organisational-level enabling components and system-level influences. The chapter then concludes by reflecting on the potential implications of quality use of research as an aspiration for improving research use within and across schools and systems.

Understanding quality use as an aspiration

Understanding quality use as an aspiration is about asking questions such as: What does it mean to use research well in education? What is at the core of using research well? And what does using research well require of education professionals, education organisations and education systems? Our answers to these questions are aspirational in nature because they are seeking to articulate what is involved in and what enables *high-quality* use of research or using research *well*. The ideas presented are also conceptual in nature because they are based on secondary (synthesis of relevant literature) as opposed to primary (investigation of relevant practice) research. However, the later chapters about quality use of research as a capacity, a culture, a practice and a system will move the discussion from the conceptual (i.e., What does quality use mean?) to the practical (i.e., What does quality use look like in practice?).

To address the above questions about quality use of research as an aspiration, we drew on and worked with the insights generated by our systematic review and narrative synthesis as described in Chapter 2. The synthesis process led to four sector-specific narratives that summarised how quality use had been described and conceptualised within the fields of health, social care, policy and education. In order to move towards a way of defining and framing quality use of research evidence that was specific for education, these sector narratives underwent two stages of analysis.

The first stage involved thematic analyses to inductively identify cross-sector insights related to quality use of research evidence across the health, social care and policy narratives. For example, as explained in Chapter 2, all of these three sectors emphasised the importance of practitioner expertise in the evidence use process and the complexity of evidence use improvement within systems. These kinds of cross-sector insights were then compared with an early framing of quality use which had been developed prior to the cross-sector review (Rickinson et al., 2020a). This process led to the early framing of quality use being modified and updated in several ways, such as the core component of "thoughtful use" being broadened to "thoughtful engagement and implementation" in order to encompass implementation explicitly, and the enabling components being organised into two levels to distinguish between individual-level and organisational-level enablers (see Appendix 1 for more details).

The second stage then involved taking this updated quality use framing and seeking to make it specific and relevant for education. Drawing on the education sector literature, each of the components of quality use of research evidence was elaborated in response to the following questions: "What is it?", "Why is it important?" and "What does it involve?". This process led to the development of the QURE Framework that is introduced in the next section. Another important part of this process was sharing our evolving ideas and framework iterations with various project partners and stakeholders locally, nationally and internationally. Feedback received through stakeholder meetings, workshops and conferences informed further refinement of the framework.

The chapter's next five sections present and unpack our understanding of quality use of research as an aspiration in terms of the:

- QURE Framework as a whole;
- core components;
- individual enabling components;
- organisational enabling components; and
- system-level influences.

The Quality Use of Research Evidence (QURE) Framework

Based on the insights generated by our systematic review and narrative synthesis, coupled with extensive stakeholder consultation, we came to define quality use of research evidence in education as:

> the thoughtful engagement with and implementation of appropriate research evidence, supported by a blend of individual and organisational enabling components within a complex system.
>
> (Rickinson et al., 2020b, p. 6)

As shown in Figure 3.1, this definition sees quality use of research evidence as:

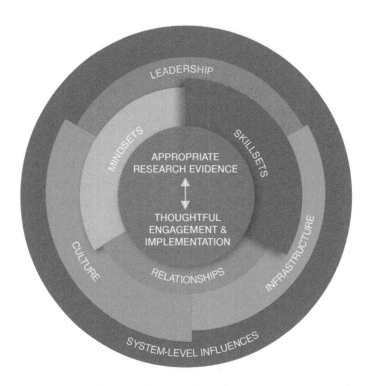

Figure 3.1 Quality Use of Research Evidence (QURE) Framework
Source: Rickinson et al. (2020b, p. 6).

- comprising two core components ("appropriate research evidence" and "thoughtful engagement and implementation") at the centre;
- being supported and surrounded by three individual-level enabling components ("skillsets", "mindsets", "relationships") and three organisational-level enabling components ("leadership", "culture", "infrastructure"); and
- being shaped by wider "system-level influences".

It is helpful to consider what this framework's different components mean at a high level. As set out in Figure 3.2, the two core components highlight the dual need for the research evidence to be appropriate and for the engagement and implementation to be thoughtful. The individual enabling components emphasise the technical, emotional and relational capacities that are required to use research well. The organisational enabling components underline the need for supportive school leadership, culture and infrastructure. Meanwhile,

CORE COMPONENTS

APPROPRIATE RESEARCH EVIDENCE

The need for research evidence to be not only methodologically rigorous, but also appropriate for the educational issue, the context and intended use.

THOUGHTFUL ENGAGEMENT AND IMPLEMENTATION

Critical engagement with the research evidence, shared deliberation about its meaning and effective integration of aspects of the evidence within practice.

ENABLING COMPONENTS - INDIVIDUAL LEVEL

SKILLSETS

The knowledge and capabilities that are required to thoughtfully engage with and implement appropriate research evidence.

MINDSETS

The dispositions, attitudes and values that are required to thoughtfully engage with and implement appropriate research evidence.

RELATIONSHIPS

The interpersonal processes and connections that are required to thoughtfully engage with and implement appropriate research evidence.

ENABLING COMPONENTS - ORGANISATIONAL LEVEL

LEADERSHIP

The organisational vision, commitments and role models that support thoughtful engagement with and implementation of appropriate research evidence.

CULTURE

The organisational ethos, values and norms that support thoughtful engagement with and implementation of appropriate research evidence.

INFRASTRUCTURE

The organisational structures, resources and processes that support thoughtful engagement with and implementation of appropriate research evidence.

SYSTEM-LEVEL INFLUENCES

The complex interactions and inter-dependencies across the education sector to support thoughtful engagement with and implementation of appropriate research evidence.

Figure 3.2 Components of the Quality Use of Research Evidence (QURE) Framework

Source: Rickinson et al. (2020b, p. 6).

the system-level influences underscore the system dimensions of quality use of research.

It is also helpful to consider what these components might involve and look like in a context of practice. The vignette below shows how several aspects of the QURE Framework can be seen within the work of a middle leader developing a new whole-school wellbeing programme.

Vignette 2 ("Looks like in practice") – "Quality use of research as an aspiration" within the work of a high school middle leader

This vignette features Claire, a middle leader who works at a secondary school. In her own practice as a teacher, Claire "love[s] the idea of research and loves learning", but when "embarking on [her] middle leadership experience [she] felt out of touch with research".

At the time of speaking with the Q Project, Claire was leading the development and implementation of a new wellbeing program across the middle years. She saw this as an important opportunity to reconnect with research. In particular, ensuring that the program "was backed with research evidence was [...] really important for its credibility and legitimacy". She explained that despite facing time deadlines which made "it tempting to not use research evidence properly [...], I really committed to it with my team and felt that that was really important".

When sourcing research to inform the programme, Claire found it challenging to know where to start looking. For this reason, she "rel[ied] pretty heavily on mentors who were able to give [...] some suggestions". This provided her with a starting point to source research that was relevant to her initiative. Yet Claire also wanted to ensure that the research was relevant to her school, noting that they "have quite a strong values framework". As a result, when appraising research, she also considered whether it aligned or "set with [the] values at our school".

At the same time, Claire also described herself as someone who has a "habit [...] of going to the end point and trying to get to the answer quite quickly". She recognised the need to "resist that temptation" and engage deeply with the research. For this reason, she sought out coaching from her principal to develop some strategies to "sit back and reflect [... as well as] read things with different perspectives". In doing so, Claire found that the research "challenged some of [... her] preconceptions" about how the programme should be designed, which she explains led to "some good opportunities" that helped to ensure it had a positive impact for the students.

Claire's vignette highlights a number of elements of "quality use as an aspiration" in practice:

- Claire recognised the need for research to be relevant to her purpose as well as her school and its values, reflecting the core QURE component of *appropriate research*. Here, the individual enabler of *relationships* was important for accessing and appraising appropriate research.
- Despite Claire's tendency to get to the answer quickly, she recognised the importance of engaging critically with research and slowly reflected on its meaning, aligning with the core QURE component of *thoughtful engagement with research*. This was supported by the organisational enabler of *leadership* as evidenced through the coaching and mentorship provided by her principal.
- Claire's approach to using research well was underpinned by a deep appreciation for the positive value of using research, which reflects the individual enabling component of *mindsets*. She also saw using research well as a means to develop her research use *skillsets* – another individual enabling component.

With this example in mind, we can now turn to a more detailed discussion of each of the framework's different components.

Core components

At the centre of the QURE Framework are two aspirations – for the research evidence to be *appropriate* and for the engagement and implementation of research evidence to be *thoughtful*. Both of these core components have links to ideas within the cross-sector literature discussed in Chapter 2. The need for research evidence to be appropriate, for example, connects to the idea of using evidence in context which was central to the importance of practitioner expertise within the health, social care and education literature.

Similarly, the need for thoughtful engagement and implementation links to calls from specific authors for evidence to be used in ways that are, for example, "conscientious, explicit and judicious" (Sackett et al., 1996, p. 71) or "deep" (Farley-Ripple et al., 2018, p. 238). It is important to stress that these two core components are highly interdependent, in the sense that deciding on what is appropriate research evidence will depend on thoughtful engagement with the evidence and engaging and implementing thoughtfully will depend on the research evidence being appropriate.

Appropriate research evidence

Appropriate research evidence is about the quality and the context-specific nature of research evidence. From a use perspective, quality research evidence needs to be not only methodologically rigorous, but also appropriate for the educational issues, the context and the intended use. As Nutley and colleagues (2013, p. 6) argued, "evidence quality depends on what we want to know, why we want to know it and how we envisage that evidence being used". This involves understanding the strengths and weaknesses of different forms of research evidence, and how well the best available research evidence relates to or is applicable to a specific context (e.g., to a specific problem, decision, student or desired outcome) (Spencer et al., 2012; Stoll et al., 2018a). Reflection on the timing of the research evidence in relation to the problem (Farley-Ripple et al., 2018), its implementation and if the evidence is still relevant to the context (Boaz & Nutley, 2019) is also important. Perhaps most critically, this component involves understanding the potential and practicality of the best available research evidence to make a difference to teaching and learning (Stoll et al., 2018a). At its heart, the core component of appropriate research evidence is about moving away from a situation where "educational decisions are made using data that are available, rather than data that are appropriate" (Earl & Timperley, 2009, p. 8).

Thoughtful engagement and implementation

Our second core component – thoughtful engagement and implementation – is about critical engagement with the research evidence, shared deliberation about its meaning and effective integration of aspects of the evidence within practice. This component reflects how "using evidence is a thinking process"

(Earl, 2015, p. 149), which demands a depth of engagement between the user, the evidence and the way it is used. This is about viewing research use as an active process of professional learning, rather than "merely bringing new information about what works to bear on professional practice" (Cordingley, 2004, p. 80). It is also about recognising that research evidence "does not speak for itself" and so educators must actively "interpret and make meaning of it in order to use it" (Coburn, 2009, p. 71). This process requires educators to combine "their understanding of school context and existing effective practice with any new perspectives […] evidence provides" (Brown & Rogers, 2015, p. 77). As noted in Chapter 2, research evidence does not replace professional expertise. Rather, using evidence involves integrating "professional expertise with the best external evidence from research" (Sharples, 2013, p. 7).

The interdependent nature of these two core components suggests that high-quality use of research evidence is a sophisticated undertaking. It is therefore important to pay attention to the factors that can enable (or impede) its achievement at the individual, organisational and system levels.

Enabling components at the individual level

At an individual level, quality use of research evidence requires educators with particular skillsets, mindsets and relationships. As with the core components, these enabling components reflect lines of thinking that were evident in the cross-sector literature review discussed in the previous chapter. For example, the critical role that practitioner expertise plays in using evidence in context was a recurring theme across the different sectors, with many studies highlighting the importance of capabilities linked to skillsets, mindsets and relationships. The same was true for some of the publications that touched on aspects of quality of use which, for example, referred to the need for particular dispositions ("an inquiry habit of mind") and social processes ("relationships of respect and challenge") (Earl & Timperley, 2009, p. 3).

Skillsets

Skillsets refer to the knowledge and capabilities that are required to thoughtfully engage with and implement appropriate research evidence. There are significant knowledge and capabilities involved in being able to translate, apply and sustainably implement evidence-informed decisions and approaches in particular contexts. Specifically, this involves being able to access research, assess its quality and understand research approaches and methods (Brown & Greany, 2018; Earl, 2015; Stoll et al., 2018a). More broadly, this involves educators' ability to draw on their professional judgement (Coldwell et al., 2017) and combine their understanding of the context and existing practice with the research (Spencer et al., 2012). It also involves capabilities in "generating ideas, challenging assumptions, testing hypotheses, formulating plans and routinely monitoring progress and making adjustments" (Earl, 2015, pp. 149–150). It takes skill "to judiciously use, apply and develop research as an integral part of one's teaching" (Evans et al., 2017, p. 404) and can be "hard because [it] requires more than just adding evidence to the conversation" (Earl & Timperley, 2009, p. 3).

Mindsets

Alongside skillsets, mindsets are the dispositions, attitudes and values that are required to thoughtfully engage with and implement appropriate research evidence. This enabling component reflects the kinds of motivations and frames of mind that are required for more thoughtful engagement with and implementation of research evidence. For example, educators with a disposition toward evidence use have a questioning mind (Earl, 2015), a conscious need to engage with research (Stoll et al., 2018a) and an awareness of their own biases and assumptions (Earl, 2015; Evans et al., 2017; Spencer et al., 2012). Earl and Timperley (2009, p. 5) argue that "the disposition to be open to a range of interpretations" is probably more important than skills in evidence interpretation. It therefore requires critical reflection when engaging with and using evidence. Mindsets also involve the need to be positive towards research use (Tripney et al., 2018) and to see it as relevant and applicable (Stoll et al., 2018a). Stoll and colleagues (2018a, p. 6) describe "an evidence mindset" as one where teachers believe that using evidence can support their own self-directed development and improve their teaching.

Relationships

In addition to skillsets and mindsets, another individual enabling component is relationships – that is, the interpersonal processes and connections that are required to thoughtfully engage with and implement appropriate research evidence. Using research evidence well is not an isolated, individual activity. It requires effective input from, and ongoing interactions with, others within and beyond the school. It is important, for example, to have "trusted colleagues to help dig deeper into understanding the [...] evidence and considering appropriate instructional, structural or policy changes" (Finnigan & Daly, 2014, p. 182). It is also important for such interactions to move "beyond superficial talk to exploring deeper meanings" (Timperley & Earl, 2009, p. 124) and to "bring to light assumptions and contribute to the development of shared understanding that move beyond individual ways of thinking" (Coburn et al., 2009, p. 83). As Coldwell et al. (2017, p. 28) explain, external research evidence "only leads to sustained change if there is time for informed debate and teachers can see the impact in practice". Relationships can also extend beyond the school to include conversations and collaborations with other practitioners, researchers and research brokers (Bryk et al., 2011; Farley-Ripple et al., 2018; Nelson & Campbell, 2019).

Enabling components at the organisational level

As well as educators with appropriate skillsets, mindsets and relationships, quality use of research also requires organisational contexts with supportive leadership, culture and infrastructure. Similar to other components of the QURE Framework, these organisation-level enabling components reflect ideas and arguments within the evidence use literature discussed in Chapter 2. The cross-sector theme about the importance of practitioner expertise, for example, included discussions about building organisational capacity to support research use and forging intentional links between research use and improvement processes.

Leadership

Leadership is about the organisational vision, commitment and role models that support thoughtful engagement with and implementation of appropriate research evidence. Leadership is central to effective evidence use at all levels of organisations and systems. At the school level, leadership was identified as a key leverage point for developing and maintaining a research-engaged school culture (e.g., Dyssegaard et al., 2017; Godfrey, 2019; Nelson & Campbell, 2019). In schools that strongly support research in the UK, for example, senior leaders were found to "play a key role, acting as intermediaries and facilitators of access to, engagement with and use of research evidence for staff in their schools" (Coldwell et al., 2017, p. 7). Importantly, though, this influence is not only about the way leaders can support others to use evidence, it is also about how they can model research engagement through their own outlooks and actions (Godfrey & Hanscomb, 2019). In addition, leadership approaches that include shared or distributed leadership models have been shown to positively influence research use (Cain, 2019; Dyssegaard et al., 2017). Middle leaders, for example, can play an important role in supporting staff to be able to access, evaluate, understand and use research evidence and research-informed practice (Cain, 2019; Stoll et al., 2018b).

Culture

Alongside leadership, culture takes into consideration the organisational ethos, values and norms that support thoughtful engagement with and implementation of appropriate research evidence. As reported two decades ago: "The main barriers to knowledge use in the public sector are not at the level of individual resistance but originated in an institutional culture that does not foster learning" (Hemsley-Brown & Sharp, 2003, p. 460). There is a need, therefore, for research use to be a cultural norm that is embedded within an organisation's "outlook, systems and activity" (Handscomb & MacBeath, 2003, p. 10). Critically important is an ethos that encourages staff to regularly reflect on their practice, take risks and try different approaches based on evidence (Brown et al., 2017). Brown and Greany (2018, p. 188), for example, describe research-engaged schools as ones with "a deliberate strategic and developmental approach toward fostering evidence-informed practices and cultures across all staff". Ultimately, a school seeking to improve its culture of research evidence use sees a shift in "teachers' beliefs about the value of systematically collected evidence, and in professional norms and discourse around the consideration of such evidence" (Parr & Timperley, 2008, p. 58).

Infrastructure

As well as leadership and culture, quality research use also depends on supportive infrastructure – that is, the organisational structures, resources and processes that support thoughtful engagement with and implementation of appropriate research evidence. There is a need for strategies such as the allocation of time, space and budget for research use, the creation of school-based research coordinators or champions, the establishment of links with external research partners and networks, and the development of formal and informal processes to support staff learning and deliberation about research and practice (Cain, 2019). These kinds of investments and initiatives are important because educators need "access to facilities and resources (both on-site and online) that support sustained engagement with and in research" (British Educational Research Association [BERA], 2014, p. 7). It is critical that staff, both individually and collectively, have the time and space to consider how research can inform their practice (Coldwell et al., 2017). Access to and use of research can also be supported by links to external research partners and intermediaries beyond the school (Farley-Ripple et al., 2018), often in connection with system-level influences.

System-level influences

System-level influences are about the complex interactions and inter-dependencies across the education sector that can support thoughtful engagement with and implementation of appropriate research evidence. Their presence within the QURE Framework reflects the cross-sector theme of systems complexity which, as discussed in Chapter 2, highlights the importance of multi-level stakeholders and processes in evidence use improvement within larger systems.

System-level influences, then, recognise that teachers, schools, evidence and its generation do not exist in isolation, but are part of a broader education system with diverse purposes and processes that can affect research use in different ways. Internationally, there is growing support for under-standing and improving evidence use through system-wide approaches that focus on building connections between evidence generation, synthesis, distribution and use to form effective "evidence ecosystems" (Boaz & Nutley, 2019, p. 251; Sharples, 2013). As Sharples (2013, p. 20) argues,

"If we are to create effective evidence ecosystems in social practice it is crucial we consider these elements as a whole".

It is also important, though, to consider system-level influences beyond the evidence ecosystem, such as the "wider political and societal systems" (Gough et al., 2018, p. 11). There is, for example, increased recognition for the (often limiting) impact that other system influences, such as accountability policies and improvement priorities, can have on research use in schools (Godfrey & Brown, 2019). That said, education systems can foster quality research use by prioritising research use at different levels such as regional, state and federal (Education Endowment Foundation [EEF], 2019; Farley-Ripple et al., 2018) and by providing funding and support to enable evidence-informed policy and practice (Nelson & Campbell, 2019). They can also embed research and data literacy training within initial teacher education, ongoing professional learning, teacher certification and professional standards (BERA, 2014; Coldwell et al., 2017; Nelson & Campbell, 2019; Stoll et al., 2018b; Tripney et al., 2018). System-level organisations can also be pivotal in supporting the synthesis and translation of research evidence for practice (Bryk et al., 2011; Farley-Ripple et al., 2017; Levin, 2013; Sharples et al., 2019; Tripney et al., 2018).

Conclusion

This chapter has put forward a way of conceptualising quality use of research evidence within education. Drawing on ideas and themes from the cross-sector review of literature discussed in Chapter 2 as well as stakeholder consultation, we have characterised high-quality research use as "thoughtful engagement with and implementation of appropriate research evidence" and argued that it is a process that requires "a blend of individual and organisational enabling components and system-level influences". Through our QURE Framework, we have set out and elaborated different elements of quality use in terms of its core components, individual-level enabling components, organisational-level enabling components and system-level influences. Taken together, these ideas about quality use of research as an aspiration have potential implications in two areas: reflecting on current approaches to using research and reviewing current efforts to support research use.

In terms of reflecting on current approaches to using research, the QURE Framework can be seen as an invitation to question current practices in various ways. For example, it can stimulate individuals, teams, organisations or systems to ask:

- How willing are we to move from talking about *whether* we use evidence to talking about *how well* we use evidence?
- How committed are we to improving not just the *quality of evidence* but also the *quality of use*?
- How curious are we about the *appropriateness* of our evidence and the *thoughtfulness* of our engagement and implementation of that evidence?

These kinds of distinctions are, of course, easy to raise but hard to address. They are not meant as either/or binaries but, rather, as both/and continua that can help teachers, school leaders, system leaders and others to become more reflective about their current approaches to research evidence and its use.

In relation to reviewing current efforts to support research use, the ideas discussed within this chapter make clear that high-quality use of research evidence is sophisticated work that needs to be supported by a range of individual, organisational and system-level factors. The QURE Framework, then, can encourage school and system leaders to think carefully about how well they are modelling and fostering the development of:

- *Education professionals* with not only the knowledge and capabilities to understand research evidence, but also the dispositions and values to be open to its meaning and the relational sensitivity and capacity to work with others to figure out how to use it in context;
- *Education organisations* with not only the structures and processes to enable staff to engage with research, but also the ethos and values to make this a cultural norm and the leadership and commitment to demonstrate and promote its significance; and
- *Education systems* that support quality use of research not only within specific individuals, institutions or contexts but through coordinated interventions across multiple levels and with varied key stakeholders.

As we see it, the above points are potentially relevant for many different groups in education such as teachers, school leaders, teacher educators, system leaders, policy makers, funders, researchers and research brokers. To give one example, the vignette below shows how the concept of quality use as an aspiration has been relevant and helpful for an education policy maker. It illustrates how the QURE Framework components provided a way for a policy team to reflect on their current evidence use practices and raise questions about how they might support future improvements.

Vignette 3 ("How is it helpful?") – "Quality use of research as an aspiration" helping a system leader to reflect on his organisation's work

This vignette features Jonas, an experienced policy maker who works in the knowledge directorate of his national ministry of education. He has worked in the ministry for over 20 years and has a long-standing interest in evidence use in education. He has been part of several international networks to support learning and exchange between different countries about evidence-based policy.

During 2022, Jonas was invited to present a case study of evidence use within his organisation as part of a learning seminar with several other countries. He decided to focus on curriculum reform and "try to deconstruct and reconstruct the way evidence was used in that policy". He wanted to "tell the story in kind of a systematic way" and it was here that the idea of quality use as an aspiration became relevant.

He used the components of the QURE Framework as a means to "analyse the way evidence was being used" in the curriculum reform process. This process helped Jonas and his colleagues "to get much more nuanced about a few things", such as:

- The evidence they use – connected to the core component of *appropriate research evidence*, they became aware "that there are lots of different kinds of knowledge being used [...] and the type of evidence being used changes at different stages";
- The way they engage – connected to the second core component of *thoughtful engagement*, they saw clearly "that the use of evidence was fragmented, pragmatic and based on policy windows [...] it was not a thoughtful engagement"; and
- *The people who are involved* – connected to the enabling components of *relationships* and *skillsets*, they realised "that the composition of the team and the knowledge within the team was

really important [...] like former teachers, former inspectors, different disciplines, etc.".

These realisations have led to further work within Jonas' organisation around:

- Human resources strategy – Given the importance of team composition for evidence use, how do we hire new staff and support and promote existing staff with these skills in mind?
- Platforms for dialogue – Given the importance of thoughtful engagement, how do we develop platforms and structures for collaborative evidence appraisal?

This vignette provides an example of how the idea of quality use as an aspiration has been relevant and helpful to an education policy maker. In particular, it shows how the components of the QURE Framework provided a lens with which to systematically review their evidence use practices and identify current strengths and areas for future improvement.

Overall, this chapter has explored "quality use as an aspiration" by presenting a conceptual framework that defines and elaborates what quality use of research evidence means in relation to education. In the coming chapters, the discussion moves from the conceptual to the practical as we begin to engage with educators' perspectives on what quality use of research looks like and involves in the school context.

References

Boaz, A., & Nutley, S. (2019). Using evidence. In A. Boaz, H. Davies, A. Fraser, & S. Nutley (Eds.), *What works now? Evidence-informed policy and practice* (pp. 251–277). Policy Press.

British Educational Research Association. (2014). *Research and the teaching profession: Building the capacity for a self-improving education system (Final Report)*. https://www.thersa.org/globalassets/pdfs/bera-rsa-research-teaching-profession-full-report-for-web-2.pdf

Brown, C., & Greany, T. (2018). The evidence-informed school system in England: Where should school leaders be focusing their efforts? *Leadership and Policy in Schools, 17*(1), 115–137. 10.1080/15700763.2016.1270330

Brown, C., & Rogers, S. (2015). Knowledge creation as an approach to facilitating evidence informed practice: Examining ways to measure the success of using this method with early years practitioners in Camden (London). *Journal of Educational Change, 16*(1), 79–99. 10.1007/s10833-014-9238-9

Brown, C., Schildkamp, K., & Hubers, M. D. (2017). Combining the best of two worlds: A conceptual proposal for evidence-informed school improvement. *Educational Research, 59*(2), 154–172. 10.1080/00131881.2017.1304327

Bryk, A. S., Gomez, L. M., Grunow, A., & Hallinan, M. T. (2011). Getting ideas into action: Building networked improvement communities in education. In M. Hallinan (Ed.), *Frontiers in sociology of education* (pp. 127–162). Springer. 10.1007/978-94-007-1576-9_7

Cain, T. (2019). *Becoming a research-informed school: Why? What? How?* Routledge.

Coburn, C. E., Honig, M. I., & Stein, M. K. (2009). What's the evidence on district's use of evidence? In J. Bransford, D. J. Stipek, N. J. Vye, L. Gomez, & D. Lam (Eds.), *Educational improvement: What makes it happen and why?* (pp. 67–86). Harvard Educational Press.

Coldwell, M., Greaney, T., Higgins, S., Brown, C., Maxwell, B., Stiell, B., Stoll, L., Willis, B., & Burns, H. (2017). *Evidence-informed teaching: An evaluation of progress in England. Research Report.* Department for Education. http://shura.shu.ac.uk/16140/

Cordingley, P. (2004). Teachers using evidence: Using what we know about teaching and learning to reconceptualize evidence-based practice. In G. Thomas & R. Pring (Eds.), *Evidence-based practice in education* (pp. 77–87). Open University Press.

Dyssegaard, C., Egelund, N., & Sommersel, H. (2017). *A systematic review of what enables or hinders the use of research-based knowledge in primary and lower secondary school.* Danish Clearinghouse for Educational Research. https://www.videnomlaesning.dk/media/2176/what-enables-or-hinders-the-use-of-research-based-knowledge-in-primary-and-lower-secondary-school-a-systematic-review-and-state-of-the-field-analysis.pdf

Earl, L. M. (2015). Reflections on the challenges of leading research and evidence use in schools. In C. D. Brown (Ed.), *Leading the use of research and evidence in schools* (pp. 146–152). Institute of Education Press.

Earl, L. M., & Timperley, T. (2009). Understanding how evidence and learning conversations work. In L. M. Earl & H. Timperley (Eds.), *Professional learning conversations* (pp. 1–12). Springer.

Education Endowment Foundation. (2019). *The EEF guide to becoming an evidence-informed school governor and trustee.* Education Endowment Foundation. https://educationendowmentfoundation.org.uk/public/files/Publications/EEF_Guide_for_School_Governors_and_Trustees_2019_-_print_version.pdf

Evans, C., Waring, M., & Christodoulou, A. (2017). Building teachers' research literacy: Integrating practice and research. *Research Papers in Education, 32*(4), 403–423. 10.1080/02671522.2017.1322357

Farley-Ripple, E., Karpyn, A. E., McDonough, K., & Tilley, K. (2017). Defining how we get from research to practice: A model framework for schools. In M. Eryaman & B. Schneider (Eds.), *Evidence and public good in educational policy, research and practice* (pp. 79–95). Springer. 10.1007/978-3-319-58850-6_5

Farley-Ripple, E., May, H., Karpyn, A., Tilley, K., & McDonough, K. (2018). Rethinking connections between research and practice in education: A conceptual framework. *Educational Researcher, 47*(4), 235–245. 10.3102/00131 89X18761042

Finnigan, K. S., & Daly, A. J. (2014). Conclusion: Using research evidence from the schoolhouse door to Capitol Hill. In K. S. Finnigan & A. J. Daly (Eds.), *Using research evidence in education: From the schoolhouse door to Capitol Hill* (Vol. 2). Springer.

Godfrey, D. (2019). Moving forward – How to create and sustain an evidence-informed school eco-system. In D. Godfrey & C. Brown (Eds.), *An ecosystem for research-engaged schools* (pp. 202–219). Routledge.

Godfrey, D., & Brown, C. (Eds.) (2019). *An ecosystem for research-engaged schools.* Routledge.

Godfrey, D., & Handscomb, G. (2019). Evidence use, research-engaged schools and the concept of an ecosystem. In D. Godfrey & C. Brown (Eds.), *An ecosystem for research-engaged schools* (pp. 4–21). Routledge.

Gough, D., Maidment, C., & Sharples, J. (2018). *UK What Works Centres: Aims, methods and contexts.* EPPI Centre. https://discovery.ucl.ac.uk/id/eprint/10055465/1/UK%20what%20works%20centres%20study%20final%20report%20july%202018.pdf

Handscomb, G., & MacBeath, J. (2003). *The Research Engaged School.* Essex County Council, FLARE.

Hemsley-Brown, J., & Sharp, C. (2003). The use of research to improve professional practice: A systematic review of the literature. *Oxford Review of Education, 29*(4), 449–471. 10.1080/0305498032000153025

Levin, B. (2013). To know is not enough: Research knowledge and its use. *Review of Education, 1*(1), 2–31. 10.1002/rev3.3001

Nelson, J., & Campbell, C. (2019). Using evidence in education. In A. Boaz, H. Davies, A. Fraser & S. Nutley (Eds.), *What works now? Evidence-informed policy and practice revisited* (pp. 131–149). Policy Press.

Nutley, S., Powell, A., & Davies, H. (2013). *What counts as good evidence?* Alliance for Useful Evidence. https://research-repository.st-andrews.ac.uk/handle/10023/3518

Parr, J. M., & Timperley, H. (2008). Teachers, schools and using evidence: Considerations of preparedness. *Assessment in Education: Principles, Policy & Practice, 15*(1), 57–71. 10.1080/09695940701876151

Rickinson, M., Sharples, J., & Lovell, O. (2020a). Towards a better understanding of quality of evidence use. In S. Gorard (Ed.), *Getting evidence into education: Evaluating the routes to policy and practice* (pp. 218–133). Routledge.

Rickinson, M., Walsh, L., Cirkony, C., Salisbury, M., & Gleeson, J. (2020b). *Quality use of research evidence framework*. Monash University. 10.26180/14071508.v2

Sackett, D., Rosenberg, W., Gray, J., Haynes, R., & Richardson, W. (1996). Evidence based medicine: What it is and what it isn't. *BMJ, 312*(7023), 71–72. 10.1136/bmj.312.7023.71

Sharples, J. (2013). *Evidence for the frontline: A report for the Alliance for Useful Evidence*. https://apo.org.au/node/34800

Sharples, J., Albers, B., Fraser, S., & Kime, S. (2019). *Putting evidence to work: A school's guide to implementation: Guidance report*. Education Endowment Foundation. https://educationendowmentfoundation.org.uk/education-evidence/guidance-reports/implementation

Spencer, T. D., Detrich, R., & Slocum, T. A. (2012). Evidence-based practice: A framework for making effective decisions. *Education and Treatment of Children, 35*(2), 127–151. 10.1353/etc.2012.0013

Stoll, L., Greany, T., Coldwell, M., Higgins, S., Brown, C., Maxwell, B., Stiell, B., Willis, B., & Burns, H. (2018a). *Evidence-informed teaching: Self-assessment tool for teachers*. Chartered College of Teachers. https://iris.ucl.ac.uk/iris/publication/1533174/1

Stoll, L., Greany, T., Coldwell, M., Higgins, S., Brown, C., Maxwell, B., Stiell, B., Willis, B., & Burns, H. (2018b). *Evidence-informed teaching: Self-assessment tool for schools*. Chartered College of Teachers.

Timperley, H., & Earl, L. (2009). Using conversations to make sense of evidence: Possibilities and pitfalls. In L. M. Earl & H. Timperley (Eds.), *Professional learning conversations: Challenges in using evidence for improvement* (pp. 121–126). Springer.

Tripney, J., Gough, D., Sharples, J., Lester, S., & Bristow, D. (2018). *Promoting teacher engagement with research evidence*. Wales Centre for Public Policy. https://www.wcpp.org.uk/wp-content/uploads/2018/11/WCPP-Promoting-Teacher-Engagement-with-Research-Evidence-October-2018.pdf

4 Quality use of research as a capacity

> **Chapter overview**
>
> This chapter explores quality use of research as a professional capacity in terms of how educators' mindsets, skillsets and relationships can support them to use research well. Drawing on educators' survey and interview responses, it shows how:
>
> - educators' views about using research well provide strong support for the importance of the three individual enablers of mindsets, skillsets and relationships;
> - quality research use mindsets are ones that value research and its potential to guide practice and approach research use in thoughtful, reflective and open-minded ways;
> - skillsets are important in enabling educators to access, read and appraise research, as well as to understand research fit when implementing research-informed changes;
> - relationships within and beyond the school support educators to engage in specific research use tasks and share knowledge that underpins the quality use of research;
> - there are strong interconnections between educators' mindsets, skillsets and relationships, with each of these elements seen as supporting each other; and

DOI: 10.4324/9781003353966-4

- conceptualising quality use as a capacity is about leveraging educators' knowledge and experiences to better target improvement efforts around research use.

Introduction

Building on the previous chapter, the discussion now shifts from the conceptual to the empirical by examining educators' perspectives on the mindsets, skillsets and relationships that are needed to use research well in practice. As discussed in Chapter 1, recent decades have seen a growth of educational reform agendas that focus on research use as a means for continuous practice improvement. Given that educators are often positioned as the 'end-users' of educational research (e.g., Clinton et al., 2018), they and their research use capacities are a common focus within these agendas. The significance of practitioner expertise was also noted within the systematic review and narrative synthesis in Chapters 2 and 3, which emphasised the critical role that practitioner expertise and capabilities play in using research and evidence in context.

This chapter builds on these discussions by exploring educators' own perspectives about the personal attributes and capacities that they see as being important for using research well. To do so, it draws on data from Australian educators' survey responses (Survey 1, $n = 492$; Survey 2, $n = 819$; Survey 3, $n = 414$) and interview discussions ($n = 27$). The chapter brings both quantitative and qualitative data into discussion to highlight educators' assessments of their own research use capacities, as well as their views about the skillsets, mindsets and relationships that are important for improving their use of research in practice (see Appendix 1 for details about methods and samples).

Following this introduction, this chapter consists of five main sections. We begin by discussing what is meant by understanding "quality use as a capacity" and how these ideas are reflected in the individual components of our Quality Use of Research Evidence (QURE) Framework: mindsets, skillsets and relationships. Then there are three sections dedicated to exploring each of the individual components and how they support the quality use of research evidence. The chapter concludes with a summary of the key points and a discussion of their implications.

Understanding quality use as a capacity

Understanding quality research use as a capacity is about asking questions such as: What does quality research use look like and involve at an educator level? What does using research well require of educators as professionals? How can quality research use as a capacity be supported and enabled? Against the backdrop of growing interest in educational research use, these kinds of questions align with increasing interest in educators' capacities to engage with research (e.g., Malin et al., 2020; Nelson & Campbell, 2019). For example, research use at the level of educators' individual practice has been discussed in terms of research 'engagement' (Brown & Greany, 2018; Gleeson et al., 2023), valuing research (Cain, 2019), beliefs about and motivation to use research (Nelson et al., 2017) or ability to collaboratively work with research (Earl & Timperley, 2009). Another line of thinking has focused on how to support and improve educators' capacities to be research-informed (e.g., Coldwell et al., 2017) or effective research users (e.g., Evans et al., 2017; Nelson & O'Beirne, 2014).

In Survey 1 and follow-up interviews, educators' views about their capacities to use research well were investigated empirically by asking open-ended questions about their experiences of engaging with research and what 'helps staff in [their] school to use research well'. Importantly, these questions did not make any specific references to the QURE Framework or the individual enabling components of mindsets, skillsets and relationships. Rather, we encouraged educators to discuss what they would 'observe' or 'experience' if research was being used well. In discussing these aspects, many educators spoke about their current research use capacities as well as those that they would like to develop to use research better. We analysed educators' responses to these questions both inductively and deductively to the QURE Framework and, as illustrated in Table 4.1, the individual components of the

Table 4.1 Number and percentage of Survey 1 respondents (*n* = 492) and interviews (*n* = 27) coded to QURE Framework individual components

Themes	Using Research Well	
	Interviews	Surveys
Mindsets	89% (24)	64% (315)
Skillsets	89% (24)	91% (447)
Relationships	96% (26)	30% (148)

QURE Framework – mindsets, skillsets and relationships – featured strongly in educators' responses about using research well, particularly in interviews.

Additional understanding of quality use as a capacity was generated by including closed-response quantitative items in each of the three Q Project surveys about the perceived prevalence, importance and value of these individual capacities in educators' own practice. Each of these survey items probed slightly different aspects of educators' capacities to use research well, where Survey 1 included items about their personal beliefs, awareness and use of evidence and research, Survey 2 asked questions about their attitudes towards and behaviours regarding sharing evidence, and Survey 3 contained items about their views on different barriers and enablers for improving their research use.

As a result, a primary aim of this chapter is to bring these quantitative and qualitative data sources into conversation to understand how we can conceptualise quality research use as a capacity. In particular, we endeavour to articulate the mindsets, skillsets and relationships that are important for using research well by drawing on educators' insights about how these capacities underpin their quality use of research. We also discuss which aspects of these mindsets, skillsets and relationships that educators see as being pertinent areas for future improvement and development efforts. This is not about framing educators' current capacities to use research from a deficit perspective, but rather highlighting their own views and calls for support to use research better.

With these aims in mind, the next sections present our findings on quality research use as a capacity in terms of educators':

- Mindsets – the dispositions, attitudes and values in relation to research and its potential value and how it can be used well in practice;
- Skillsets – the knowledge and capabilities required to access, read and appraise research, as well as understand if research is appropriate when implementing research-informed changes; and
- Relationships – the variety of research use relationships that educators see as important, and how sharing knowledge within these relationships supports the quality use of research.

Although these aspects of quality use as a capacity will be discussed separately for ease of illustration, they are, in practice, closely imbricated (Rickinson et al., 2021). For this reason, as a prelude to our discussion of each aspect, the following vignette highlights how one primary school teacher leveraged all three when implementing a research-informed change to better support "students from poverty backgrounds".

Vignette 4 ("Looks like in practice") – "Quality use of research as a capacity" in the work of a primary school teacher

This vignette features Alex, a specialist teacher for students with disabilities at Park Walk State School. Working with many "students from poverty backgrounds", Alex and the school principal, Phoebe, wanted to use research to inform new trauma-related teaching practices. As Alex explained, though, to implement such change, both he and his colleagues needed to engage with research "properly" to achieve the improved student well-being and academic outcomes that they were seeking.

For Alex, quality research use starts with the right mindset. Alex describes himself and Phoebe as "self-starters" who are "very curious, adventurous people". These dispositions held them in good stead as they explored different research for its relevance to their school context. Alex also emphasised the importance of questioning, critical thinking and reflection when engaging with research. For example, he used guides and frameworks provided by his state-based Department of Education to interrogate poverty-related research for evidence of impact, potential transferability to his context, and credibility and rigour. He also reflected on what aspects of certain research studies could be easily "adopted" by his colleagues.

These types of dispositions were also important to foster in others. Alex felt that unless he "flip[ped] [his colleagues'] thinking" from seeing research use as a "burden" to their current workloads to something that would "make their life easier", the school would not embrace new ways of teaching and not achieve their intended goals. Alex then invested time in building relationships with his colleagues, focusing on understanding their openness to change to avoid "overwhelming them" with new ideas. He prioritised listening to them, seeking their input and scaffolding their engagement with selected research to help trial and implement the new teaching practices.

While mindsets and relationships were critical to using research well, Alex observed that certain skillsets were necessary to effectively implement research-informed change. In particular, he emphasised the importance of identifying a specific issue to address, staying focused on that single issue and using school data and evidence, alongside research, to fully understand the extent of the issue. Alex highlighted that "choosing the right research is at the heart of [using research well]". By applying certain appraisal skills, Alex ensured that the research they used to underpin their new teaching practices was "fit for purpose".

Alex's vignette highlights several elements of "quality use as a capacity" in practice:

- Before selecting certain research, Alex emphasised the importance of having the right *mindset* in being curious and open to thinking about how research might be relevant to his school context and intended practice change.
- Alex drew on data literacy and critical appraisal *skills* when engaging with school data to clearly identify a practice issue and before appraising research in relation to this issue. This helped Alex to select *appropriate research* (a core component of the QURE Framework) that was relevant, could be adapted and used easily by a range of staff.
- Using research well relies on the capacities of educators to build and sustain *relationships*, particularly in Alex's case as he collaborated with his colleagues to understand their openness to the research-informed change as well as to find and appraise research, understand it, apply it in practice and then evaluate the success of their efforts.

Mindsets

Many educators emphasised how their mindset was seen as a foundational capacity for quality research use and was especially "key to making it stick" in practice (middle leader, interview[1]). When they discussed their mindsets in relation to using research well, educators emphasised their beliefs, views and dispositions towards research and its potential impact and how research is used in practice.

Mindsets about research and its potential impact

In general, educators demonstrated positive mindsets about research and its contribution to their practice (referenced in 89% of interviews, 64% of surveys[2]). They characterised these mindsets as being "open to research" (senior leader, interview) and "see[ing] the value of it" (senior leader, interview) to inform professional decision making. When educators saw research as valuable, they described feeling passionate and excited about its use in practice, as one middle leader explained in an interview:

> I've been appointed into the [research lead] position, which I'm really excited about because I really love the work. I feel like this is the type of thing that I want to continue doing and direct my energy towards because I really see the value in it and the potential for this to have an impact.

The connection between educators' positive mindsets and their use of research in practice was also evident in their survey responses. For example, in Survey 1, 83% of educators 'agreed' or 'strongly agreed' that 'research will help improve student outcomes'. Educators who held this belief were significantly more likely to indicate that 'when confronted with a new problem or decision, [they] look for research that might be relevant' (69% vs. 43% for those who did not believe in the value of research, $p < .001$). These educators were also significantly more likely to report regularly using research to inform their practice (47% vs. 22%, $p < .001$).

For a few educators, their positive dispositions towards the value of research were related to their personal passions or their subject area (37% of interviews, 3% of surveys). To provide two examples, during interviews, one middle leader exclaimed, "I love research and I love thinking and reading. I always use it in my teaching practice", while a teacher reflected:

> I believe in evidence and research [...] and I would like to use it wherever possible. [...] I think my personal values come into it [...] that drive me to use evidence where possible. I'm a science teacher as well, so, that's what I teach the students, that you have to have evidence for what you're trying to claim.

73

However, educators' positive mindsets were largely based on how they saw research as complementing their professional knowledge and supporting their growth as an educator (81% of interviews, 63% of surveys). In Survey 3, for example, 86% of educators 'agreed' or 'strongly agreed' that they 'believe[d] in the benefits of using research' and 79% indicated 'want[ing] to complement [their] knowledge and experience with research'. Notably, 88% of educators who believed in the benefits of using research also wanted to complement their existing knowledge with research, suggesting a significant relationship between these two dispositions ($p < .001$). When educators felt that research supplemented their professional experience, they described it as strategically supporting their work. For example, one senior leader explained in an interview:

> I've got to do that professional reading that informs my practice, so that I know the practice and I know that what I'm doing is the right thing to do […] I've got the knowledge then to be able to do the strategic planning I do.

This idea was also seen in Survey 3, where educators most commonly indicated that 'using research [was] worthwhile' because it 'helps [them] make informed decisions' (82% 'agreed' or 'strongly agreed', most strongly endorsed item), 'complements [their] teaching experience and practice' (81%, equal 2nd endorsed item) and 'increases [their] professionalism' (80%, 3rd).

Finally, a number of educators also described how they adopted an openminded and inquisitive disposition towards research and how this can deepen their thinking (30% of interviews, 11% of surveys). In a survey response, one senior leader explained that using research well required "a community which is curious and engaged, where deep learning is occurring". Similarly, another senior leader explained in an interview that the "number one [disposition for using research well is] being curious about what it is [you're] trying to look into […] and I keep using the word 'inquiry' […] having the willingness to go forward with inquiry-oriented action into exploring what that research is". For these educators, being inquisitive involved using research to "challenge mental models […] and trial approaches in the classroom" (teacher, survey) by "finding new ways to think about existing practice [and] combining this thinking with contextual experience to design and evaluate next [steps in] practice" (middle leader, survey). As hinted in these quotes, these inquisitive dispositions about research were also related to the second way that educators' discussed quality use mindsets: their dispositions about how research is used in practice.

Mindsets towards how research is used in practice

Building on educators' curiosity towards and valuing of research as discussed above, they also spoke about being curious in terms of how it is used and approaching its implementation in thoughtful ways that "brought the research to life" (middle leader, interview). Key to this aspect of mindsets was educators seeing value in the processes of professional enquiry associated with quality research use, rather than just focusing on the outcomes of a research-informed initiative. For example, one senior leader described in a survey response that using research well involves:

> [Supporting] staff understanding of the research [...] [rather than] just implementing programmes; engaging and investing long term for improved outcomes not just a quick fix; matching site goals to the research and practice; [and] reflecting on the outcomes within the school context.

This notion of avoiding "a quick fix" mentality was reiterated in a survey response by another senior leader who reflected on her own journey of using research well which "rather than tak[ing] a 'solutions stance' and 'find [ing] a quick fix' [...] [involved taking] the time to inquire, learn and grow as a school community to ensure [the] approach would suit the school's unique context".

In this sense, educators emphasised approaching the use of research in a thoughtful and reflective manner, where engaging with research aimed to "prompt personal reflection and questioning" (senior leader, survey). In contrast, when research was used poorly, it was often described in terms of an "ad hoc approach with limited reflection" (teacher, survey). The value of these thoughtful and reflective mindsets was reinforced in Survey 3, where, when asked about the most important ways to improve their use of research, educators' two most strongly endorsed approaches were acts of reflection. Specifically, 73% indicated that it was 'important' or 'very important' to 'reflect on [their] own learning", while 79% saw it as important to 'reflect on students' learning outcomes'.

In connection with being thoughtful, open-minded and reflective, educators also emphasised how their approach involved engaging with research "very dynamically to make sure that we were [...] looking widely and thinking widely" (middle leader, interview). Their descriptions of this dynamic process often spoke about the need to critically engage with research by "using a critical mind" (other role, survey[3]) and "being willing to question" different aspects of the research base (teacher, survey). In a particularly notable example, one senior leader explained in an interview how he and his colleagues practised being open-minded by actively seeking out and critically engaging with research that made competing claims:

> We build from [our current practices] and we tend to focus on readings that support that [...] [but] then we try to read things that are against it and see where the differing views are. So, we're not just reading things to back up what we found. We also try to read the other side as well to see what the differences are and [...] to make sure [our practices] are reliable in terms of [the] research evidence.

Inherent in much of the discussion of educators' mindsets above is a focus on actively putting research-informed ideas into practice. Many identified with this disposition, with 62% of educators in Survey 3, for example, 'agreeing' or 'strongly agreeing' that they 'want to experiment with and trial new research ideas and knowledge'. When explicitly articulated, a number of educators spoke about the importance of having an aptitude towards experimentation and informed risk-taking in practice (30% of interviews, 8% of surveys). Common descriptions included being "pretty open [...] [and giving] things a good go" (senior leader, interview), "trying and being open to new ideas" (middle leader, survey) and "experiment[ing] within the classroom [by] taking risks within evidence-informed practice" (teacher, survey).

Importantly, educators emphasised that during these processes of experimentation it was "OK to try and fail" (senior leader, survey) because it is possible to "learn from successes and failures" (middle leader, survey). In this sense, experimenting with research was seen as one way to determine whether a research-informed initiative was worth investing in. As one teacher explained in an interview: "Having those little tries [...] being able to just do a little bit of a try with something to see if it works or doesn't work [...] [is how] we can see how things would be [...] and [determine] the work that we can use".

In the main, this section has illustrated how educators valued research and its contribution to practice in how it complemented their professional knowledge and supported their professional growth. In doing so, they also highlighted the value of approaching its use in open-minded and inquisitive ways by asking questions of research, reflecting on their practice and engaging in informed risk-taking. Mobilising these dispositions to use research well in practice, however, is a skilful undertaking to which we now turn.

Skillsets

Educators were clear that using research is highly skilled work (in 89% of interviews, 91% of surveys). In some cases, the skill-intensive nature of research use posed barriers, as just under half of educators (48%) in Survey 3 'agreed' or 'strongly agreed' that they 'find it easy to use research'. As might be expected, educators who felt that using research was not easy were significantly less likely to report regularly engaging with research (27% used it regularly) than those who found it easy to engage with (42%, $p = .001$). Despite these challenges, though, the overwhelming majority of educators were clear about the research-related skills required to use research well (81% of interviews, 85% of surveys). This section explores educators' discussions of these skills in relation to accessing, reading and critically appraising research, as well as understanding research fit when implementing research-informed changes.

Skills involved in accessing, reading and appraising research

As a first step towards using research well, many educators discussed the knowledge and skills regarding "avenues to access research" (senior leader, survey), being able to "access multiple sources of information" (other role, survey), and being able to locate research in ways that were "available, accessible, appropriate and efficient" (teacher, survey) (67% of interviews, 37% of surveys). Educators' emphasis on these skills is perhaps unsurprising given the barriers they face in relation to accessing research, as discussed in Chapters 5 and 7. For example, in Survey 1, just 32% of educators 'agreed' or 'strongly agreed' that they 'have sufficient access to research evidence'. As a result, they often described relying on alternative avenues for accessing research such as leveraging "'critical friend' access via a university" (middle leader, survey), "ringing one of my colleagues and hav[ing] a conversation" (middle leader, interview) or through "studying in university [...] [with] access to a wonderful library" (senior leader, interview).

A number of interviewees also spoke about the skills and knowledge that supported them to feel "more equipped [...] to select relevant readings" (middle leader, interview) (33% of interviews). Specifically, they emphasised that locating appropriate research did not occur in simple, ad hoc ways, but rather was a planned and involved process. For example, one teacher interviewee described their "structured approach" to accessing relevant information sources:

> We would [...] [determine] what our starting point was. So as a school, we talk a lot about [our jurisdiction's school improvement strategy] and so we might just go straight there [...] and then, when you look at that sort of information, there's internal links from that information to external sources [...] and so, you follow a bit of a chain from your starting point.

Similarly, a middle leader interviewee described the "active process" of "trawling to see if [...] [the research] answers the question that you had or solves the problem that you had". To do so effectively, educators explained that they required the technical skills to "access databases [...] [and] search for key terms" (senior leader, interview) alongside the capacity to select suitable research based on their broader knowledge of "what research there is" (senior leader, interview).

Notably, educators' survey responses indicated that they were confident in their knowledge of different research sources, with two-thirds of educators in Survey 1 (65%) indicating that they 'kn[ew] where to find relevant research that may help to inform [their] teaching practices'. However, they also pointed to challenges in navigating and dealing with the large amounts of information available via these sources (22% of interviews, 4% of surveys). During interviews, for example, one senior leader described being "quite overwhelmed with the volume of literature out there", while a middle leader noted how "the volume of research that does exist" was "a hindrance sometimes" because it made it difficult to locate appropriate research. Evidence of these challenges was also seen in educators' responses to

Survey 1, where just 36% of educators 'agreed' or 'strongly agreed' that they can 'find research that addresses [their] specific practices, context or needs'.

A further complicating factor in navigating these large amounts of information was that educators recognised that they would likely come across "poorly designed research" (middle leader, survey) and "research [that] is not credible [and] therefore ineffective" (senior leader, survey). As a result, they emphasised "researching with critical eyes [...] not trust[ing] everything you read, but question[ing] and analys[ing] it" (teacher, survey). Educators described how this process relied on their critical thinking skills to determine whether certain research publications provided "an in-depth study that has got the right controls and structures in place [...] [to be] credible" (senior leader, interview), as well as if they provided "reasonable proof that the results are positive" (teacher, interview). The importance of these critical appraisal skills was also inferred in Survey 1 when educators were asked to rank how they 'assess the quality of information'. Educators' most common assessment approaches involved questioning how well the source was 'backed by academic research' (68% ranked in top five approaches/10 approaches) and considering the 'available evidence of impact of the information' (67%).

While a number of educators explained that they understood what constitutes a high-quality research design, they also expressed that they were not completely confident to draw on this knowledge and "discern between what is really good and what's not" (senior leader, interview). For example, in Survey 1, just over half (56%) of educators indicated that they were 'confident in how to judge the quality of research evidence'. Those educators who were not confident to judge the quality of research were significantly less likely to rank 'assessing academic backing' in their top five approaches to appraising the quality of research (59% vs. 74% of educators who were confident, $p = .001$). Rather, these educators were significantly more likely to rank 'source credibility' in their top five assessment approaches (65% vs 49%, $p < .001$). That is, they relied more on their contextual and professional knowledge of the education landscape by appraising whether research has "been viewed/critiqued by colleagues [...] [and] ensuring that the author is credible" (senior leader, survey).

Many of the research skills involved in accessing, reading and appraising research also played a role in how educators understood the "fit" of research and implemented research-informed changes. As one senior leader described in a survey response, "being data and methodology 'literate' [is] to be able to assess the validity *and* 'fit' for research" (emphasis added). The skills involved in these processes are taken up in the next section.

Skills involved in understanding research fit when implementing research-informed changes

When discussing how they considered the fit of research, educators spoke about how they used their skills for three key purposes. First, they explained how they used reflective thinking skills to engage with "research and try to get deeply into the [implications for] [...] what we do at school" (senior leader, interview) (44% of interviews, 56% of surveys). This is well illustrated in one middle leader's interview description of how her team engaged with research to reflect on their school's approach to teaching reading:

> So obviously reading is a big multi-faceted area to tackle and the more that we read, the less we could see a neat solution. So, the research has been invaluable in that the more that we dug, the more resonances we saw across things and went, "Okay, so these things keep popping up, they're clearly important." And now we're starting to think, "Well, how does that work in our context?"

Underpinned by the knowledge that the findings of research are not universally applicable, this process of considering how research fitted with their practice involved needing to "unpack why it works and how it will work in our context" (middle leader, survey). To do so, educators often drew on their professional knowledge to consider how research aligned with the culture, values and vision of their school. This knowledge, as one senior leader explained in an interview, was used as "a lens" with which to critically appraise the research:

> It's understanding the context and part of that is the culture of the school [...] and the vision and values that we work within. For us, when we're looking at any of the research that we bring into the school, we're also then putting a lens over that of "How does this fit within what we value?"

This aspect of research use appears to be a task which educators were largely comfortable applying their skills to, with the majority of educators in

Survey 1 (68%) indicating that they 'feel confident analysing and inter-preting research for [their] own teaching context'. These feelings of confi-dence appear to be an important enabler of quality research use as they were associated with significantly higher rates of regular research use in practice, where 50% of educators who felt confident analysing and inter-preting research used research regularly, compared with 29% of those who did not feel confident ($p < .001$).

Second, educators discussed research fit in relation to their capacity to "determine whether/how research is applicable to the problem that you are trying to solve" (senior leader, survey) (7% of interviews, 14% of surveys). This capacity related to how educators drew on their professional reflection and data literacy skills to develop a "critical understanding of the [research] evidence and being able to integrate or apply it where appropriate" (teacher, survey) (22% of interviews, 11% of surveys). Part of this process also involved engaging with research to illuminate practice problems in different ways, as one senior leader reflected in an interview:

> [It's] a deliberate and focused approach to finding out something about learning [...] [an] approach to finding out more about [an issue], [...] why it might be happening, what you can do about it [...] Reading to see what's out there to help me address what I think is happening in my classroom.

Third, educators considered the 'usability' of research and the skills involved in "applying and modifying the evidence to the [staff] cohort" (teacher, survey). They emphasised the need for relational and collaboration skills to network, share research and consider how it "might need to be translated/interpreted to suit" their approach (senior leader, survey) (52% of interviews, 21% of surveys). One senior leader described this in an interview as:

> A process: research of the research; reading and discussion of the research; looking at its applicability to our context; then trying to distil it into something that is meaningful to us and to our teachers; and then basically sharing that practice.

As alluded to in the quote above, this process required skills and knowledge related to adapting, repackaging and sharing research in ways that did not "dumb the research down [...] [but] fram[ed] it for teachers in a way that's accessible, easy to access, something that they can discuss and then gives them a launching pad into their own classroom" (senior leader, interview).

Despite these clear views about approaching these fit considerations, educators' responses to Survey 3 suggested that they see this capacity as a priority area for further skill development. For example, when asked to rank the 'skills [they] would most need help with' to improve their use of research, the most common skills to be ranked in the top five positions (out of eleven options) were: 'identify[ing] specific school-based challenges that research could help with' (43% ranked in top five), 'assess[ing] whether research is usable' (42%), 'assess[ing] the research for fit to context' (41%) and 'collaborat[ing] with colleagues about adapting and/or connecting the research with context' (39%).

In contrast, skills related to implementing research, such as 'conduct[ing] small-scale trials of the research' (31%, ranked 10th) and 'evaluat[ing] and refin [ing] the research based on trial outcomes' (29%, ranked 11th), were not seen to be as critical. When educators discussed the skills involved in implementing research-informed changes, they emphasised their abilities to "implement targeted changes in a logical, practical way" (teacher, survey) and engage in planning to "guide us in the right direction of implementation" (teacher, survey) (41% of interviews, 64% of surveys). Specifically, they drew on their own professional judgement and planning skills, often because they felt that implementation considerations were not clearly outlined in research:

> Being clear with your area of research […] and using the evidence to actually form a plan of attack or strategies to improve/support findings. A lot of research states findings but does not go further to give the actions needed.
>
> (senior leader, survey)

> Coming up with a plan about how to actually implement it. So, it's all very well to read about it, and have a better understanding of the theory, but often it's hard to translate that into a classroom scenario, or into practice. And so, having a proper plan about how to implement it in actual practice.
>
> (teacher, interview)

Overall, when discussing these skills, a number of educators positioned themselves as "researchers in their own classroom" (senior leader, interview) and spoke about how they draw on research-related skills to develop a "hypothesis or research question" (middle leader, survey). These skills were important because they allowed educators to consider "what worked and what the outcomes were" (other role, survey), "the conditions under which adjustments can be made" (senior leader, survey) as well as how "things might need tweaking to work in your own setting" (middle leader, survey). In doing so, educators felt that these skills allowed them to move beyond "just reading the research, but actually trialling it in the classroom" (teacher, survey) to "drive change [...] [and] ongoing improvement of teacher practice" (middle leader, survey).

Relationships

Although the previous two sections have drawn on findings about educators' mindsets and skillsets primarily from an individual perspective, both of these enablers were strongly connected with the final enabling component outlined in the QURE Framework – relationships. When educators described the social aspects that underpinned using research well, they discussed the variety of relationships within and beyond their school that supported specific research use tasks, as well as how sharing knowledge within these relationships underpinned their quality use of research. These two themes are discussed in turn.

The relationships and collaborations that support quality research use

Overall, relationships featured strongly in educators' descriptions about using research well (96% of interviews, 30% of surveys) as well as how they typically used research in their daily practice. For example, of the educators in Survey 1 who had indicated using research in the last 12 months, 76% indicated using it to 'discuss best practice with colleagues'. This way of collaboratively engaging with research to inform practice was slightly more common than individual uses of research that served similar aims, such as 'to improve my own knowledge of a topic or subject' (72%, 2nd most commonly selected) or 'to reflect on my own practice' (67%, 3rd). In interviews, one middle leader reinforced the value of encouraging "professional dialogue" among educators in order to support the quality use of research:

I think about the teams in our school that are high performing [...] They have, almost like debates about what's the best way to do things and what's going to work well [...] We can't just say to someone, "This piece of research looks good, why don't you read about it and see what you can do about it". That's never going to work. So, the biggest thing would have to be the collaboration.

Most commonly, when speaking about the relationships that supported them to use research well, educators referred to relationships within their school (81% of interviews, 29% of surveys). For example, they described how research featured in staff or team meetings (63% of interviews, 11% of surveys), during professional discussions (52% of interviews, 20% of surveys) and when seeking opinions from others (26% of interviews, 7% of surveys). Although being less common in educators' survey responses, some educators also spoke about relationships that extended beyond their school (78% of interviews, 2% of surveys). In interviews, educators often reflected on how they supported research use by building collaborations between two or more schools (44% of interviews), partnering with universities (44% of interviews) and/or fostering consultation with experts (41% of interviews).

When explaining why relationships were important for using research well, educators often referred to how these collaborations supported them to undertake specific tasks, such as understanding and appraising research (see Table 4.2). For example, one senior leader explained in a survey response how research "should be studied and examined carefully in a collaborative way so that it is not one person's interpretation". Similarly, a teacher explained in an interview how formal relationships, such as "when the principal and classroom teachers [...] meet for an hour each week", helped to ensure that research was appropriate for her school context because they could "spend more time unpacking [the research] [...] so, we're able to think about it, 'How could it be used? What's the difficulties with it?'"

Notably, though, there was a level of nuance in how educators participated in these relationships depending on the research use task at hand, with collaborations becoming more important and involved as educators moved through the research use process. For example, when accessing research, educators often described more 'light touch' and informal relationships, such as using "recommendations from colleagues or people who I respect" (middle

Table 4.2 Examples of collaborations around specific research use tasks

Finding research	**Appraising research**
"We found the research through networking with other schools [and seeking out] a variety of sources [including] university and professional recommendations [and] external agencies who are elite in their niche". (teacher, survey)	"Research from [both] internal and external sources should be studied and examined carefully in a collaborative way so that it is not one person's interpretation". (senior leader, survey)
Understanding and implementing	**Adapting and trialling**
Using research well means "unpacking the research together to gain a common understanding. [We] would be working together to plan and implement the research effectively in the classrooms". (senior leader, survey)	Using research well involves "subsequent debriefing along with colleagues after a suitable trial period and trial of other methods to gather group evidence of what works or not". (teacher, survey)

leader, interview), "chat[ting] with people in the Twitter network that I have" (senior leader, interview) or "ring[ing] one of my colleagues and hav[ing] a conversation" (middle leader, interview). In many cases, these 'light touch' relationships leveraged educators' existing social, professional and school networks as sources of information and ideas about research use initiatives. As an illustration, one senior leader explained in a survey response how, when looking for research that might be relevant to their context, "they wanted to see what other schools were doing". For this reason, they drew on their local networks and "visited other schools to see their programmes […] [and] connect[ed the] research to [their] own context through engaging with the research in discussions with colleagues and other leaders [from the school]".

In contrast, when trialling and implementing research, educators referred to more formal and in-depth relationships, such as "reciprocal relationship[s]" (senior leader, interview). This often involved "modelling, coaching, having rich professional dialogue[s] with the teachers, walking with them […] and team teaching" (middle leader, interview) in order to "pull the staff team together […] on one improvement journey" (senior leader, survey). For these tasks, educators more commonly discussed purposefully building new partnerships to address a specific need, as one senior leader reflected in an interview: "We've partnered with an academic mentor […] to put in place a whole series of data collection measures […] to measure the impact of [our efforts]".

These partnerships were seen as fostering educators' collective capacities and establishing a sense of common purpose to help ensure that their efforts were sustainable over time. This point highlights how educators not only shared their knowledge about research evidence, but also shared their broader capacities related to using research well: an idea that is developed in the next section.

Sharing knowledge within relationships as a key support for the quality use of research

Overall, educators' survey responses indicated that leveraging relationships to share knowledge was important to them. For example, when they were asked how they collaborated with others for research use tasks, educators indicated that their relationships most commonly involved 'sharing each other's knowledge and opinions' when finding and selecting (67%), assessing (55%), adapting (49%) and/or implementing (50%) research. When educators spoke about how sharing knowledge supported them to use research well (41% of interviews, 12% of surveys), they explained that "when you talk [...] and you share the information, it just gains a life of its own" (senior leader, interview). This section explores the three main ways that educators spoke about sharing knowledge and how this was seen to support their quality use of research.

First, educators discussed sharing knowledge about research articles and publications that they felt were relevant to their colleagues. For example, in an interview a middle leader discussed how she and her colleagues "go away, do their own finding out, soul searching, finding information and then we come back and we share it and discuss it". Along similar lines, a senior leader equated being a 'team player' among the leadership at her school with sharing research readings:

> So, we share educational readings or articles that have a link or through line to what we're currently working on, and then each of us, we call them players and members of our team, [...] are expected to be looking at best practice, they are expected to be using evidence to support that and then sharing that with the rest of the leadership team.

In Survey 2, educators indicated that sharing and receiving research was a relatively common practice, with 29% of educators who received evidence from others specifying that this occurred at least weekly, and 41% reporting that this occurred fortnightly to monthly. Most commonly, educators reported that it was their school leaders (77%) and teaching colleagues (74%) who shared evidence with them, with 75% believing that this was occurring because sharing research 'is an important part of being an educator'. Notably, educators who indicated receiving evidence more often were significantly more likely to regularly use research in their practice (40% of those who received weekly used regularly, 37% of those who received fortnightly to monthly, 26% of those who received less often, $x^2 = 12.984$, $df = 2$, $p = .002$). A possible reason for this can be seen in educators' responses to Survey 3, where educators were 'more likely to trust' research that was 'recommended by fellow teachers/colleagues' (79%) or 'recommended by [their] school leaders/principals' (70%). This was also noted in an interview by a teacher, who explained: "If it's come from a source that you can trust [...] where you know that they wouldn't [share it] unless they had done some background research, then that can give you some confidence in using [the research]".

Second, educators spoke about how "they share [their] professional knowledge" (senior leader, interview) about curriculum content, pedagogical principles and classroom practice as part of their collective engagement with research. Collaboratively engaging with research was described as an avenue for educators to mobilise their professional knowledge in order to unpack specific research publications and consider the complexity of applying these to their practice. This process was evident in one middle leader's interview:

> We get together, we talk about [research related to supporting students' literacy skills], we share, we've sort of built up a bank of expert knowledge, I guess you could say, with the three of us – the speech pathologist, the support teacher [who] has just done a course on sounds, [and myself]. [The relationship] delves deeper into linking it all together. So, the phonics, the writing, the reading, the vocab, and it's more of a holistic approach that we were looking for in the beginning. So, we've done a lot of discussion.

As illustrated in the quote above, in these knowledge-sharing relationships, research did not replace educators' collective expertise but, rather, was brought into conversation with their professional knowledge. As one senior leader explained in an interview, research was seen as "one tool that you can use [...] we still [need to use our knowledge] of good pedagogy [...] because like any good tool, there's always gaps".

Third, educators discussed sharing knowledge in relation to how they "share their expertise" (senior leader, interview) around the processes of using research. The value of these knowledge-sharing relationships rested on the understanding that "teachers all have different ideas [...] and varying degrees of knowledge" (teacher, survey) around research use. As a result, being able to "sit down as a group to be able to talk about things, to explain things and to go through the bits of research slowly" is valuable for supporting the collective quality use of research (teacher, interview). This was also seen in Survey 3 where 63% of educators indicated that 'sharing knowledge within the school' was 'important' or 'very important' for improving their use of research. As this statistic may suggest, the benefits of engaging in these expertise-sharing relationships were not only emphasised by educators who saw themselves as beginners in using research. Rather, educators who considered themselves experienced research users also advocated for opportunities for a "range of views [to be] discussed" (middle leader, survey) and harnessing educators' collective "wealth of professional knowledge" (teacher, interview).

Across educators' descriptions of the ways that they shared knowledge, it was also noted how these sharing opportunities were seen to foster collective buy-in and understanding of the value and purpose for using research well. As a middle leader explained in an interview, because of the "collegial discussions [...] [we were having], we're all picking up on the same sort of things as well, that sort of solidifies that, 'Okay, we're all thinking in a similar way now'". Recognising the value of this, she also discussed how her school had formalised opportunities for the sharing of knowledge about research-informed practice. She noted how this fostered interest in research use across the school:

> We have a sharing afternoon in term four, where all of the groups that have been researching different ideas or exploring different ideas, share that learning with other colleagues. Through that, then we got a lot of other people interested.

As will be discussed further in Chapter 5, the importance of these formalised opportunities for knowledge sharing and collaborative learning were emphasised in educators' responses to Survey 3. In particular, 68% indicated that 'internal professional learning communities and/or collaborative learning opportunities' were 'important' or 'very important' for improving their use of research and 60% indicated the same for 'external professional learning communities and/or collaborative learning opportunities'. However, when asked about the quality of the provision of these supports in their school, only 51% and 36% of educators respectively rated the provision as 'good' or 'very good'. As a result, it is perhaps unsurprising that in interviews, educators – and notably, senior leaders – called for greater opportunities to share knowledge both within and beyond their school:

> So, I guess more opportunities, either from the non-profit sector that really want to support in education, or the education department themselves, making opportunities for schools to actually share and look at what other schools are doing based on good research.
>
> (senior leader, interview)

> I would like us to base all of our decision making [...] on a blend of evidence [...] [but] we haven't had an opportunity to get teachers to work together, to examine how research impacts their classroom or how their classroom is impacted by research.
>
> (senior leader, interview)

Overall, this section has illustrated how relationships are an important capacity that supported educators to use research well, especially in how they fostered the sharing of research knowledge, pedagogical expertise and know-how about research use processes. It has also explored how educators spoke about engaging in different kinds of research use relationships depending on the specific research use task at hand. In light of this discussion, the final section considers the way in which the three individual enablers presented in this chapter are interconnected.

Conclusion

This chapter has explored how the quality use of research can be understood at an individual level in terms of educators' mindsets, skillsets and relationships. Our findings illustrate how the quality use of research relies on educators holding positive beliefs about research and its potential impact, as well as drawing on reflective, open-minded and thoughtful dispositions to guide how they use research in practice. It is also clear how using research well is highly skilled work. Educators emphasised the importance of research skills that allowed them to access, read and critically appraise research and ensure that there is alignment and fit between the research and proposed research-informed changes. And finally, our findings signal the importance of relationships in supporting educators to undertake specific research use tasks and engage in knowledge-sharing that underpinned their quality use of research.

Individually, the findings presented in this chapter articulate what might be considered the key capacities for using research well. Yet, when educators spoke about these capacities, they were also quite reflective about their current capacities to use research well, often making personal judgements on how they could work towards these key capacities. Our intention in presenting these views therefore is not to portray educators from a deficit perspective, but rather to draw on their own views about what they see as key priorities for capacity development. Educators' interview and open-text survey responses, for example, highlight opportunities for skill development in navigating the volume and varying quality of available research. Our quantitative survey data also suggest that identifying whether a school-based challenge warrants a research-informed response, determining the usability and contextual fit of research, and collaborating with colleagues to adapt research are seen by educators as other key areas for capacity building. We argue that it would be remiss to overlook these perspectives, particularly given the role they could play in moving the focus of improvement efforts from supporting the *increased use* of research, to supporting the *improved use* of research.

It is also important to emphasise that in educators' responses about what it means to use research well, their views were not limited to what might be considered immediately and solely research-focused capacities. For example, our findings indicate that relationships are seen as an important capacity for quality research use because of how they allow educators to share knowledge. While it is true that educators leveraged these relationships to share knowledge about research publications and/or expertise around research use processes, these relationships also enabled educators to share their professional knowledge about curriculum, pedagogy and classroom practice. By sharing this knowledge within research use relationships, educators brought their professional expertise *into conversation with* research evidence, as opposed to *being replaced by* it. While a similar line of thought in the literature recognises the importance of practitioner expertise when using research, the focus is often how educators use their knowledge to balance research use and policy demands, consider the differing needs of different stakeholders, and/or determine the applicability of research to educational situations. Our findings here provide a slightly different perspective by emphasising how the sharing of professional knowledge within relationships is an important means to support educators' thoughtful, considered and reflective engagement with research.

In a similar vein, this discussion of educators' capacities to use research well also provides insight into the core components of the QURE Framework. For example, this chapter has begun to illuminate how educators understand appropriate research evidence in exploring the skillsets and knowledge they draw on to consider the fit of research to the school context, the problem at hand and/or its usability. Similarly, the ways in which educators leverage purposeful relationships and adopt reflective, critical and inquisitive mindsets help to highlight what is involved in thoughtful engagement with and implementation of research in practice.

This chapter has also helped to show how these individual capacities are deeply interconnected and mobilised collectively in order to support the quality use of research in practice. These interconnections were illustrated in the ways educators spoke about working collaboratively to undertake specific research use tasks. For example, 'light touch' and informal collaborations or networks were viewed as important relationships for supporting educators' skills and capacities to access, understand and appraise appropriate research. Similarly, purposeful partnerships and coaching relationships were seen as valuable ways to address skill gaps related to implementing and measuring the impact of research-informed changes. Relationships were also seen as an avenue for fostering educators' quality research use mindsets. As put by two senior leaders in their survey responses, relationships were important for building "a community which is curious and engaged" with research where they could "inquire, learn and grow as a school community". By the same token, educators also spoke about the ways that mindsets and skillsets were important for supporting productive research use relationships.

To further illustrate the interconnections between these individual enablers of quality use of research, the vignette below explores the motivations and considerations of a school team attending professional learning to develop their research use capacities.

Vignette 5 ("How is it helpful?") – "Quality use of research as a capacity" motivating a school team to improve their research use skills, knowledge and attitudes

This vignette features a team of four school staff (i.e., two senior leaders, one middle leader and one teacher) who were keen to develop their own research use skills and knowledge. The team participated in the Q Project's professional learning (PL) programme related to quality research use and were motivated to do so for their own development, as well as to improve how they led and encouraged others to use research well at their school.

As a team, they were cognisant that unless they had the right research use capacities – particularly, skillsets and mindsets – they would not be in a position to role model effective research use to others. Teresa, the school's Research Lead and an instructional coach, stated that she "felt it was important to walk the talk" so she could better influence others. While Gina, Deputy Principal of Learning and Teaching, felt that it was critical she undertake the training as well: "It's not okay for me to just say, 'Well, you go off and do it [...] and tell me about it'". More specifically, they felt that by undertaking professional learning they could better champion the school's strategic investment in research use for improved teaching practices. Gina went on to explain, "What we're trying to do here is align everything with our strategic plan around continuous school improvement. So, this [professional learning] was ideal".

While the PL programme helped to "upskill" the team, its focus on "challenging [their] mindsets around what's possible in a classroom" helped to reinforce the idea that professional learning is "not something that's done to you. It's something you engage in continually". The team came away from the programme motivated to influence their colleagues' views that professional learning on research use was not an "add-on", rather it was a core part of their professional capacities and work as educators.

When applying the learnings from the PL programme, two collective capacities of their team helped to ensure the success of their actions:

- The team understood the "importance of contextual factors" when finding research and considering whether it was appropriate. Consequently, they engaged in professional discussions that combined their critical appraisal *skills*, knowledge of their school and the research use processes discussed in the PL programme. This allowed the team to view new ideas "through a different lens" and consider which would "fit where we're at", rather than "flop and [not] have the success we'd hoped for".

- Drawing on the aspects of the PL programme which highlighted the importance of connecting research use *skillsets*, *mindsets* and *relationships* in practice, the team translated learnings from other school examples to their own project work throughout the programme. In particular, they used their *relationships* to share practitioner case studies which captured educators' voices to influence their colleagues' *mindsets* and "to get them thinking about what might work" as well as how research might support their professional decision making.

This vignette provides an example of how the concept of quality use as a capacity has been relevant and helpful to a school team. In particular, it shows how a focus on leveraging the individual components of the QURE Framework, particularly research use skillsets and mindsets, are not only critical to the improvement of educators' own professional capacities but are important ways to develop collective leadership capacities to support others to use research well in practice.

This chapter has illuminated how we can conceptualise "quality use of research as a capacity" and what it requires of individuals. At the same time, though, we recognise that educators' capacities alone do not fully account for their quality use of research in practice (Plant et al., 2022). For this reason, this individual perspective of "quality use as a capacity" should be situated within a nuanced understanding of how research is used well within specific social and institutional contexts. This challenge is taken up in the next chapter, which explores the "quality use of research as a culture".

Notes

1 Throughout this book, parentheses following quotes indicate the type of educator being quoted, and whether the quote comes from an interview or an open-text response in Survey 1.
2 Throughout this book, when percentages are introduced as 'XX% of interviews, XX % of surveys', this is referring to the prevalence of qualitative themes in educators' interview responses and answers to the open-text questions in Survey 1. All quotations of survey items that use single inverted commas in-text pertain to educators' responses to quantitative items. Quotations that use double inverted commas in-text relate to educators' comments within interviews or written survey responses.
3 'Other role' refers to survey respondents who were in a role within a school other than teacher, middle leader or senior leader (see Appendix 1, Table 9.2 for full survey sample details).

References

Brown, C., & Greany, T. (2018). The evidence-informed school system in England: Where should school leaders be focusing their efforts? *Leadership and Policy in Schools*, *17*(1), 115–137. 10.1080/15700763.2016.1270330

Cain, T. (2019). *Becoming a research-informed school: Why? what? how?* Routledge.

Clinton, J. M., Aston, R., & Quach, J. (2018). *Promoting evidence uptake in schools: A review of the key features of research and evidence institutions*. University of Melbourne. 10.4225/49/5aa61c6c75a9e

Coldwell, M., Greany, T., Higgins, S., Brown, C., Maxwell, B., Stiell, B., Stoll, L., Willis, B., & Burns, H. (2017). *Evidence-informed teaching: An evaluation of progress in England*. Department for Education. https://assets.publishing.service. gov.uk/government/uploads/system/uploads/attachment_data/file/625007/Evidence-informed_teaching_-_an_evaluation_of_progress_in_England.pdf

Earl, L. M., & Timperley, T. (2009). Understanding how evidence and learning conversations work. In L. M. Earl & H. Timperley (Eds.), *Professional learning conversations* (pp. 1–12). Springer.

Evans, C., Waring, M., & Christodoulou, A. (2017). Building teachers' research literacy: Integrating practice and research. *Research Papers in Education*, *32*(4), 403–423. 10.1080/02671522.2017.1322357

Gleeson, J., Cutler, B., Rickinson, M., Walsh, L., Ehrich, J., Cirkony, C., & Salisbury, M. (2023). School educators' engagement with research: An Australian Rasch validation study. *Educational Assessment, Evaluation and Accountability*, *35*, 281–207. 10.1007/s11092-023-09404-7

Malin, J. R., Brown, C., Ion, G., van Ackeren, I., Bremm, N., Luzmore, R., Flood, J., & Rind, G. M. (2020). World-wide barriers and enablers to achieving evidence-informed practice in education: What can be learnt from Spain, England, the

United States, and Germany? *Humanities & Social Sciences Communications*, 7, Article 99. 10.1057/s41599-020-00587-8

Nelson, J., & Campbell, C. (2019). Using evidence in education. In A. Boaz, H. Davies, A. Fraser, & S. Nutley (Eds.), *What works now? Evidence-informed policy and practice* (pp. 131–150). Policy Press.

Nelson, J., Mehta, P., Sharples, J., & Davey, C. (2017). *Measuring teachers' research engagement: Findings from a pilot study*. Education Endowment Foundation. https://educationendowmentfoundation.org.uk/public/files/Evaluation/Research_Use/NFER_Research_Use_pilot_report_-_March_2017_for_publication.pdf

Nelson, J., & O'Beirne, C. (2014). *Using evidence in the classroom: What works and why?* National Foundation for Education Research. https://www.nfer.ac.uk/publications/impa01/impa01.pdf

Plant, B., Boulet, M., & Smith, L. (2022). *A behavioural approach to understanding and encouraging quality use of research evidence in Australian schools: Final report*. BehaviourWorks Australia. 10.26180/21530658.v1

Rickinson, M., Gleeson, J., Walsh, L., Salisbury, M., Cutler, B., & Cirkony, C. (2021). *Using research well in Australian schools: Discussion paper*. Monash University. 10.26180/14783637.v2

5

Quality use of research as a culture

Chapter overview

This chapter explores how quality use of research can be enacted and supported at an organisational level through a school's culture, leadership and infrastructure. Drawing on educators' survey and interview responses, it shows how:

- understanding "quality use as a culture" is about examining what quality use of research involves at the school level and what it requires of schools as organisations;
- educators' accounts of using research well in practice strongly endorse the importance of the three organisational enablers of culture, leadership and infrastructure;
- a supportive school culture is one that encourages collective or collaborative research use and feels trusted and safe when staff take informed risks;
- a supportive leadership is one that models quality research use in their own practice and promotes such use in the work of others across the school;
- a supportive infrastructure is one that provides developmental support through professional learning and material support in terms of time and research access;

DOI: 10.4324/9781003353966-5

- fostering quality research use within organisations requires integrating culture, leadership and infrastructure in multi-faceted, dynamic and multi-layered ways; and
- thinking about the influence of, and connections between, culture, leadership and infrastructure can help leaders to support quality research use at the school level.

Introduction

In Chapter 4, we discussed quality research use as a capacity and highlighted how educators needed research-engaged mindsets, skillsets and relationships. This perspective focused on educators as individuals, but needs to be complemented by an institutional-level perspective focused on schools (Rickinson et al., 2022). That is, an approach that considers how research use is "collective and embedded" at the organisational level (Nutley et al., 2007, p. 306). The limitations of a solely individual approach to understanding research use have been increasingly acknowledged in recent decades (e.g., Hemsley-Brown & Sharp, 2003; Levin, 2013; Nutley et al., 2007). Subsequently, a substantial body of work focused on the leadership and organisational aspects of 'research-engaged schools' has emerged (e.g., Brown & Greany, 2018; Cooper & Levin, 2013; Godfrey, 2016; Godfrey & Brown, 2019). This work has shed light on the key organisational enablers that can facilitate and sustain educators' use of research. It has also helped to support the argument that, while there are steps that educators can take to increase and improve their own use of research, these need to be connected with and amplified by structures and supports at the school and system levels (e.g., Coburn, 2005; Cordingley, 2008; Levin, 2013; van Schaik et al., 2018).

However, such work has tended not to focus on using research well, and therefore little is known about the organisational aspects of quality research use in schools. With this need in mind, this chapter discusses the key organisational enablers that interconnect and encapsulate quality research use as a culture. Drawing on data from Australian educators' survey responses (Survey 1, $n = 492$; Survey 3, $n = 414$) and interview accounts ($n = 27$), (see Appendix 1 for details about samples and methods), it highlights the key cultural principles, leadership practices and infrastructural supports that are needed for quality research use to develop.

This chapter has five main sections. The next section explains what we mean by understanding "quality research use as a culture" and how our ideas are reflected in the organisational components of the Quality Use of Research Evidence (QURE) Framework – culture, leadership and infrastructure. There are then three sections that detail the perspectives of educators on how quality research use is supported by each of these organisational enablers. The chapter concludes with a section that considers how the connections between culture, leadership and infrastructure can help leaders to support quality research use at the organisational level.

Understanding quality use as a culture

To understand quality research use as a culture we must ask questions such as: What does quality research use look like and involve at a school level? What does using research well require of schools as organisations? How can quality research use be supported and enabled within schools? In our work, these questions were addressed empirically by probing educators' per-spectives and experiences of using research well in schools and then ex-amining if and/or how the organisational enablers of culture, leadership and infrastructure from the QURE Framework, discussed in Chapter 3, featured within their accounts.

In Survey 1 and the follow-up interviews, for example, we asked open-ended, broad questions about practitioners' use of research in order to gain practical insights into the different "drivers and shapers" of research use on the ground (Davies et al., 2019, p. 381). To give shape and form to how schools can enable quality research use, we also asked open questions about what educators would 'observe' or 'experience' in their school if research was being used well. Educators' responses to these survey and interview questions were then analysed inductively as well as deductively in relation to the organisational enablers of the QURE Framework in order to gain insights into whether and/or how school culture, leadership and infrastructure can contribute to using research well. Additional insights into quality use as a culture were gained by asking closed-response questions about certain organisational barriers and enablers to research use in Survey 1 and specific organisational resources and supports in Survey 3. Analysis of

Table 5.1 Number and percentage of Survey 1 respondents (*n* = 492) and interviews
(*n* = 27) coded to QURE Framework organisational components

Themes	Using research well	
	Interviews	Surveys
Culture	96% (26)	40% (196)
Leadership	89% (24)	72% (355)
Infrastructure	93% (25)	39% (192)

responses to these questions generated insights into the perceived importance and impact of different kinds of organisational influences.

Overall, the analysis of educators' views provided rich insights into the
roles that culture, leadership and infrastructure can play in facilitating the
development of quality research use within schools. As shown in Table 5.1,
all of the QURE Framework organisational enablers featured within educators' interview and survey responses, particularly that of leadership. Indeed,
as the subsequent sections within this chapter will show, educators made
clear that, at the organisational level, quality research use depends on a
school culture that enables research use to be collaborative and safe, school
leadership that practises and promotes using research well and school
infrastructure that provides developmental and material support for
research use.

In understanding quality research use as a culture, though, it was
important to be open to several ways in which the organisational aspects of
using research well could be conceived. One way was to consider the
tangible aspects of quality use as a culture – what educators might be doing
or have access to when research was being used well and/or what was
observable in the school that supported quality research use. Also important
were the *intangible* aspects of quality use as a culture – what educators
might be experiencing or feeling when using research well and how these
experiences and feelings were influenced by an overarching ethos within
the school. In addition, there were the *temporal* aspects of quality use as a
culture – how research can be used well over time and how these changing
or evolving ways can influence collective research use practices across the
school community.

With these points in mind, the next three sections elaborate on the
development of quality research use within schools from the perspectives of:

- Culture – in particular, the underpinning principles of collective or collaborative research use, and the need for a trustworthy and 'safe' school environment.
- Leadership – in particular, leaders' own research use practices, and their promotional practices that encourage research use by others.
- Infrastructure – in particular, developmental support through collaborative professional learning opportunities, and material support in the form of time and access.

Before considering each of these organisational enablers individually, though, it is helpful to look at how they might play out in combination in the context of a specific school. The vignette below highlights how aspects of culture, leadership and infrastructure featured within the development of quality research use within a primary school.

Vignette 6 ("Looks like in practice") – "Quality use of research as a culture" within a primary school's overall approach to research use

This vignette captures Central River Public School's story of building a quality research use culture. When speaking with the principal, Imogen, and members of her leadership team, all emphasised that cultural change starts with them as leaders. They have a clear school vision for research use that involves themselves, as a leadership team, investing in weekly research-based collaborative professional learning sessions. These sessions facilitate their collective buy-in to certain research so that they can role model effective use and support other staff to use research well. They are also clear that in trying to achieve their vision, "it is not just one thing" that they do, rather, it is a combination of several deliberate strategies related to embedding research use supports and resources within the infrastructure of the school. They are also clear that "it is about consistency"; it is not about "'What do we need to do next?' [...] it is about 'How does it need to evolve?'"

One of these strategies is focused on allowing teachers time to engage with research. For example, the school "buys additional time" by recruiting casual staff so that the timetable can be organised to provide teaching teams with 80 minutes of scheduled time away from face-to-face teaching each week. Alongside this is an evaluation strategy, where teachers self-report how effective they believe this time has been in helping them to achieve their professional development goals and in positively affecting student learning outcomes. To facilitate this time provision certain activities, such as music and library classes, have been reassigned from teachers to other specialists.

Within the school, there are also senior leaders who act as dedicated research leads or champions. Amongst other responsibilities, these leaders are charged with identifying and curating research, ensuring that research is appropriate and linked to their school's strategic aims and School Excellence Framework, and coaching and supporting staff via structured inquiry cycle processes and classroom observations to understand, interpret, implement and evaluate the research. They have also developed an "effective practice hub", which is an online platform that houses research, advice and guidelines, professional learning examples, practice approaches and case studies, amongst other helpful information.

This vignette highlights a number of elements of "quality use as a culture" in practice:

- The way the leaders ensured that research use was purposeful and clearly linked to the school's strategic plan is illustrative of the QURE Framework's core component of *appropriate research*. This approach was also supported by the leadership team's efforts to prioritise principles of consistency, persistence and collaboration, which reflect aspects of the organisational enabler of *culture*.
- The leadership team made clear that if a research-engaged culture was to be built and sustained within the school, then they needed not only to have the *skillsets* and *mindsets* themselves to use research well, but also to role-model quality use to staff. These beliefs and actions reflect the importance of the individual enablers of quality research use, as well as the organisational enabler of *leadership*.
- Central River Public School also exemplifies the organisational enabler of *infrastructure* by embedding research use in school schedules and timetables, professional learning and coaching processes, accountabilities of key leaders and supporting resources.

Culture

When educators described a culture of quality research use, two under-pinning principles were identified as key: A focus on collective or collab-orative research use, and the need for a trustworthy and 'safe' environment when using research together.

A focus on collective or collaborative research use

Educators explained that cultivating a collective or collaborative culture around using research well involved establishing a collective research-engaged language, so that research use became an intrinsic part of everyday practices, processes and decision making (referenced in 85% of interviews, 15% of surveys) and collaborating around research use (59% of interviews, 11% of surveys).

In the same way that educators highlighted the importance of individual mindsets, educators viewed culture as a 'collective mindset' that enabled quality research use. When describing using research well, educators spoke about it as an 'ethos' within the school or an intrinsic way of doing things, where they "talk[ed] [research] all the time" (middle leader, interview) or it was in "every breath we take" (middle leader, interview). Educators em-phasised the principle of collective research use when they explained that "you can't have just one teacher [using research] [...] in isolation, it has to be a collaborative approach" (senior leader, interview), with "everybody talking the same language [and] moving the same way" (senior leader, interview). In Survey 1, another senior leader captured these ideas when they stated that using research well involved "[d]eveloping a collaborative learning culture across the school [...] with common goals, consistent ways of working and a common language. Everyone [is] rowing the boat together, not just sitting in it or having one leg in".

Working together to share knowledge was seen as an important aspect of a quality research use culture. In Survey 3, most educators (81%) indicated that 'a culture of knowledge sharing' was 'important' or 'very important' for supporting their improved use of research. In addition to viewing this cul-ture as important, most expressed wanting to be active participants in it. For example, involvement in school practices such as 'sharing knowledge about practice within the school' (63%) and 'generating new knowledge about teacher practice' (63%) were viewed as 'important' or 'very important' for educators' improved use of research. Less popular was involvement in collective research use activities external to or beyond the school, including 'sharing knowledge beyond the school' (40%) or 'developing collaborations with external partners' (37%).

Sharing ideas from research in group settings, such as team meetings, staff presentations or reading circles, was viewed as a helpful way to build a quality research use culture. Educators explained that these types of col-laborative settings helped to "[get] a lot of other people interested" (middle leader, interview) and "snowball or [create] a swell of support" (senior leader, interview) for greater and improved research use. During their interview, one senior leader explained how a year-level learning area leader in his school contributed to a collaborative culture of using research through knowledge sharing:

> She was very, very used to using research. She was also doing further study, and so she did an inquiry into knowledge and thinking curriculum. So, she used a lot of external research and then applied it with internal research to come up with the best way to support our Year 7 [students] to learn and retain learning in Humanities. Then she would have people within her learning area team in [other] faculties giving her feedback, but also applying the research in the classroom […] that started to develop a collaborative approach [to research use] and a shared learning approach.

A trustworthy and safe environment

Along with, and connected to, a collective approach to research use, was a second principle related to the importance of trust and 'safety'. A trust-worthy environment was viewed as one that supported and encouraged research use (56% of interviews, 14% of surveys) and valued the research use related opinions and actions of staff (37% of interviews, 6% of surveys). In Survey 3, 'having trusted relationships between staff and leadership' was viewed as the most important aspect of a school's culture to enable im-proved research use (82% rated as 'important' or 'very important'). An en-vironment of respect was also needed, with leaders who trusted teachers and 'encouraged them to exercise judgement when using research' viewed as important (76%). During interviews, one senior leader described how mutual trust underpinned critical discussions and decisions in their school about a particular research-informed curriculum initiative:

> [We've been taking] a more proactive approach. So, trying to empower all the staff and get them on the same page has been what we have tried to do [...] Twelve months ago, I was the face of [the initiative] and I've deliberately tried to step back and go "It's not about me. It's about the collective and empowering staff to get on board" [...] There have been a lot of discussions [particularly] with learning leaders. I've been challenged by them. So, it's a culture of mutual trust [...] and we have made some changes [to the initiative] based on staff challenging some decisions. [There is a culture] of healthy respect and the healthy advice has been very much appreciated.

A trustworthy research use school environment was also one that was perceived as "safe" (senior leader, interview). Educators valued a school culture "where informed risk taking [was] encouraged and reflected upon to inform decision making" (teacher, survey) or where there was "risk taking [and it was] OK to try and fail" (teacher, survey). Educators emphasised that a safe and trusting culture was needed to engage in collaborative "critical open discussions" (senior leader, survey) about research, as well as to ask questions and debate its relevance (63% of interviews, 21% of surveys). For example, in Survey 1, one middle leader used the idea of there being an "open-door policy" to describe a supportive cultural attitude towards questioning and debating research. They described using research well as:

> New ideas and practice are encouraged. Risks are taken, [and] there is [an] appropriate amount of time to see the new practices come into fruition and see if they work well. [There is] an open-door policy, [with] good debate and discussion in staff meetings.

In contrast, an 'unsafe' school culture was associated with poor research use, with the same middle leader explaining, "Staff are scared to take risks and there is no new [research-informed] practice. [There are] closed doors and no discussions". In Survey 3, these types of ideas were reinforced, with a majority of educators indicating that 'a respect for differences in opinions about research' (73%) or leaders 'encouraging questions and debate about research' (72%) were 'important' or 'very important' aspects of school leadership.

Overall, educators highlighted a collective, collaborative approach and a trusting, safe environment as important underpinnings of a quality research use culture. They were clear in their views, though, that such a culture could not be cultivated in schools without the explicit commitment and practices of leaders and leadership.

Leadership

When educators described the leadership necessary for a quality research use culture, they highlighted the importance of two types of leadership practices: Leaders' own personal practices around using research that they role modelled to others, and their promotional practices that envision and direct the use of research by others.

Leaders' own research use practices

Educators explained that they expected leaders to help them develop greater understanding of research and its use and that leaders' own personal practices were key to facilitating this (67% of interviews, 31% of surveys). These practices involved the ways in which leaders role modelled using research well themselves, including being able to "model that [research-informed practice] rather than just describe it" (senior leader, interview), "get [staff] on board [by] going through things in a way that explains [the research]" (teacher, interview) and "walk the talk and model its implementation" (teacher, survey). During interviews, one senior leader explained the influence of role modelling: "Always know that you've got to be ready for learning [any] time. I've got to model that behaviour that I want my teachers to show myself". In Survey 3, these modelling practices were also viewed as important, with a majority of educators indicating that improved research use was facilitated by 'leaders demonstrating and role modelling research use and implementation' (75% rated as 'important' or 'very important'). In Survey 1, one teacher described what good role modelling looked like to them:

> Leaders are able to not only "quote" the relevant research but are able to match it with what is happening in the school and then model the application of that research to all teachers, staff and students.

In contrast, from the same survey, one middle leader described what poor research use entailed and, in doing so, highlighted the importance of leaders "knowing the research themselves":

> Leaders make loose claims such as "the research says", but are not able to articulate specifics nor apply recommendations or gather and analyse data from replicated studies or use research in their [own] work.

Role modelling quality research use also involved leaders making visible to others their own beliefs in the value of research use, including seeing themselves as "learners" (senior leader, interview), and "prioritising" use as a personal practice (teacher, interview). Responses suggested that if these types of personal leadership practices were evident, then research use "could become part of the school's routine and be demonstrated as something that's really a value, and really valued by the school's leadership" (middle leader, interview). During interviews, this point was captured well when one senior leader described her assumption that she was accountable to use research well in her practice, particularly if she expected others to do so. As she explained:

> My responsibility is to absolutely keep abreast of all educational research and to keep in touch with developments in [particular] fields and make sure that I'm using [research] to inform my own thinking about education at my school. [For example], to review and evaluate procedures and programmes that we might be doing, and then also to look at future initiatives that we might engage in. So, I've been engaged in always making sure I look at research around leadership qualities and change of strategic improvement and things like that. So, I definitely use [research in these ways].

Promotion of research use across the school

Quality research use leadership was also described by educators as those practices that promoted the use of research across a school community. These included overseeing engagement with and implementation of research (41% of interviews, 36% of surveys) and promoting a vision for research use (41% of interviews, 35% of surveys).

At the outset, educators reported that using research to underpin practice and knowledge improvement was very important, and they looked to leaders to drive the use of research in their schools. For example, a majority of Survey 3 respondents (74%) believed that it was an 'important' or 'very important' aspect of school leadership for 'research to be used to inform decision making'. Additionally, in Survey 1, those educators who believed that their schools ensured 'research was referred to when deciding which programmes or initiatives to implement' regularly used research significantly more often in practice (48%) when compared with those who did not believe that their schools used research to inform decision making (20%, $p < .001$). These ideas were captured by one middle leader who, during an interview, described how using research was not only an important part of accountability in leadership, but was integral to better decision making and contributed to improved student outcomes in their school:

> The decisions we make as a leadership team are from a research and evidence base. They're not from a random selection of things, and I think that's definitely a problem in education. There are lots of "shiny things" and not all of them are actually evidence-based. So, I would say that I feel like our culture here as a leadership team is to use evidence and research to make any decisions that we're making as a school.

Educators' responses indicated that for research to be used well, there was also a strong need for school leaders to provide a clear vision and purpose for research use. Teachers, in particular, looked to leaders to "explain the why" (middle leader, survey) behind research priorities and decisions, and to "unpack why [the research] works and how it will work in our school context" (middle leader, survey). During interviews, one senior leader outlined the types of questions she would ask of others when trying to understand the rationale for using certain research. In so doing, she highlighted the importance of quality research use needing to be purposeful:

> [I would want to understand] if they're implementing [the research] authentically, if there's certain procedures or directions or structures [we] have to follow, that it's thought out, it's planned. That there's reasons why [we're] doing it. [For example], "Why are you doing it? Why are you doing it with this student? What are you hoping to get

from it? Is it fitting into your routine? How are you managing it in the classroom? Is it impacting on other students?" There has to be a real thought-out process. It can't just be "kids are just going to do this, and we'll hope for the best". It has to be planned and purposeful.

The need for a clear vision and purpose around research use was reinforced in Survey 3, with a majority of educators indicating that it was 'important' or 'very important' for leaders to 'be transparent about the source and reasons for research use' (76%), 'support educators' understanding of 'what the research means for practice' (73%) and 'have a clear vision and language about research use' (70%).

In contrast, if educators perceived that research use was *not* purposeful, then it may not be used at all. For example, in Survey 3, those educators who 'agreed' or 'strongly agreed' that there was not 'a clear purpose for using research' (48%), were less likely to regularly use research in practice (30%) when compared with those who did believe there was a clear purpose (38%). These same educators were also significantly more likely to believe in the value of using 'teachers' experience and knowledge over the use of 'research' (73% vs. 50%, $p < .001$).

In essence, educators' perspectives on using research well make clear that leaders are critical to the development of a quality research use culture in schools. Leaders' own commitment to research use and personal practice are important but so too are the ways in which they envision and promote the use of research within their school communities. Ensuring research informs school decision making and providing a clear vision and purpose for research use are two valued leadership practices. Educators are clear, though, that they also look to leaders to ensure that research use is supported developmentally as well as materially – which brings us on to the question of infrastructure.

Infrastructure

When educators described the infrastructure necessary for a quality research use culture, two types of support were identified as key: Developmental support through collaborative professional learning opportunities and material support in the form of time and access to engage with research.

Developmental support for collaborative professional learning

Within the school environment, educators emphasised that the availability of support and resources was critical to help them use research well (81% of interviews, 18% of surveys). In particular, educators wanted support in the form of collaborative professional learning that allowed them to improve their research use skills and mindsets. As educators explained, such developmental support helped them to create "a learning community" where they "were very keen to learn [...] [until research use has] become embedded in what we do" (senior leader, interview), or learn from each other so that they could "build up a bank of expert knowledge" (middle leader, interview).

The need for developmental support was also reflected in survey responses. For example, in Survey 3, a majority of educators (80%) believed that a school culture that 'focused on continuous learning and improvement' was 'important' or 'very important' for improved use of research. Similarly, educators indicated that the most important types of professional learning for them to improve their research use included 'professional learning communities and/or collaborative learning' (68%), 'peer-led demonstration of using research' (67%) and 'participating in cycles of inquiry and reflection' (64%).

These types of learning opportunities were also found to be strongly connected with educators' more frequent research use. In Survey 3, for example, those who believed that there were adequate opportunities to 'participate in inquiry cycles' at their school were more likely to regularly use research (45%) than those who did not believe that there were adequate opportunities to take part in inquiry cycles (26%, $p < .001$). In Survey 1, those educators who 'agreed' or 'strongly agreed' that their school 'facilitated a professional learning community or supported collaborative learning' (87%) were significantly more likely to use research regularly (45%) than those who did not believe that their school supported collaborative learning (30%, $p = .029$).

Connected to the importance of collaborative professional learning, educators also valued developmental support in the forms of "instructional leaders, demonstrating lessons for them, showing them what [the research] would look like in the classroom" (senior leader, interview) or "a growth coaching model to help [teachers] set goals, improve elements of their practice, or essentially through coaching conversations, work through particular issues" (middle leader, interview). The need for these types of support was also reflected in survey responses. For example, in Survey 3, educators believed that 'in-school instructional leaders' (75% rated as 'important' or 'very important') and 'research use mentors or coaches' (70%) were important supports that a school could provide to help them to improve their research use. During an interview, one middle leader explained how she intended to utilise coaches and instructional leaders within her school as a way to support teachers during the implementation of a new research-informed teaching approach:

> Next year I think we'll be about working with coaches and also, we've got heads of learning […] I think that they're going to be our biggest advocates [of the research-informed change]. We really need to work with them, not just in learning the […] process, but I really believe that we need to build capacity in actually engaging with research. One proposal I have is that we bring [a jurisdiction expert] in for a session with our leaders and [focus on] up-skilling […] I think we need to be upskilled in just what we will probably be exposed to in academic research.

Educators highlighted several key conditions of effective developmental support. First, the individual professional learning needs of teachers needed to be prioritised, with professional learning opportunities structured as both flexible and continuous to sustain improvement. During an interview, one senior leader commented:

> The more fundamental problem I'm trying to work on in this school is having an infrastructure for ongoing professional learning, where we can identify what the needs are of our staff to improve their performance, and then be able to bring in research at those key points and examples of practice so we can model that rather than just describe those practices to help have that sustained improvement. We're not [just] talking about a research use issue, we're also talking about structural issues.

Secondly, educators valued opportunities to participate in research use related decision making and viewed these as key ways to "feel empowered" (middle leader, interview) and develop their skills. Such development was also associated with more frequent use of research in practice. For example, in Survey 3, educators were more likely to regularly use research in practice when they were involved in school decisions regarding the selection (63% used regularly), assessment (59%), adaption (61%) or implementation (48%) of research compared with those who felt that they were not involved in these processes (30%, 29%, 27% and 27% respectively, all $p < .001$).

Finally, providing multiple and connected learning opportunities was also viewed as important, with one middle leader describing the multiple ways in which teachers were supported to implement a particular research-informed initiative in her school:

> [Our] professional learning team meetings after school were dedi-
> cated to [our initiative] [...] interpreting the data [from implementa-
> tion], reading all the research and reading all the information about
> [the initiative] from a content perspective and a pedagogical
> perspective. Like it was massive. We really worked it to the ground.
> [Another leader] and I went in classrooms modelling, coaching,
> supporting, having rich professional dialogue with the teachers,
> walking with them [...] having those conversations [about the
> research] with them during the lesson and team teaching. So yeah,
> it was heavily supported.

Material support for time and access

As well as the need for developmental support, educators also stressed the importance of material support for improved research use. The two most critical forms of such support were educators having sufficient access to research and scheduled time during school hours to engage with it. During their interviews, educators explained that they wanted scheduled time where "there's no admin[istration], no marking, nothing like that. It's only meant for that practice improvement and in that context, you reference your research that's relevant to your question" (middle leader). They explained that "if [access to research and its use] was structured into what we're doing, then it makes it easier to find the time to do the reading" (middle leader).

These sentiments were reflected strongly in survey responses. For example, in Survey 3, a majority of educators believed that it was 'important' or 'very important' for the school to 'build time into staff schedules for reading, discussing and understanding research' (72%) and to provide 'access to online research databases and/or journals' for their improved research use (64%).

A school's provision of these supports was also connected with educators' regular use of research in practice. Those educators in Survey 1 who believed that their school 'made sufficient time available' (55%) regularly used research in practice significantly more often (52%) than those educators who believed that they were not provided with sufficient time (33%, $p < .001$). Similarly, in Survey 3, while only 37% of all educators believed that their school often provided 'structured time dedicated to reading, discussing and understanding research', these educators were significantly more likely to regularly use research in practice (48%) than the nearly two-thirds (63%) of educators who did not believe that they were provided with sufficient time (26%, $p < .001$). With regards to access, while only 37% of Survey 3 respondents believed that their school provided adequate 'access to online research databases and/or journals', these educators were significantly more likely to regularly use research in practice (46%) when compared with those who did not believe that they had adequate access (28%, $p < .001$).

Having sufficient access and time to engage with research were acknowledged as challenges by most educators. For example, in Survey 1, a majority of educators felt that they had 'did not have adequate time' to engage with research (76% 'agreed' or 'strongly agreed') and 'found it difficult to keep up with new research' (76%). More than two-thirds did not believe that they 'had sufficient access to research' (68%). In Survey 3, while nearly half of all educators wanted to 'invest time in research use' (46% 'agreed' or 'strongly agreed'), a greater number indicated that using research was *not* worthwhile because of the 'significant time needed to access, read and put research into practice' (61%). Educators' excessive workloads were viewed as one reason that research was not accessed or used frequently in practice, with several leaders acknowledging that "we do have some very well-intentioned staff who do want to try [using research], but feel so burdened by documentation" (middle leader, interview) or "time is such a huge issue and unfortunately we get so caught up in busy work, admin[istration] stuff, that people can't find time to do development work" (middle leader, interview). During interviews, one teacher explained the challenge of finding sufficient time in her day to engage with research:

Time is a big [barrier]. If I have the resources, and if I have the time allocated outside of my day-to-day duties to actually put the time in to do it properly, and actually gather the information and the research and that sort of thing, that's probably going to be a big factor.

Lack of access to research databases and libraries was another reason for infrequent use, with one middle leader observing during interviews: "Schools simply [don't] have the access that we would require to make our teachers understand the importance and relevance of [research]". A newly qualified teacher echoed this perspective during interviews when she explained:

When I was at university and an enrolled student, it was really easy to access information that I knew was peer reviewed because they've got all these databases available. And since I've left that lovely environment where all this information is available really easily, I've found it more difficult to know where to look to find that information, because half the time you have to pay for a particular paper, which I'm perhaps not willing to do, or all those databases that made it really easy are not accessible anymore, and then I'm not sure if what I'm accessing is a valid source of evidence. So, I've noticed that over the last couple of years, since I haven't been at university, and so the access is different, and much, much less, I feel.

Overall, having quality infrastructure for improved research use was viewed as essential by educators. In particular, having developmental support in the form of professional learning opportunities and material support, such as sufficient access to research and scheduled time to engage with it, was highly valued. Yet, like the cultivation of a research-engaged culture, the provision of adequate infrastructure was connected with the commitment and practices of leaders. With this in mind, the final section considers the ways in which the three organisational enablers can be interconnected.

Conclusion

This chapter explored how the quality use of research can be enacted and supported at an organisational level through a school's culture, leadership and infrastructure. Our findings suggest that using research well relies on key principles such as the notion of collective or collaborative research use and the need for a trustworthy and safe environment when working together. Using research well also requires leaders to adopt certain personal practices that they role model to others, as well as promotional practices, such as providing a clear vision for research use, that encourage research use across a school community. And finally, our findings suggest that using research well requires the school to make available developmental and material support in the forms of collaborative professional learning, as well as scheduled time and access. While each of these organisational enabling factors is important, it is the ways in which they can interconnect that really help to bring quality use of research as a culture to life.

Firstly, these factors do not operate independently in practice. Fostering quality research use within a school is multi-faceted and requires different aspects of culture, leadership and infrastructure to work in concert at any point in time. For example, our findings highlight that leaders are critical to setting and prioritising an agenda for research use in a school and ensuring that how, when and why research is used is clear and embedded in the school's operations. However, unless leaders empower the school community to not only follow this agenda, but make it their own, quality research use will not transfer and be adopted by the collective, and the research-engaged culture of the school will struggle to develop. Even though research might inform school decision making and be obvious within certain school processes, our findings suggest that educators might be reluctant to truly engage with the idea of quality research use themselves if, for example, "someone in power gets a bee in their bonnet about a new research idea and foists it on the entire school community with no ownership or engagement of the teaching body as a whole" (teacher, survey).

Secondly, the development of quality research use is dynamic in terms of time, effort and impact. Without a developmental, long-term view of quality research use, our findings suggest, for example, that there is a risk that "things would be quickly trialled and abandoned, practice would stay overall the same, [and] teachers [would be] saying things like 'Research is all well and good, but it doesn't work like that in the classroom'" (teacher, survey). Capturing the essence of our core QURE Framework components – thoughtful engagement with and implementation of appropriate research – we suggest that a research-engaged culture within a school is a process that builds over time, rather than an event that happens instantaneously. It takes time for a school team or community as a whole to identify a need to be informed by research and then find, assess and interpret appropriate research. Time and consideration are also needed when thoughtfully trialling, implementing and evaluating the impact of the research-informed approach or decision. Additionally, at different points in the research implementation process, thought will need to be given to different leadership actions and school community involvement that may be required, or to different supports and resources that may also be necessary. Throughout this process, individuals' research use skillsets, mindsets and relationships will likely evolve, as will the collective nature of these. This evolution will require an ongoing consideration and re-evaluation of the most appropriate and relevant cultural principles, leadership practices and school support to continually foster improved research use.

Finally, quality research use is multi-layered, as it can be considered at various levels of the school organisation and involve different or all educator cohorts. As elaborated further in Chapter 7, it can also be considered at a system level that extends beyond the school. A quality research use culture is therefore complex and multi-contextual because different research may be assessed and applied in different settings within a school to address different needs at any point in time. Further, the cohorts involved in each setting may be different and/ or overlap with other settings and may be at different points in their research use journey, in terms of either their own capacities to use research and/or where they are in their research implementation process. Our findings suggest that educators want "to be heard" and have research "adapted to meet [their] own needs" (teachers, survey), which means that a quality research use culture needs to be flexible and adaptable, as much as it needs to be cognisant of its different internal contexts, as well as those external to the school.

Taken together, these three points – about quality research use being multi-faceted, dynamic and multi-layered – can help leaders to consider how best to support quality research use at the organisational level. The idea of quality research use being multi-faceted, for example, can help leaders to consider what combinations of action they can take at any point in time to support research use. Meanwhile, the idea of quality research use being dynamic can help leaders to consider planning and evolving research use over time so that it is sustainable and embedded in the processes, operations and culture of the school. Along similar lines, the idea of quality research use being multi-layered can help leaders to implement different initiatives that involve and/or are targeted to different cohorts within a school but contribute to overall school improvement and professional development.

As an example of how thinking about the influences of, and connections between, culture, leadership and infrastructure can be helpful to leaders, the vignette below focuses on a secondary school early in its quality research use journey. It shows how the school's improvement team used the QURE Assessment Tool[1] to guide their plans to improve research use across the organisation.

Vignette 7 ("How is it helpful?") – "Quality use of research as a culture" helping to guide research use improvement plans across a school

This vignette features the school improvement team at Malahide College and how they utilised the QURE Assessment Tool to support their plans for improving research use in their school. The team is responsible for designing and implementing learning and assessment strategies, guides and tools across the school, and have set themselves the goal of using research, alongside school data, to inform their work. Their newly-developed learning and assessment framework is a good example of a research-based resource that has been well received by staff for both its clarity and understandability. As a part of their remit, they see themselves as role models of quality research use and are accountable for promoting and encouraging research use within the school.

Marcus, Assistant Principal Learning and Teaching, and leader of the team, explained that they initially thought improving staff's skills on how to use research was a priority. However, when using the QURE tool to complete a group assessment, their team's scoring profile indicated that culture was an area that needed immediate improvement. The scoring profile also showed that individual team members had different perceptions of their own and the school's research use capacities. These differences allowed the team to discuss what they meant by "using research well", which highlighted the importance of establishing common understanding and language regarding quality research use. The scoring profile also helped them to see that being united as a team and communicating consistent messages about research use to others were important first steps to get right.

The team reflected on how closely infrastructure and leadership were related to building a research-engaged school culture. They viewed the tool as a useful way to gather data from the school community about their research use capacities that could inform infrastructure improvements. Marcus explained, "That would give us data that would be really interesting for how we plan, say, internal professional development, and also how we talk to our learning area leaders". Maya, another team member, commented that tool data may help to guide the implementation of structured research-informed staff meetings and inquiry cycle processes as ways to improve staff's research use. Angie, also a team member, felt that the tool could be "useful as a teaching tool" and help to inform practice improvement processes. Overall, the team felt that the practitioner case studies, embedded in the scaffolds available in the QURE Assessment Tool, would provide productive tips for how to build a cultural improvement plan that would suit their school's context.

This vignette provides an example of how the concept of quality use as a culture has been relevant and helpful to a school improvement team. In particular, it shows how the inter-connected organisational QURE components of *culture, leadership* and *infrastructure* were influential on one team's discussions about quality research use and ideas about priority actions to improve their own collective *leadership* of research use, and the broader research-engaged *culture* of the school.

As a whole, this chapter has shed light on what quality use of research involves at the school level and what it requires of schools as organisations. It highlights ways in which leaders of all kinds and at all levels within schools can support quality research use. However, this organisational perspective on "quality use as a culture" needs to connect with and be informed by, a deep understanding of what is discussed in our next chapter: What quality use of research involves as a practice.

Note

1   The QURE (Quality Use of Research Evidence) Assessment Tool is an online tool based on the QURE Framework that enables educators, as individuals or as a group, to assess their current research use practices and gain feedback and scaffolded resources for future improvement.

References

Brown, C., & Greany, T. (2018). The evidence-informed school system in England: Where should school leaders be focusing their efforts? *Leadership and Policy in Schools, 17*(1), 115–137. 10.1080/15700763.2016.1270330

Coburn, C. E. (2005). The role of nonsystem actors in the relationship between policy and practice: The case of reading instruction in California. *Educational Evaluation and Policy Analysis, 27*(1), 23–52. 10.3102/01623737027001023

Cooper, A., & Levin, B. (2013). Research use by leaders in Canadian school districts. *International Journal of Education Policy & Leadership, 8*(7). 10.22230/ijepl.2013 v8n7a449

Cordingley, P. (2008). Research and evidence-informed practice: Focusing on practice and practitioners. *Cambridge Journal of Education, 38*(1), 37–52. 10.1080/0305 7640801889964

Davies, H., Boaz, A., Nutley, S., & Fraser, A. (2019). Conclusions: Lessons from the past, prospects for the future. In A. Boaz, H. Davies, A. Fraser, & S. Nutley (Eds.), *What works now? Evidence-informed policy and practice* (pp. 369–382). Policy Press.

Godfrey, D. (2016). Leadership of schools as research-led organisations in the English educational environment: Cultivating a research-engaged school culture. *Educational Management Administration & Leadership, 44*(2), 301–321. 10.1177/ 1741143213508294

Godfrey, D., & Brown, C. (Eds.) (2019). *An ecosystem for research-engaged schools: Reforming education through research*. Routledge.

Hemsley-Brown, J., & Sharp, C. (2003). The use of research to improve professional practice: A systematic review of the literature. *Oxford Review of Education, 29*(4), 449–470. 10.1080/0305498032000153025

Levin, B. (2013). To know is not enough: Research knowledge and its use. *Review of Education, 1*(1), 2–31. 10.1002/rev3.3001

Nutley, S., Walter, I., & Davies, H. T. O. (2007). *Using evidence: How research can inform public services*. Policy Press.

Rickinson, M., Walsh, L., Gleeson, J., Cutler, B., Cirkony, C., & Salisbury, M. (2022). Using research well in educational practice. In OECD (Ed.), *Who cares about using education research in policy and practice? Strengthening research engagement* (pp. 182–199). OECD Publishing. 10.1787/65aac033-en

van Schaik, P., Volman, M., Admiraal, W., & Schenke, W. (2018). Barriers and conditions for teachers' utilisation of academic knowledge. *International Journal of Educational Research, 90*, 50–63. 10.1016/j.ijer.2018.05.003

6 Quality use of research as a practice

Chapter overview

This chapter explores how the quality use of research evidence can be conceptualised in terms of educators' enacted practices. Drawing on educators' survey and interview responses, it considers how:

- the practices involved in using research are little explored, especially in relation to using research well;
- using research well can be conceptualised as an individual practice, a shared practice and an invested practice;
- as an individual practice, the quality use of research is driven by educators' curiosity and connected to their sense of professionalism;
- as a shared practice, the quality use of research involves collective engagement and needs to be embedded within educators' ways of working;
- as an invested practice, the quality use of research must be guided by a clear purpose and take time and effort;
- these three lenses on quality use as a practice are interconnected and link with the core, individual and organisational components of the Quality Use of Research Evidence (QURE) Framework; and

DOI: 10.4324/9781003353966-6

- quality use as a practice is not about prescribing what it must 'look like', but about understanding how it can be enacted across different contexts.

Introduction

As noted throughout this book, the quality use of research to inform educational decision making is a complex and "sophisticated undertaking" (Rickinson et al., 2022, p. 143). While there is a growing understanding of the individual, organisational- and system-level elements that can support educators to use research well, the practices of such use (i.e., how educators conceptualise, relate to and enact quality research use) are not as well understood. This reflects a shortcoming in the educational research use literature more broadly, where "little attention has been paid to *the practice* of evidence use" (Farley-Ripple et al., 2018, p. 236, emphasis original). This chapter aims to address this gap by conceptualising the quality use of research as a practice.

In service of this aim, this chapter draws on qualitative data from Survey 1 ($n = 492$) and interviews ($n = 27$) with Australian educators about their perspectives of what it means to 'use research well' or 'use research poorly'. To conceptualise "quality research use as a practice", we analysed educators' responses using a thematic approach, focusing on how they envisioned and enacted using research well in their day-to-day practice. This analysis process differed slightly from Chapters 4, 5 and 7 which involved both inductive theme generation alongside deductive coding of educators' responses to the QURE Framework. Whereas, here, we solely coded educators' responses in terms of new inductively-generated codes and themes relating to "practices of quality research use". This process generated six characteristics that aimed to capture the commonalities in how educators practised the quality use of research despite them approaching it differently across the diverse educational contexts in which they worked. The discussion of these characteristics is complemented with quantitative data from Survey 3 ($n = 414$) that aimed to gather educators' perspectives about the barriers, enablers and practices involved in using research well (see Appendix 1 for more details about samples and methods).

Following this introduction, this chapter is structured into five main sections. The next section positions our understanding of quality research use as a practice within the broader literature and highlights how this connects with the perspectives discussed in previous chapters, as well as the QURE Framework. Following this, there are three sections that draw on educators' perspectives to articulate quality research use as an *individual* practice, a *shared* practice and an *invested* practice. The chapter then concludes with a section that summarises the key points and draws out what we see as being important implications from these findings.

Understanding quality use of research as a practice

With an increased focus on supporting educators' use of research, we have seen an increasing recognition that "the use of research in practice is complex" (Farley-Ripple et al., 2018, p. 235). In response to this complexity, Ward (2019) notes that frameworks and models of research use processes are useful tools for deepening our understanding of research use practices. However, there are relatively few frameworks that are grounded in the context of contemporary education systems (Ward, 2019) and those that are tend to outline different types of research use, as opposed to the practices that underpin different ways of using research (Farley-Ripple et al., 2018). For example, Weiss and Bacuvalas' (1980) typology of instrumental, conceptual, strategic and imposed research use is often used to discuss the ways in which educators use research (e.g., Penuel et al., 2016). Yet, because such typologies are focused on the *types of use* rather than the *practices of use*, they are not generally attuned to the complexities of how teachers understand, relate to and enact these practices as part of their professional identity and pedagogy. As Cain (2015, p. 490) has argued, while such typologies can help to inform a broad understanding of research use practices, they are "less helpful for describing teachers' use of research from a practitioner perspective". This is particularly true against a backdrop where wider work on research use in policy and practice tends to be more theoretical than empirical (see Oliver et al., 2014).

Turning our attention to understanding what is meant by the quality use of research evidence, these theoretical and conceptual contributions do have their place. As noted in Chapter 2, the lack of sustained theoretical discussion of quality use is an important gap to address and looking across different sectors (e.g., policy, social care, health) can provide valuable conceptual tools for this task. Similarly, we explored in Chapter 3 how conceptual clarity is important for articulating quality use as an aspiration for educational practice. However, when "theoretical talk [...] is too distanced from the real-world problems faced by practitioners" (Tseng & Gamoran, 2017, p. 2), it can be dismissed as being of little relevance to educators. This highlights the need for ways of understanding the quality use of research that speak to the complexities and realities of educators' daily practices (Gleeson et al., 2023; Rickinson et al., 2017).

In particular, Ward (2019, p. 180) notes that "it is through the interplay of theoretical frameworks and practical experiences that we are most likely to come to a clearer understanding of how best to support evidence-informed practice in education and beyond". This book, more broadly, has taken up this aim and has drawn on educators' perspectives to further our conceptual and empirical understanding of the QURE Framework in practice settings. For instance, previous chapters explored the individual (e.g., mindsets, skillsets and relationships) as well as the organisational (e.g., culture, leadership and infrastructure) components that support the quality use of research evidence in practice. There are definitely connections, for example, between quality research use as an individual capacity in Chapter 4 and quality research use as an individual practice as it is discussed here. There are also conceptual links between quality research use as a collective practice and quality use as a culture as discussed in Chapter 5. Yet, much like the broader research base on educators' and policy makers' use of evidence (e.g., Innvær et al., 2002; Ion & Iucu, 2014), these previous chapters articulated educators' perspectives in terms of specific barriers and enablers of quality research use, rather than their understandings of different actions and behaviours that can constitute the practices of using research well across different contexts.

As a point of difference, this chapter focuses explicitly on how educators described the practices that they associate with using research well. We conceptualise 'practice' to encompass not only what educators physically do when engaging with research (Farley-Ripple et al., 2018), but also how they understand these actions and the motivations behind why they are considered important. This is particularly useful in helping us to illuminate the core components of the QURE Framework, such as thoughtful engagement with and implementation of research by exploring how educators' quality research use is invested with a clear sense of purpose and practiced in collective and shared ways. Thus, in taking this perspective, our aim here is to provide a "fine-grained, closer-to-practice understanding that will help education professionals make sense of and reflect critically" on the quality use of research evidence in their setting (Rickinson et al., 2017, p. 187).

However, we do not intend for this chapter to be read as prescribing what the quality use of research *must* look like in practice. Underpinned by the appreciation that there is no 'one size fits all' approach to using research, our conceptualisation of quality use as a practice aims to move beyond trying to translate single "exceptional cases of research use" across different settings (Boaz & Nutley, 2019; Oliver et al., 2014, p. 4). This is important because while it is widely recognised that quality research *evidence* must be specific to the educational context (e.g., Drill et al., 2013; Gore & Gitlin, 2004), the same is not often stated for quality research *use*. For this reason, as shown in Table 6.1, this chapter identifies six common characteristics that were evident in educators' varied descriptions of quality research use across their different educational settings.

These characteristics can be conceptualised under three broad themes related to how they speak to the quality use of research:

- An individual practice – where quality use of research is driven by curiosity and connected to educators' professionalism.
- A shared practice – where quality use is collective and embedded.
- An invested practice – where quality use is purposeful, and time- and effort-dependent.

Table 6.1 Number and percentage of Survey 1 respondents (*n* = 492) and interviews (*n* = 27) coded to the characteristics of quality research use practices

Characteristics	Using research well	
	Interviews	Surveys
Purposeful	89% (24)	81% (398)
Embedded	85% (23)	75% (367)
Collective	81% (22)	35% (171)
Supporting professionalism	81% (22)	50% (246)
Curiosity-driven	78% (21)	64% (313)
Time- and effort-dependent	56% (15)	55% (271)

Before exploring each of these practices in detail, it is beneficial to briefly illustrate how they may be observed in educators' day-to-day work. The vignette below highlights how aspects of quality use as an individual, shared and invested practice featured in the work of one primary school middle leader.

Vignette 8 ("Looks like in practice") – "Quality use of research as a practice" within the work of a primary school middle leader

This vignette features Tracie, Head of Curriculum at Baltimore School, and describes how she uses research well in her everyday practice. At the outset, Tracie has an open and curious mindset about research: "I love research. I just think it has such a positive impact [and] if you can prove that it works elsewhere, then that's what you should be using". She connects research use with her professionalism as an educator and not only looks for ways to continuously improve her practice but seeks to influence others to do so as well. She believes that you can turn around colleagues who may initially be "negative" towards research use if you "listen […] take their ideas on board and coach [them] through what it might look like". She emphasises that trust is key, as is "not throwing away what [people] know and where [they] feel safe". In her experience, research use is most effective when it is used as part of broader school improvement processes, where research is connected with school data and is integrated with educators' professional experience and knowledge.

Relationships, therefore, are very important to Tracie. She believes that collaboration is fundamental to identifying relevant research and applying it well in practice. She explains that "the more […] that you are doing that consultation and collaborating with people, the more convincing it is [to use research]". But, she explained, building these relationships is not a quick and simple process. Quality research use takes effort and time: "It's not a fast journey. It has taken a long time to gain the trust of other people on staff that you are that open person that they can talk to". She also emphasises that quality use needs to "have a purpose – that would be number one". Pulling these ideas together, Tracie suggests that other schools looking to improve performance and embed research use into practice might start with "finding something [to change], then build your relationships and then just bite it off slowly

---

bit by bit [...] make sure there is a purpose [...] then be helpful to others with the backing behind [you]".

Tracie's vignette highlights a number of elements of "quality use as a practice":

- First, Tracie engages in quality research use as an *individual practice*. She has positive views about how research can support her practice and supports others to be curious about research use. Tracie's use of research is also closely linked to her sense of professionalism where she integrates research knowledge with her own experience as a form of continuous professional development.
- Second, Tracie establishes and promotes *shared practices* around using research. Her work relies on core principles of collaboration, knowledge sharing and facilitation of open and safe conversations in order to bring her colleagues on a collective research use journey. Tracie also values embedding research alongside engagement with other forms of evidence as part of broader school improvement processes.
- Finally, quality use as an *invested practice* is evident in Tracie's views that using research well takes time and effort. She believes that "rushing things" can result in research being "poorly instigated in practice". Similarly, Tracie emphasises that quality research use should begin with identifying an issue in practice and then considering how research might support a purposeful and targeted change.

Quality use as an individual practice

At an individual level, educators practised the quality use of research in two primary ways: first, their engagement with research was driven by a disposition of curiosity, and second, they saw research use as underpinning their sense of professionalism.

Curiosity as a driver for quality research use

Educators explained how being curious was a core practice of using research well because it guided how they approached and engaged with research (78% of interviews, 64% of surveys). When educators were curious about research, they described themselves as being "open to listening and looking at evidence" (senior leader, interview) and taking that evidence into their practice in several ways. This way of working included using research to reflect on their practice, engage with new interpretations of problems they were facing and provide ideas about different teaching practices that they could apply in their classroom. Across each of these instances, being genuinely curious about research meant that it was applied in ways that deepened or challenged educators' thinking. In contrast, when research was used without this guiding sense of curiosity, educators described how it was used to "back up what was already being done" (teacher, survey) or to "support a pre-existing view" (middle leader, survey).

Being curious was also important for how educators saw themselves as being open-minded in their use of research in practice. For instance, in Survey 3, when asked about 'how they think about research', 88% of educators 'agreed' or 'strongly agreed' that they were 'open-minded to new research ideas and knowledge', while 73% saw themselves as 'curious and inquisitive about different research'. There was a statistically significant relationship between these two dispositions, with 97% of educators who indicated being 'curious and inquisitive' also indicating that they were 'open-minded' ($p < .001$). While being open-minded was seen as important for engaging with research more broadly, it was particularly important in relation to the specific research use tasks of accessing, interpreting and adapting research. For example, when describing the creation of a research-informed instructional model, one middle leader interviewee explained the importance of looking and thinking "widely":

> It [involved] high levels of research, both looking at other schools but also looking at best practice across the world. [...] So, we spent a lot of time and [...] it was being led very dynamically to make sure that we were doing it [properly]; looking widely and thinking widely about what [...] our own school [model] would look like.

In drawing out how they practised curiosity in their use of research, it is notable that a number of educators made connections to various pedagogical models of inquiry. They explained how the processes of using research well mirrored the staged and iterative processes of "inquiry spirals" (senior leader, survey), "inquiry cycles" (senior leader, survey), "inquiry-based project learning" (other role, survey) and "appreciative inquiry" approaches (middle leader, survey). For educators who indicated that using research was not yet an established practice for them, these pedagogical models provided familiar and accessible ways to approach quality research use. For instance, when describing how they approached a practice change, one middle leader explained in their interview:

> I have a bit of a habit of kind of going straight to the end point and trying to get to the answer quite quickly. I resisted that temptation and tried to do some reading before, I guess, deciding what this exactly was going to look like and let the reading go a little bit. [...] [My principal is] always telling me that I need to, you know, sit back and reflect and think a little bit more before I take action on things because I just like getting stuff done. And so, I [...] [used] de Bono's hats [to] look at things from a variety of different perspectives.

By following these models, educators not only felt more comfortable in the fact that they were "implementing real inquiry" (senior leader, interview), but it also provided an important opportunity for them to demonstrate the curious mindsets that they aimed to instil in their students. In particular, one leader of an International Baccalaureate (IB) school explained in their interview that using research well allowed her colleagues to role model the principles of the IB to their students: "So understanding inquiry from the first instance, and the teachers being role models of inquiry for the students, has really helped that inquiry process and to look beyond what's going on in the school". In making these connections to pedagogical and inquiry models, educators also saw themselves as ongoing learners in the sense that "we're always [...] encouraging the children to ask questions about their learning, but we're constantly learning as well" (senior leader, interview). This line of thinking highlights the connection of curiosity with the second characteristic of quality use as an individual practice, which is about research use underpinning educators' views of their own professionalism.

Supporting educators' professionalism and professional identity

Although educators often discussed the various benefits of research use, it was clear that the practice of using research well had significant implications for

127

how educators understood their own professionalism and enacted their professional identity (81% of interviews, 50% of surveys). For example, one senior leader described in their interview how engaging with research was "the bread and butter of [their] role" where it was important to "keep abreast of all educational research and to [...] make sure that [they're] using that to inform [their] own thinking". In this sense, the practices of staying up to date with research and using it as a stimulus for reflection were important for the ongoing development of educators' knowledge and skills. Some also saw research and evidence use as being part of their ethical obligations and professional conduct. For instance, another middle leader explained in their interview how they felt that it would be "careless and wrong professional conduct if we [did] not reach or try to gain as much evidence [...] as we could".

These views about the practice of research use point to an underpinning professional motivation to make well-informed decisions about classroom practice. In Survey 3, educators' responses suggest that these motivations are particularly important reasons for using research. For instance, when asked 'what makes research use worthwhile', 82% of educators 'agreed' or 'strongly agreed' that it 'helps me make informed decisions'. This was the most strongly endorsed item, closely followed by 'it influences my practice' (81%, equal 2nd most strongly endorsed), 'it increases my professionalism' (80%, 3rd), and 'it empowers me and my practice' (77%, 5th). There were also statistically significant relationships between these items, with 90% of educators who indicated that research helps them to 'make well-informed decisions' also indicating that it 'increase[d] [their] professionalism' ($p <$ .001). Similarly, 87% of educators who believed that research helped them to 'make well-informed decisions' also felt that research 'empowers me and my practice' ($p < .001$).

In interviews, educators explained that using research empowered them in their professional practice because it helped to ensure that "nothing [was] left to chance" (senior leader, interview). They were "drawn to" the "robust, reputational credibility" of research to inform their professional decision making because they did not want to be seen as "just [...] willy-nilly suggesting something that is purely anecdotal" (senior leader, interview). A number of educators with many years of experience explained the importance of such research-informed prac-tices with reference to how their practice "used to be". To quote one middle leader interviewee:

The vast majority of my day would be driven by research and that's really something that's changed. I've been teaching now for close to 20 years [...] it used to be a lot more "choose your own adventure", and it used to be more what's being passed on from one generation of teachers to the next one, what was, what would work or not. Whereas now, I find that [we] emphasise [...] the importance of using evidence-based practice, a) to achieve better outcomes and b) to have consistency of practice.

When explaining how these practices related to their sense of professionalism, many educators highlighted how they saw themselves as being a researcher of their own practice in the classroom. For one senior leader interviewee in particular, using research to "problematise their own practice [and] [...] be researchers in their classroom" was a foundational way of understanding their practice that "strongly [came] from [...] [their] formative years as a teacher". Yet, being a researcher in the classroom not only encompassed how educators understood their professional identity, but also how this identity was enacted in the classroom, with the same senior leader explaining:

Teachers [need] to see themselves as researchers in their own classrooms, to be able to find their own problems, frame those problems, collaboratively work to resolve those problems through trial and error and experimenting, and that might mean then using other people's research as a touchstone or some stimulus or inspiration.

In essence, educators cared deeply about practising quality research use and were clear in how they understood it at an individual level as being central to their professionalism and underpinned by a sense of curiosity about research. However, at the same time, educators emphasised that the quality use of research was not wholly an individual practice, but also a shared one.

Quality use as a shared practice

Alongside individual practices, using research well is also underpinned by two key practices that require the cooperative engagement of groups of staff. First, educators spoke about working collectively to engage with research, and second, they described how research use was embedded in their shared ways of working with colleagues.

Collective ways of working with research

Working collectively with others was discussed as a crucial way of prac-tising quality research use, particularly in interviews (81% of interviews, 35% of surveys). Without a collective approach, educators not only felt that it was not possible to use research well, but that "inconsistent and disjointed approaches [would cause] conflict and confusion" (senior leader, survey) amongst staff teams. For this reason, educators highlighted both the need to develop "a collective understanding of what we're trying to do" (senior leader, interview) at the beginning of a research-informed change and the importance of implementing the change "consistent[ly] across the school" (senior leader, interview).

To illustrate this point, some educators shared how a collective approach to research use allowed their school to shift from what could be understood as poor use to quality use. For example, in an interview, one senior leader shared their experience of implementing a school-wide initiative to support the consistent use of research. They explained that prior to the initiative, research use was "problematic, because people are working incredibly hard, [but] if everybody's got different pedagogies and different ways of doing it, then we're not a team working together". However, after creating whole school goals to support educators' collective and unified engagement with research, they noticed a substantial change:

> We had our leadership team meeting last night and everybody checked in about where their learning areas were, actually, and everybody was talking the same language, moving the same way, and there feels this incredible momentum [...] I think before that, people were knowledgeable about lots of different evidence-based practices and what good teaching was [...] but I don't think they were getting traction, because we were working independently, even though we were talking about the same theories and ideas.

In other words, the quality use of research as a practice gained "traction" and "momentum" when educators were working with the same goal in mind, but also when they had the opportunity to share their knowledge with others.

As discussed in Chapters 4 and 5, sharing knowledge with others was seen to be an important component of educators' collaborative research use practices. For example, in Survey 2, when asked how they collaborated with others for different research use tasks, most often educators indicated 'sharing [their] knowledge and opinions' irrespective of the research task they were engaged in (i.e., 67% indicated sharing their knowledge and opinions when finding research, 55% when assessing research, 49% when adapting research, 50% when implementing research). Notably, though, the collective sharing of their knowledge was not just an aspect of how educators practised quality use of research, it was also seen as a means to support and improve it. When asked how important certain actions were for improving their use of research, 63% of educators indicated that being involved in 'sharing knowledge about practice within the school' was 'important' or 'very important'. This was third only to being involved in 'reflecting on students' learning outcomes' (79%) and 'reflecting on [their] own learning' (73%).

By coming together to collectively engage with research, educators are able to draw on their understanding of students' learning, the school context and their own professional values to make collective decisions about the quality use of research. For example, one senior leader reflected in an interview on their approach to collective consultation around a research-informed change to writing at their school:

> We looked at 17 different [research-informed] approaches to writing. [...] We put them up all around the walls of a room and [...] asked our teachers to look at them all. It blew us away [...] they could get rid of five approaches straight away. [...] We sat down and unpacked that as the teaching staff. It really came back to, "Well, this is the vision of the school, these are our values" and so, therefore, if we have these very strongly within us, then this is part of our consideration when we consider what we're going to use in relation to research.

She noted that this collective process formed the "foundation and the common knowledge and understanding of us all" and although individual teachers "might delve off" to adapt the research to their individual classroom, they "have a foundation or common understanding from the starting point".

This school leader was not alone in emphasising the importance of these consultative processes. Several others also described how such processes were important opportunities to have "rich dialogue[s]" that drew on the staff body's collective professional knowledge (middle leader, interview). For this reason, it was common for many senior and middle leaders to discuss how they had incorporated these collective processes into the schedules and operation of their school, which highlights the connection with the second characteristic of quality use as a shared practice: research use being embedded in the school context.

Embedding research use in shared ways of working

Educators saw the quality use of research as embedded when it was positioned as a central aspect of the shared practice within their school (85% of interviews, 75% of surveys). When educators saw the practices of quality research use as "embedded in the culture" (senior leader, interview) of their educational setting, they specifically referred to how it had "become a priority [...] and [was] demonstrated as something that's really a value" (middle leader, interview). In many cases, as discussed in Chapter 5, educators' descriptions often referred to the role that school leadership teams played in building these cultures. For example, one senior leader noted in an interview how at their school, the "culture as a leadership team is to use evidence and research to make any decisions that we're making as a school and then that flows down to [...] [the] professional learning communities". This quote suggests a natural permeation of these shared practices throughout the school. However, other educators emphasised that embedding quality use as a shared practice was an active process that was achieved by bringing research use into different activities within the school. Such efforts created the space and opportunity for educators to collectively engage with research despite their busy schedules. For example, one middle leader interviewee reflected on "redesign[ing] part of our annual review meetings [...] [so staff can] talk about a piece of reading", while another discussed how they used "professional learning teams on a fortnightly cycle [...] [to conduct] a joint book study and discuss strategies recommended in the book".

As also noted in Chapter 5, the value of such practices was supported by Survey 3 responses, where 66% of educators indicated that it was 'important' or 'very important' for improving their use of research that it was 'incorporat[ed] [...] into school processes, activities and practices'. To better understand 'the best activities to incorporate research discussion and engagement', respondents to Survey 3 were asked to select up to five activities from a list of 14 options (or suggest their own). The most popular activities included 'scheduled staff professional development (PD) meetings/working sessions' (selected by 56%), 'organised whole of staff days' (52%), 'staff development planning sessions (e.g., goal setting)' (44%), and 'structured school time dedicated to [...] research' (36%). They were then asked how often their school currently embeds research in these selected activities. Notably, educators who indicated that their schools 'often' or 'always' discussed research during any of these activities were all significantly more likely to regularly use research in their practice (PD sessions, $p < .001$; staff days, $p = .001$; staff development planning, $p < .001$; structured time, $p < .001$).

Capturing the essence of quality use as a culture, several educators' descriptions went beyond the practical elements of school organisation structures. In these cases, educators instead focused on how they and their colleagues embodied the practice of quality research use. For example, one educator observed that "using well means it's intrinsic in your language, it's intrinsic in your approach [...] we talk [research] all the time" (middle leader, interview), while another explained that research was embedded when it became part of "every breath we take" (middle leader, interview). These statements reflect instances where research use was such a strongly shared practice that "it just informs [educators'] thinking about [their] approaches on a day-to-day basis" (senior leader, interview).

In short, when quality research use was discussed as "improving our collective practice" (senior leader, interview) or "embedded in what we do" (senior leader, interview), educators were describing quality research use as a shared practice. These descriptions highlight how using research well is a deeply relational and collaborative practice if it is to be sustained and have a positive impact on students' learning and teachers' development. Yet, in order for educators' efforts, both at an individual and shared level, to make a difference, they were clear that quality research use was also a practice that required investment.

Quality use as an invested practice

Using research well is a complex and sophisticated practice. For this reason, educators spoke about quality use of research as a practice that requires investment in two main ways: first, it needed to be purposeful to ensure meaningful buy-in; and, second, it required the investment of time and effort to be effectively realised.

Having a clear purpose to establish buy-in

When educators spoke about the quality use of research being a purposeful practice, they often discussed how their personal investment was connected to the research-informed change having a clear purpose (89% of interviews, 81% of surveys). For example, one educator noted that by "coming up with something that's really specific and focused [...] [that's when] people are invested" (senior leader, interview). In another instance, when reflecting on the success of a research-informed programme in an interview, one senior leader remarked that because educators "saw the value of the programme, they had the buy-in [...] they want[ed] to drive it and they want[ed] to make it great". In other words, when educators saw that the use of research had a clear purpose, they were more likely to invest themselves in how it was practised.

In contrast, when educators described what it looked like to use research poorly, many of their descriptions highlighted instances where the practice of using research lacked clear purpose. For example, it could involve using research in an "ad hoc way" (senior leader, interview), or "just read[ing] [research] for the sake of filling in time at a staff meeting" (teacher, survey). When research use was viewed in these ways, educators described it as not "worthy of attention" (senior leader, survey). These descriptions emphasise that 'purposefulness' is not an inherent characteristic of research use, rather it was something educators actively invested in research depending on how they were engaging with it. This not only related to how research was used to address practice problems but that it also played an important role in understanding them. As one middle leader explained in an interview, research was helpful "not just [to] fix the problem, but [also to] give us that background into why we're seeing what we're seeing [...] [to] enrich our understanding and help us make a decision".

Educators' views about quality use needing to have a clear purpose were also evident in their Survey 3 responses. For instance, to improve their use of research, 70% of educators indicated that it was 'important' or 'very important' that their school had 'a clear vision [...] about research use'. Similarly, almost half of all educators (48%) 'agreed' or 'strongly agreed' that 'using research is *not* worthwhile' when 'it doesn't always have a clear purpose for its use'. These educators were significantly less likely to also indicate that they were willing to 'invest time in research use' (indicated by 39%, compared to 52% for those who saw research use as worthwhile even without a clear purpose, $p = .010$). This finding suggests that educators weigh up the purposefulness of research use when determining how much of themselves to invest in this practice.

Such a perspective was exemplified in one middle leader's survey response which equated "weighing up the purpose of the research [with] conducting a 'cost-benefit' analysis" in order to determine whether they implemented specific research-informed strategies in their classroom. Following this reasoning, another educator explained that a "really purposeful" use of research was expected to have a "really high impact" in the classroom (senior leader, interview). In this sense, purposefully engaging with research well was seen by educators as an investment in their students and their learning. However, the important point here is that the connection between impact and purposefulness is not solely a characteristic of the research, but also the way in which it was practised and enacted in the school context. For example, one educator explained: "If it's not done in a way where it has meaning and leads to something else, then it could be a really well researched, documented, [and] evidenced approach. But if it's not done well and given the time to be able to devote to it, then it might become [purposeless]" (senior leader, interview). This quote highlights how educators not only see the quality use of research as a practice that is invested with a purpose, but it also requires an explicit investment of resources.

Requiring investment of time and effort

Educators also emphasised that practising the quality use of research involves an explicit investment of their time and effort (56% of interviews, 55% of surveys). Without this investment, educators described research use as being "superficial, [where] you go through the motion [...] and so there is not really that deep learning [...] [because you] cut corners" (middle leader, interview). This was also seen in educators' survey responses where they articulated research use without the investment of time or effort as being "rushed, tokenistic" (teacher, survey), "watered down" (middle leader, survey) and having "no real impact or change" (teacher, survey). In contrast, when educators made these investments, they felt that they were able to "learn more deeply about [the research]" (senior leader, interview) and "unpack the evidence in a way that can be discussed and implemented effectively in classrooms" (senior leader, survey). These investments were important, too, for the sustainability of research-informed changes. For instance, one educator explained that if research use was "going to be sustainable and have a long lasting, powerful impact on student outcomes [...] you need to take your time and you really need to explore things carefully" (senior leader, interview).

Given the importance of this investment in quality research use as a practice, several senior and middle leaders highlighted how they did not expect teachers to make these contributions on their own and aimed to support them with school infrastructure. As one middle leader explained in an interview: "Carving out time [...] is so important, and we appreciate the impact it can have. We must make time, we cannot presume that people will just [engage with research] out of goodwill, of their own accord." Yet, as discussed in the previous chapter, despite these good intentions, this support was not always necessarily sufficient, with one senior leader stating in their interview:

> While we do have our collaborative planning each week during school time, and we do give teachers time during the day, every now and then for research [...] [where] they come off class [...] that's a very tiny amount of all the hours that are put in for the research.

For these reasons, a number of educators explained how they looked to their *personal* time (i.e., out of school hours) to make this investment, with one middle leader explaining in an interview:

> I would say that most staff, we would work in excess of a 55- or 60-hour week [...] And so, I just don't actually know where I would fit in any more academic reading [...] I could be listening to more like

podcasts or something else when I drive. But literally, my driving time is about the only time where I could fit in more work.

There was also evidence of educators making these investments of personal time in their responses to Survey 3. Almost half of the educators (46%) expressed that they 'want to invest time in research', yet just 37% indicated that 'school time dedicated to reading, discussing and understanding research' was 'often' or 'always' provided. We asked those who engaged with research during the school term when and where they did this, with the most common times and locations being at school, during school hours (81%), at home, on weekends (69%) and at home, after school hours (59%). Notably, educators who were willing to invest time in research were significantly more likely to indicate that they invested their personal time in research use. This included using research at home, on weekends (78% compared with 62% for educators not willing to invest, $p < .001$) as well as at home, after school (69% compared with 50%, $p < .001$). Given this finding, it is perhaps unsurprising that 72% of educators in Survey 3 indicated that it was 'important' or 'very important' to build 'time into staff schedules for reading, discussing and understanding research'. Educators saw these investments as valuable because they believed that the time and effort that they put into the quality use would pay off in the long term:

> There are times when we need to slow down, refocus and then continue on. Because we live in this fast-paced way that we work [...] I think that concept of slowing down to then help you speed up is something that we might need to do a little bit more of.
>
> (senior leader, interview)

In summary, educators are clear that the quality use of research is a complex practice that requires substantial investment. Not only did educators emphasise that research use has to have a clear purpose in order to be a practice worth investing in, but it also requires an explicit investment of time and effort to be realised – preferably by schools, but more commonly by themselves. Viewing the quality use of research at the personal and shared levels, as well as an invested practice, highlights some important considerations in how it can be understood and supported to which we now turn our attention.

Conclusion

This chapter explored how the quality use of research is a complex and sophisticated professional practice. At an individual level, using research well is driven by a disposition of curiosity and underpins how educators understand and enact their professional identity. Using research well requires educators to work collectively and for these collective processes to be embedded in the shared way of working in schools. At the same time, while the practice of quality research use needs to be purposeful to foster educators' buy-in, it also requires an explicit investment of educators' time and effort to lead to impactful and sustainable change.

While these characteristics have been presented separately in this chapter for ease of interpretation, in practice, they are likely to be interconnected. For example, if educators are to follow their curiosity and engage deeply with research, this requires an investment of time and effort. Similarly, if research use is to become embedded within the practice of a whole school community, it needs to be purposeful and connect to that community's shared vision, values and aims. In both of these cases, the enactment of the former practice is connected to the latter. We see these connections as highlighting the multi-faceted nature of quality research use as a practice. For example, when Cook and Brown (1999, pp. 386–387) explain practice as encompassing the "activities of individuals and groups […] [as] informed by a particular organisational or group context", we see the connections between individual and shared practices. From this perspective, the complex and dynamic ways in which these aspects are connected and embodied in educators' practice can provide a useful frame to understand, articulate and support the quality use of research.

In pointing to this complexity, we aim to highlight that the quality use of research as a practice is not a "single exceptional way of using research" that can be simply translated into other educational settings (Boaz & Nutley, 2019; Oliver et al., 2014, p. 4). Rather, it is practised in very different ways depending on the context. The connecting thread, however, between these different ways of enacting quality use is the shared meanings behind each of these practices. In light of Cook and Brown's (1999) point that it is the meaning and value behind actions that substantiate them as practices, we argue that articulating these aspects is important for introducing the quality use of research as an educational practice. We also concur that it is the meaning and value behind these actions that substantiate them as practices.

For example, this chapter has not just illustrated how educators have practised the quality use of research, but also how certain meanings and values informed these actions. This is particularly evident in relation to how educators imbued quality research use with a sense of purpose or related using research well to their sense of professionalism. It became clear that educators did not see the quality use of research as "just another one of those things, that research is an add-on and that after we tick this box, we can get back to the real teaching" (middle leader, interview). Nor is it viewed as "extra work", as one senior leader explained during an interview: "It's actually asking [educators] to think more deeply about the work that they do".

Many readers may also be rightly seeing connections between these practices and components of the QURE Framework presented earlier in this book. For instance, quality use as an individual practice connects strongly with the individual enabling component of mindsets as discussed in Chapter 4. Quality use as a shared practice connects with the individual enabler of relationships, as also discussed in Chapter 4, and the organisational components of culture and leadership, as discussed in Chapter 5. Quality use as an invested practice has strong links to the organisational enabler of infrastructure, also discussed in Chapter 5. Finally, each of the individual, shared and invested practices of quality use can illuminate the varied ways in which educators approach the core component of thoughtful engagement with and implementation of research, as presented in Chapter 3.

We see these connections as offering a way to ground the QURE Framework in "the fine-grained realities of evidence-use within the real-life processes of educational practices" (Rickinson et al., 2017, p. 186). In doing so, though, we do not wish for this exploration of quality use as a practice to be considered as fully exhaustive or prescriptive. Articulating quality use as a practice, for example, is not about stipulating how educators should approach research use with curiosity or embed it in their shared ways of working, but about underscoring the importance of these practices. For this reason, we encourage educators and researchers to adapt and build on our understanding in their own work. As an example of this, the following vignette illustrates how a team of three educators at a science learning centre used the idea of quality use as a practice to guide their approach to a sustainable and impactful research-informed change.

Vignette 9 ("How is it helpful?") – "Quality use of research as a practice" informing three educators' approach to a research-informed change

This vignette features Natalie, Barry and Chris, a group of lead educators at a science specialist learning centre. They are responsible for supporting a team of 'science mentors' who deliver small-group interactive learning experiences for "different cohorts of students who visit the centre each day". To support the quality of the learning experiences provided by the science mentors, Natalie, Barry and Chris undertook a small organisation-based research use project as part of the Q Project's professional learning (PL) programme. In the following vignette, we explore how they took up the key practices of using research well (introduced as part of the PL programme) and enacted them to support a high-quality research-informed change in their context.

First, as they thought about the reason for engaging with research, Chris noted how the science mentors "are skilled scientists, [but] they're not trained educators". For this reason, they felt that introducing the science mentors to educational practices in a research-informed manner would appeal to their sense of *professionalism and professional identity* as scientists. Natalie, Barry and Chris then undertook "anecdotal observations [...] [to understand] that the mentors tended to do most of the talking, mainly teaching by instruction". This allowed them to determine that the *purpose* of their research-informed change would be to support the mentors to "ask questions that could facilitate dialogic teaching".

Natalie, Barry and Chris then used the resources from the PL programme to search the academic literature. *Driven by their curiosity,* they consulted a wide range of academic sources, including theoretical and philosophical works that informed their conceptual understanding, as well as case studies and empirical investigations of different strategies. To determine which strategies would be suitable, Natalie, Barry and Chris then *worked collectively* with the science mentors to generate evidence about their current dialogic interactions with the students. Together, they developed an observation tool, and mapped the frequencies, directions and types of interactions between mentors and students.

The evidence they generated suggested the need to diversify the types of questions that mentors asked, for which they felt that 'talk moves' (see NSW Department of Education, 2021) would be useful as a strategy. Natalie, Barry and Chris then incorporated these strategies into an "instructional playbook" which they believed was a "digestible form" to help *embed* the 'talk moves' in day-to-day "discussions among the science mentors and [lead] educators". In doing so, the lead educators recognised that supporting the mentors' uptake of these strategies was a *time- and effort-dependent* task, and consequently, allocated some "in-programme time" to modelling and discussing the strategies. Over time, Natalie, Barry and Chris began to "monitor the impact" of their research-informed change. Early signs indicated that they were moving towards their goal of fostering conversations where "we would like to hear and value students' questions more than our own".

This vignette provides an example of how the dimensions of quality use as a practice were helpful in guiding three lead educators to implement research-informed change with the science mentors in their particular context. It also points to the potential relevance of these practices in diverse educational contexts beyond the traditional classroom setting.

On a final note, while this chapter addresses an important gap in the literature by "describing teachers' use of research from a practitioner perspective" (Cain, 2015, p. 490), it should not be interpreted as foregrounding educators' individual practices at the expense of broader shared and invested practices. This chapter makes clear that the quality use of research is a necessarily collective practice which takes place across, and requires investment from, multiple levels of the education system (e.g., at school, jurisdiction and national levels) if it is to be impactful and sustainable. For these reasons, in framing quality use in terms of individual, shared and invested practices, we aim to invite reflection from educators, researchers and system actors alike on how well education systems as a whole are practising and supporting the quality use of research. In the next chapter, we dive further into understanding the quality use of research from a systems perspective.

References

Boaz, A., & Nutley, S. (2019). Using evidence. In A. Boaz, H. Davies, A. Fraser, & S. Nutley (Eds.), *What works now? Evidence-informed policy and practice* (pp. 251–277). Policy Press.

Cain, T. (2015). Teachers' engagement with research texts: Beyond instrumental, conceptual or strategic use. *Journal of Education for Teaching, 41*(5), 478–492. 10.1080/02607476.2015.1105536

Cook, S. D. N., & Brown, J. S. (1999). Bridging epistemologies: The generative dance between organizational knowledge and organizational knowing. *Organization Science, 10*(4), 381–400. 10.1287/orsc.10.4.381

Drill, K., Miller, S., & Behrstock-Sherratt, E. (2013). Teachers' perspectives on educational research. *Brock Education Journal, 23*(1), 3–17. 10.26522/brocked.v23i1.350

Farley-Ripple, E., May, H., Karpyn, A., Tilley, K., & Mcdonough, K. (2018). Rethinking connections between research and practice in education: A conceptual framework. *Educational Researcher, 47*(4), 235–245. 10.3102/0013189x18761042

Gleeson, J., Rickinson, M., Walsh, L., Cutler, B., Salisbury, M., Hall, G., Khong, H. (2023) Quality use of research evidence: Practitioner perspectives. *Evidence & Policy, 19*(3), 423–443. 10.1332/174426421X16778434724277

Gore, J. M., & Gitlin, A. D. (2004). [RE]Visioning the academic–teacher divide: Power and knowledge in the educational community. *Teachers and Teaching, 10*(1), 35–58. 10.1080/13540600320000170918

Innvær, S., Vist, G., Trommald, M., & Oxman, A. (2002). Health policy-makers' perceptions of their use of evidence: A systematic review. *Journal of Health Services Research & Policy, 7*(4), 239–244. 10.1258/135581902320432778

Ion, G., & Iucu, R. (2014). Professionals' perceptions about the use of research in educational practice. *European Journal of Higher Education, 4*(4), 334–347. 10.1080/21568235.2014.899154

NSW Department of Education. (2021, December). *Talk moves*. NSW Department of Education. https://education.nsw.gov.au/teaching-and-learning/curriculum/literacy-and-numeracy/teaching-and-learning-resources/numeracy/talk-moves

Oliver, K., Lorenc, T., & Innvær, S. (2014). New directions in evidence-based policy research: A critical analysis of the literature. *Health Research Policy and Systems, 12*(1), 34. 10.1186/1478-4505-12-34

Penuel, W. R., Briggs, D. C., Davidson, K. L., Herlihy, C., Sherer, D., Hill, H. C., Farrell, C. C., & Allen, A-R. (2016). *Findings from a national survey of research use among school and district leaders*. National Center for Research in Policy and Practice. https://files.eric.ed.gov/fulltext/ED599966.pdf

Rickinson, M., Cirkony, C., Walsh, L., Gleeson, J., Cutler, B., & Salisbury, M. (2022). A framework for understanding the quality of evidence use in education. *Educational Research, 64*(2), 133–158. 10.1080/00131881.2022.2054452

Rickinson, M., De Bruin, K., Walsh, L., & Hall, M. (2017). What can evidence-use in practice learn from evidence-use in policy? *Educational Research, 59*(2), 173–189. 10.1080/00131881.2017.1304306

Tseng, V., & Gamoran, A. (2017). *Bringing rigor to relevant questions: How social science research can improve youth outcomes in the real world*. William T. Grant Foundation. http://wtgrantfoundation.org/digest/bringing-rigor-relevant-questions

Ward, V. (2019). Using frameworks and models to support knowledge mobilization. In J. Malin & C. Brown (Eds.), *The role of knowledge brokers in education: Connecting the dots between research and practice* (pp. 168–181). Routledge. 10.4324/9780429462436

Weiss, C. H., & Bucuvalas, M. J. (1980). *Social science research and decision-making*. Columbia University Press.

7 | Quality use of research as a system

Chapter overview

This chapter explores the system aspects of quality research use by considering system influences, system supports and system practices. Drawing on data collected from educators and system actors, it reports how:

- to understand quality use as a system, we must probe what quality use of research requires of system actors in terms of their practices and their provision of support;
- the findings shared here represent early insights that are based more on the views of educators than the views of system actors;
- system-level influences do not feature frequently in educators' accounts of using research well in school and, when they do, are cited as barriers more than enablers;
- there are calls for improved system support through removing barriers to research use and providing targeted skill development in research use;
- system actors' own practices are characterised by variable levels of research use and variable involvement in evidence sharing;
- the potential of system actors to enable and support quality use of research within and across schools is yet to be fully realised; and

DOI: 10.4324/9781003353966-7

- key priorities are strengthening system actors' involvement in research use, system role modelling of quality use, and system-level support for research use.

Introduction

Much of the discussion so far in this book has focused on the research use capacities of educators and those enablers at individual and organisational levels that improve educators' use of research. However, it is also important to consider wider system-level factors which, as discussed in Chapter 3, are another potential influence on how well research is used (Rickinson et al., 2022). This chapter therefore explores the system dimensions of quality use of research.

Over the past decade, the importance of thinking about research use in education from a systems perspective has gained greater attention (Boaz & Nutley, 2019; Boaz et al., 2022). Work in and across other sectors has influenced this thinking, such as the conceptual shift towards relationship and systems models of knowledge mobilisation described by Best and Holmes (2010) in their work in the health sector. By definition, these systems models recognise the multiple actors, processes and relationships involved in the production, diffusion, dissemination, and use of research and evidence, and the ways that these are individually and collectively shaped by the social, physical and political contexts in which they exist and interact (Best & Holmes, 2010). Connected to, and illustrative of, these shifts in thinking is an increasing emphasis in many jurisdictions internationally on developing national and/or federal infrastructures for research use in education that rely on effective system-wide collaboration (Malin et al., 2020). Additionally, there have been recent calls, such as that of the Global Commission on Evidence to Address Social Challenges (2022), for system actors in different sectors, such as education, to work in concert and take whole-of-system approaches to improving the use of research evidence for better policy, practice and social outcomes.

Despite the growing importance of system perspectives, there is a paucity of analytical work regarding the effect of different system-level enablers and barriers on research use in education (Levin, 2013; Nelson & Campbell, 2019).

Further, what has been conducted has tended not to focus specifically on using research well, and therefore little is known about the system features of quality research use. With this shortcoming in mind, this chapter discusses different system actors and their activities that influence quality research use within and beyond schools. Drawing on data from educators' (Survey 1, $n = 492$; Survey 2, $n = 819$; Survey 3, $n = 414$) and system actors' (Survey 2, $n = 158$) survey responses, educators' ($n = 27$) interview accounts, and contributions from participants in our professional learning co-design process (educators, $n = 27$; system actors, $n = 28$) (see Appendix 1 for details about samples and methods), this chapter highlights those system-level factors that start to give shape to what constitutes "quality research use as a system".

Following this introduction, this chapter has five main sections. The next section explains our framing of quality research use as a system and how it builds on related issues raised in previous chapters. The proceeding three sections then detail our findings, based on data from Australian educators and system actors, about the wider education system in terms of system influences, system support, and system practices. The chapter concludes with a final section that summarises the key points and provides consider-ations for strengthening quality research use from a systems perspective.

Understanding quality use as a system

In Australia, similar to other countries and jurisdictions, the education system comprises a number of actors that are external to schools, as well as schools themselves and school community members including students, parents and staff. With regard to research use in educational practice, system actors external to schools include government education depart-ments and governing jurisdictions, national and state-based education agencies, universities and academics, research organisations, research brokers and professional learning providers, amongst others. Their actions and outputs are varied and wide-ranging and include the production and dissemination of educational policy, guidelines and standards, professional resources, and learning supports, to name a few. Taking a systems per-spective, as discussed in Chapter 3, means considering the actions of and relationships between these actors at a system level, and how they influence the use of research by schools, at an organisational level, and educators, at an individual level.

Understanding quality use as a system, then, is about asking questions such as: What does quality research use look like and involve at different levels of the system, as well as across the system as a whole? What does using research well require of different system actors and in what ways are these connected? And how can quality research use be supported and enabled by system actors so that educators in schools can use research in improved ways? In our work, these questions were addressed in four ways.

Firstly, they were addressed by probing in exploratory ways into educators' perspectives and experiences of using research well in schools, and then examining if and how system-level influences featured in their accounts. As outlined in previous chapters, open-ended questions asked of educators in Survey 1 and interviews were analysed inductively as well as deductively in relation to the Quality Use of Research Evidence (QURE) Framework components (in this case 'system-level influences'). None of these survey or interview questions made any direct reference to system-level influences, so any insights gained about such factors were volunteered by educators as they described what using research well or poorly looked like in their schools.

Secondly, additional insights into quality research use as a system were gained by asking educators closed-response questions in Survey 1 and Survey 3 about their consultation with, assessment of and trust in different evidence types and sources. Some of the types and sources were specifically related to system-level actors or processes, such as research produced and disseminated by academics, universities, educational research organisations, government education departments or national- and state-based education agencies. Analysis of responses to these kinds of survey questions therefore generated quantitative insights into the perceived importance and impact of system-related research use activities and influences.

Thirdly, the system dimensions of quality use were also covered to some extent in Survey 2, which involved system actors as well as educators being asked closed-response questions about their research and evidence use behaviours and attitudes. The Survey 2 sample included four types of system actors: those working in higher education institutions; those working in national or state-based education departments; those working in organisations specialising in service provision to school students; and those working in organisations specialising in service provision to teachers. Analysis of responses to these questions generated quantitative insights into the research use practices of different actors at the system level.

Finally, information related to quality use as a system was also gleaned by examining data generated during the co-design process. The co-design process involved bringing together varied education stakeholders for two workshops about ways to improve research use in schools, the second of which was focused on system-wide possibilities for action (Cirkony et al., 2022). Analysis of participants' ideas and suggestions from these workshops provided qualitative insights into system-level enablers to support educators' quality use of research in schools.

In highlighting the above sources of data related to the system dimensions of quality use, it is important to note that they originate from a project that was focused primarily on research use at the school rather than the system level. This means, for example, that our insights into research and evidence use practices at the system level are based on a much smaller survey sample of system actors ($n = 158$) than the equivalent for educators ($n = 1,725$). Similarly, it means that our insights into system influences on quality use are based on a smaller number of data collection processes with system actors (i.e., Survey 2; co-design process) than were undertaken with educators (i.e., Surveys 1, 2 and 3; interviews; co-design process). These points are important to bear in mind in relation to the findings presented within this chapter, which need to be seen as the start of an understanding of quality research use as a system.

That said, the ideas that are presented in this chapter connect with, and build on, a number of points that have been raised in earlier chapters about the system dimensions of using research well. In Chapter 2, for example, we noted a cross-sector theme of system complexity that informed our conception of system-level influences within the QURE Framework in Chapter 3. In Chapter 4, the ways in which educators described their research use relationships suggested that a wider landscape of networks and collaborations beyond schools was needed to enable quality research use. In Chapter 5, educators' needs for developmental and material support to use research well suggested the potential for system-level interventions. Finally, in Chapter 6, quality research use as a shared and invested practice suggested that for research to be used well, varied actors, both within and beyond schools, needed to work together to support educators' improved use of research.

The ideas presented also reinforce the QURE Framework core and enabling components previously discussed and provide further insights into what these enablers involve. For example, the expectations that educators

Table 7.1 Number and percentage of Survey 1 respondents (*n* = 492) and interviews (*n* = 27) coded to the QURE Framework component of 'system-level influences'

QURE Framework component	Using research well	
	Interviews	Surveys
System-level influences	33% (9)	3% (17)

have of system actors to use relevant and methodologically robust research to inform policies and guidelines elaborates the core component of appropriate research. Additionally, calls made by educators for system actors to practise and role model quality research use themselves reflect the need for effective leadership at all levels of the system, not just at the school level.

Overall, though, the analysis of educators' and system actors' responses in this chapter suggests that the system dimensions of quality use of research are underdeveloped. As shown in Table 7.1, for example, there were very few references to 'system-level influences' within educators' survey and interview responses when they were asked about using research well. These infrequent references to system-level influences, which are in stark contrast to more frequent references to the individual and organisational enablers discussed in earlier chapters (see Table 4.1 in Chapter 4 and Table 5.1 in Chapter 5), suggest that there is more work to be done at the system level to support quality research use. Indeed, as the subsequent sections in this chapter will show, there are several ways in which a range of system actors can improve how they use research themselves, as well as how they can support educators' use of research.

The next three sections, then, elaborate on quality use of research as a system in terms of:

- System influences – in particular, educators' varied perceptions of system influences, and how these were viewed more as barriers than enablers to using research well.
- System support – in particular, educators' need for system actors to remove barriers to research use, and to provide targeted skill development.
- System practices – in particular, system actors' variable research use dispositions and practices, and variable evidence-sharing practices.

To help visualise what system-level influences might look like in practice, the vignette below highlights how one school principal interacts with different system actors beyond her school and, in so doing, creates her own system of research use support.

Vignette 10 ("Looks like in practice") – "Quality use of research as a system" within the work of a primary school principal

This vignette features Bianca, Principal of South Harbour Public School, and "the journey [her] school went on to create [their] own system" that supported the development of a school learning culture. Bianca admittedly "loves to network" and has actively reached out to others in her own networks to develop her ideas about effective learning environments and using research well. For example, she participates in several external professional development programmes that have exposed her, over several years, to different research studies and best practice education approaches. These programmes involve workshops, partner school visits, keynote expert presentations, mentoring and project work. Through these programmes, Bianca has developed strong relationships with other school leaders and an external coach, all of whom she learns from and shares knowledge with about research-informed ideas.

Bianca is also an active participant in different professional associations and has cultivated a close relationship with her Education Director (state-based Department of Education) to seek guidance around school improvement. Bianca explained that these types of relationships not only helped her to "think outside of the box" and develop as a leader, but also critically informed the cultural transformation of her school community. Connections between schools and system actors, she believes, are key to quality research use in practice. She suggested that system actors, such as universities, professional associations and governing jurisdictions and Departments of Education, could better initiate and facilitate such connections with and/or on behalf of schools.

Two key challenges Bianca has faced as she has developed a learning culture within her school are sufficient time and budget for staff to engage with research and embed its use within processes. While Bianca has "created a professional learning model that includes using [research] evidence in practice" across 5-week cycles of inquiry, she has been challenged by the small budget she is allocated for teachers' professional learning. To allow teaching teams scheduled release time away from the classroom to engage in the inquiry cycle process, she has "paid" for relief teaching staff. This has had significant implications for her overall school budget and she explained that system actors could help to support schools better with additional budget and/or staff allocations. Coordinated support between different system levels and across the system as a whole, she suggested, is critical for quality research use.

Bianca's vignette highlights three key elements of "quality use as a system" in practice:

- Schools can be systems themselves, with quality use of research enabled by how well a school leader supports this within their community, but also by how well the leader facilitates connections with system actors beyond the school. Bianca demonstrates that the QURE enabling components of *relationships*, *leadership* and *culture* can be leveraged to create a school ecosystem for using research well.
- Schools can also collaborate and form their own clustered system where knowledge is shared and research is used to improve professional expertise. Again, Bianca drew on *relationships* and *leadership* as key enablers when establishing her own network of school leaders.
- Reflecting the QURE component of *system-level influences*, Bianca's work also signals how system actors can impact the quality of educators' research use in practice. For schools to use research well, educators need developmental support, as well as material support in the form of time and budget to engage with research. System actors can also play active roles in making system connections with and on behalf of schools.

System influences

A systems approach calls for a better understanding of the activities and interactions that shape the production, dissemination and use of research amongst actors (Hill, 2022; Torres, 2022). A deeper understanding of these activities and interactions will improve education system awareness of the different actors that exist, their contexts, and the ways in which their roles, accountabilities and practices influence educators' use of research in schools. When the educators in our study described such system actors and influences, two points were identified as key: such influences and actors were variously conceived, and when described, were viewed more as barriers to quality research use than as enablers.

Varied perceptions of system influences

When system influences were spoken about by educators, they were described in varied ways. These ways included describing a range of system actors external to their school contexts, including those within: federal or state-level government Departments of Education or governing jurisdiction bodies; official education bodies; national or state-based research and evidence organisations; universities; research brokers; professional development service providers and state-based teaching academies; and professional associations.

The activities undertaken by different system actors that impacted schools, or the expectations that different actors were perceived to have of schools and their performance, were also described. Examples included: the reporting and compliance requirements of schools as specified by different governing jurisdictions and/or Departments of Education; specified curriculum or syllabus content and changes made to these by relevant national or state-based government education authorities; specified school improvement frameworks that included guidance and standards regarding research and evidence use; national teaching standards as governed by official education bodies; research conducted and disseminated by universities, academics and research organisations; and research prioritised, summarised and disseminated by government Departments of Education, governing jurisdictions, national or state-based research organisations, and research brokers.

Another way in which educators spoke about system influences was by referring to their own school as a system itself, or as one part of a wider education system. As discussed in Chapter 5, school leaders were viewed as largely accountable for driving research use within their school system. They were also viewed as being responsible for managing interactions with different external system actors on behalf of the school, and for crafting "solutions" (senior leader, survey) to issues arising from tensions between system influences and school operations.

System influences as barriers more than enablers

When educators spoke about system influences, particularly during interviews, they were not often considered as enablers of quality research use (33% of interviews, 3% of surveys). One reported system-level enabler of quality research use was collaborations between system actors and schools or educators. For example, some educators appreciated collaborative situations involving governing jurisdictions or state-based Departments of Education where "our Regional Director might suggest a book to us […] that might get us interested in reading" (senior leader, interview), or having "[helpful] conversations […] with the Regional Office – just to ask them 'What are other schools doing in our area?'" (teacher, interview). Educators described other enablers as governments' provision of "professional learning support" where "[teachers] can access the same sorts of research that leaders have access to through the Department" (senior leader, interview), or the provision of "reviews of research" (senior leader, interview) or "[research-based] guidebooks" that help inform "strategies for teacher action" (senior leader, interview). Other key actions at a wider system level that were viewed as enablers included official education bodies' provision of teaching and leadership standards that included links and references to research use (7% of interviews, 1% of surveys).

While not occurring often, some educators described positive interactions with other types of system actors as enablers of quality research use including universities, professional learning providers, or educational consultants. These interactions or "partnerships" were viewed as important, particularly as an avenue for schools to access external expertise to "up-skill in just what we will probably be exposed to in academic research" (middle leader, interview). They were also viewed as a way for educators to expand their professional research use-related networks beyond the school. During interviews, one middle leader emphasised:

> Schools generally don't have access to the kinds of databases that universities do, and so sometimes when it is a very specific question, or it's quite a broad question and you need to know how to narrow it down, access to that can sometimes be a problem. But you can do that through your [university partnership] network [...] once you've got that network, you can keep going back to those people and if they don't know, then they'll know someone in their research teams or universities that will be able to connect you.

System influences, though, were more often described as barriers to quality research use (74% of interviews, 4% of surveys). Educators described these barriers in three main ways. Firstly, barriers were viewed as a lack of activity or attention that was at odds with educators' expectations of certain system actors. A lack of access to research was considered a key concern (44% of interviews, 2% of surveys), as was a lack of sufficient scheduled time during school hours to engage with research. Educators' responses indicated that they wanted system support to resolve these issues, which is discussed in the next section. Educators also described a lack of interconnection or collaboration between different system actors as a barrier to quality research use in schools, particularly between schools or governing bodies and universities. These disconnects impacted educators' abilities to access appropriate research or gain knowledge about available current or 'best practice' research-informed ideas. One senior leader, participating in the co-design process, made the following observation:

> Is [the lack of research use] inferring that we schools, we are the ones who need fixing? I'm just asking the question. Or is the real issue the lack of interface between schools and researchers?

Secondly, barriers were viewed as poorly executed system activity, with production and dissemination of appropriate research described as a key issue (63% of interviews, <1% of surveys). For example, while educators appreciated the dissemination of research by governing jurisdictions or state-based Departments of Education, at times, they described such dissemination processes as a barrier to quality research use because they were "political" and "depended on which government was in power and what the flavour is coming through the [state-based] Department of Education" (senior leader, interview). Their views also indicated a lack of trust in disseminated research, at times, because it "followed a fad" (middle leader, interview), or had been "[made] defunct, because that tends to be what happens with the [state-based] Department" (middle leader, interview). These actions then caused educators to feel "a bit jaded by new source[s] of research that seem to come out in a cycle every two years and [we're] a bit research-fatigued" (senior leader, interview). Again, educators described their need for system support to resolve this issue.

Finally, barriers were described in terms of the "wide range of demands" (middle leader, interview) made by governing jurisdictions or state-based Departments of Education that educators reported as impediments to their capacities to use research well in practice (33% of interviews). These included changes in policy, approaches, curriculum content or syllabus decisions by governing jurisdictions and state-based Departments of Education that caused change fatigue and workload issues. They also included performance delivery and reporting requirements. For example, some educators' responses suggested that the "performative culture [in which] we exist" created "tensions" for them about putting in place a "quick fix" (senior leader, interview) or "band-aid solution" (middle leader, interview) that might not be well-researched versus taking "more of an inquiry stance whereby you take the time, you work through, you read, you research and then you make some decisions about that and go longer term, look to the long game" (senior leader, interview). Educators also described how the "demands" on them to deliver "success" that were focused on "how busy I am and how much work we do versus how much of an impact we make" were not only "difficult [...] to navigate [...] within an institutional structure" such as a school, but impeded their capacities to use research well (senior leader, interview).

Overall, when educators described quality research use as a system, they identified a range of system actors. Educators viewed these actors as external to the school, with interactions between them and schools seen largely as linear or one-way in direction. This meant that the activities of system actors, or in some cases, their lack of activity, were depicted by educators as doing things to or affecting schools that mainly hindered their capacities to use research well. Educators made clear suggestions, though, about how system actors could play a role in removing these barriers and better supporting their research use, and it is to such system support that we now turn.

System support

Within the complexity of education systems, it is imperative that system actors understand key leverage points and intervene so as to reduce the number of barriers to educators' research use, as well as to provide co-ordinated and targeted support for improved use (Torres, 2022). When the educators in our research described the system support that they wanted for quality research use, they highlighted two key needs: for system actors to remove barriers to research use, and for system actors to provide targeted skill development.

Removing barriers to research use

In both the preceding section and Chapter 5, several barriers to educa-tors' quality research use at a school level were noted. In particular, there were difficulties due to: a lack of access to appropriate research, including access to research in 'usable' formats; a lack of sufficient scheduled time within school hours to engage with research; and unreasonable or unclear demands made of schools that impeded research use. Educators not only looked to their school leaders to help them with these issues, but they expected system actors to take actions to reduce or remove these barriers. When expressing their expectations, educators spoke about the need for system actors, particularly governing jurisdictions and state-based Departments of Education, to change or improve the ways in which they were supporting schools, and actively participate in co-constructing sustainable solutions. Participants in the co-design process elaborated this need further, explaining that "aca-demic research isn't really baked into our system" (teacher), and so needed to be embedded in system processes and artefacts, such as policy documents, school strategic and improvement planning cycles, and performance development plans.

In their descriptions, educators provided clear cues about how system actors could remove research use barriers. For example, educators viewed access to appropriate research as a barrier that could be addressed by system actors in several ways.

Firstly, educators made clear that system actors had a role to play in improving physical access to sources of research. During interviews, a middle leader and a senior leader from the same school explained the challenging nature of sourcing research through university partnerships or academic databases as follows:

> If you're talking about a hindrance, sometimes what gets in the way is being able to easily access [research]. [...] Establishing [access to academic databases and/or university partnerships] in the first place actually takes resources in itself. So, I think that is a big challenge for schools, and there would be things that departments and systems could do, just like there's things that I think senior leaders in schools need to do to help.

These leaders went onto explain how system actors, particularly governing jurisdictions and state-based Departments of Education, could help by: introducing and/or connecting schools with university partners around specific topics; hosting university-school networking events; or government/ jurisdiction research representatives visiting schools (or clusters of schools) to share research-informed ideas. Universities had a role to play as well in initiating or facilitating partnerships with schools more widely. In support of this, for example, nearly two-thirds of Survey 1 educators responded that they wanted 'opportunities to work with academic researchers' (62% 'agreed' or 'strongly agreed'). This point was reinforced by participants in the co-design process, who specifically called out the need for universities to initiate partnerships with schools to provide access to research itself and/ or academic experts who could support educators in their improved use of research.

Other leaders spoke of the need to be connected with professional as-sociations as a source of research, and/or for professional associations to coordinate with governing bodies to promote the importance of using research well in schools. These ideas were further reinforced by co-design process participants. For example, one participating system actor observed:

> School networks or principal networks could embed some sort of research discussion in those networks, where principals can discuss [the] latest research or information they may have come across. I think that's a very good, useful and easy-to-achieve action.

Overwhelmingly, though, most educators recommended that a greater financial investment in access to online databases for schools was a necessary and worthwhile change that needed to happen. Connected with this issue of physical access to research, was the need for educators to be able to access curated or synthesised research. This suggestion did not necessarily mean that research had to be summarised; educators expressed strong desires to interpret the contextual relevance and applicability of research for themselves. Rather it meant access to a research platform or system whereby research could be filtered and curated based on educators' specific needs, with the potential for professional associations, research organisations or research brokers to play facilitating roles. For example, one system actor participating in the co-design process commented:

> Realistically, unless you have that dissemination worked out, teachers cannot access some of this research. Even if they can, so much is there, there must be filters, where you can filter down to whatever teachers want to do. Because otherwise, a teacher, as a practitioner, will never be able to link up with the research basically.

Secondly, educators highlighted the importance of trust and the need for system organisations to share and enable access to trustworthy research. For example, in Survey 3, educators' responses indicated that system actors external to the school were their *least trusted* sources of research, including 'academics' (60%, 7th most strongly endorsed/10 items), 'educational research organisations' (59%, 8th/10), 'professional associations' (58%, 9th/10), and 'government Departments of Education' (54%, 10th/10). Additionally, when asked how often they consulted different evidence sources, Survey 1 respondents indicated that research-related sources external to the school were some of the least consulted, including 'research disseminated from universities' (43% consulted 'often' or 'always'), 'university-based advice or guidance' (36%), and 'online evidence platforms' (31%). 'Endorsement from professional bodies' was one of the lowest ranked reasons for sourcing and using different evidence types (22%, 10th ranked in top five reasons/19 items), as well as one of the least used methods for assessing the quality of evidence (48%, 7th ranked/10 items). With regard to the specific use of research, 'endorsement from professional bodies' was also one of the weakest influences (23%, 10th ranked/14 items). Educators' responses suggest that all system actors needed to have a mind to producing and disseminating quality research that was perceived as "trustworthy", "credible", "rigorous [in method]", and "showed evidence of impact".

Finally, educators emphasised the need for access to research that is usable in practice. Educators' responses indicated that all system actors could produce and/or disseminate research in formats that were more considerate of educators' contexts, skill-levels and time. For example, during interviews, one senior leader explained how researchers could improve the ways in which they conducted and presented their research findings:

> The thing that's missing from educational research is more of the teacher's voice, written in a way that resonates with other teachers, that captures the dynamics of a classroom, the complexities of a classroom, and I think that's why some educational research is not accessible by some teachers because it's just not written in a way that they can see themselves relating to or connecting to the question that the researchers are exploring in the first place.

This idea was reinforced by co-design process participants, who emphasised the need for educators to have more influence on research agendas. They commented on the benefits that would derive if universities and research organisations focused on "specific question[s] that school[s] have" (system actor), and for these questions to underpin future projects. The topics of school improvement and connections between improved practice and better student outcomes were viewed as good examples of immediate research priorities.

During interviews, two senior leaders pointed out how universities, state-based education departments and governing jurisdictions can play a more active role in supporting and brokering the use of research in practice:

> What happens a lot is universities will come up with all these wonderful ways forward for education and we all just buy the program and bring it into the school, despite where the school is at that point in time. And [universities] then just expect, without any support, that [schools] will be able to actually take it on board and run with it for the benefit of our students. That's what happens typically.

> I find, though, that with the Department's packaging of research, they lose a sense sometimes of who their audience is […] teachers are very much looking for a practical technique described in a way that they

could think about "Yes, I could see this reason for using this technique with my students", and then take it into the classroom tomorrow, try it, trial it again, experiment with it, monitor the impact on their students learning, that sort of thing. The Department never quite takes the research to that point.

Other types of accompanying support described by educators and co-design process participants included: complementary videos and/or podcasts; in-person researcher or expert presentations at conferences or within schools to explain the research and its application to practice; and research-informed programme implementation guidelines.

Alongside the challenge of limited access, another barrier that educators wanted system actors to address was the lack of sufficient scheduled time during school hours to engage with research. Many educators commented that "time is always a limiting factor. None of us ever get enough time to do as much as we want, that's just the nature of the work we do" (senior leader, interview). Educators spoke about time from two key perspectives. Firstly, time was an issue of insufficient resources or funds to 'create' scheduled time for individuals or teaching teams to engage with research. Many educators suggested that governing jurisdictions and national or state-based Departments of Education had accountability for providing additional, but equitable, funding to support research use in schools. But, as highlighted by one senior leader participating in the co-design process, school leaders needed "to be convinced" that prioritising funding for research use was "worth doing".

Secondly, time was an issue related to administrative and compliance workload pressures that eroded available time while at school for research use. Again, many educators wanted governing jurisdictions and national or state-based Departments of Education, to reduce the workload associated with administrative and compliance reporting, and/or financially support additional staff in schools to undertake this type of work, thereby freeing up educators' time. As one middle leader reflected during interviews:

Time is a huge issue for us […] I think it raises questions that there are issues with our system, and what it is that we can do to support this. What can we do from a [system] leadership perspective to reduce this busy work, because ultimately our goal is to improve student outcomes? We know that teachers are one of the biggest influences in that, so how can we [as a whole] support them to continue to develop? And, if time is the biggest issue, I would say bigger than [teachers'] mindset here, because we do have some very well-intentioned staff who do want to try, but feel so burdened by documentation.

Connected with this issue of time were educators' perceptions that unreasonable demands from governing bodies acted as a barrier to quality research use. These demands might take the form of compliance with education policies or recommended approaches, where educators felt that "we're told to do something, we wouldn't have any choice" (middle leader, interview). These were viewed, at times, as creating "tension" if they were perceived as poorly conceived or lacking a sufficient research-informed rationale. This made it challenging for educators to decide whether to use research that they felt was more appropriate or follow the dictates of their jurisdiction leaders. During an interview, one middle leader explained:

I'm not sure policies are always developed with a research base, so there can be a gap, and that's a space that the senior leadership team has to try and navigate [...] Sometimes I look at a document and I'm like, "Where's the research that supports that? Tell me where the evidence is?" As a school, you have to filter a little bit - we know that there isn't research to support that, [so] are we willing to go down that road? Or do we take the essence of that [policy] and use [other] research to support the decision we do want to make as a school?

Similar to their need for trustworthy and credible research, educators made clear that they wanted system actors to provide them with unambiguous but evidence-based policies and guidance that helped to improve practice.

As discussed in the previous section, unreasonable demands could also take the form of unrealistic performance delivery expectations of schools. Many educators spoke of the need to take research-informed change "slowly" so as to "get things right" (senior leader, interview), yet felt that they were not afforded such time when trying to meet reporting deadlines. During an interview, one middle leader spoke of the support that system actors, particularly governing jurisdictions and state-based Departments of Education, could provide in terms of greater time affordances to implement and evaluate research-informed initiatives. He described how this type of support would help educators to be open to using research to improve practice:

> The time frame needs to be taken into account when it comes to change. I see that teachers, especially teachers who have been in the profession for a long time, find this shift challenging and find this transition very challenging.

Providing targeted skill development

Alongside wanting system actors to remove barriers to quality research use, educators also wanted system actors to make available targeted research use skill development. Across all three surveys conducted, educators ($n = 1,725$) reported having strong beliefs in the value of research use, particularly 'how research will help to improve student outcomes' (81% 'agreed' or 'strongly agreed'). Additionally, in Survey 3, a majority of educators 'believed in the benefits of research' (86%), with a similar number reporting that they were 'open to changing practice and/or their thinking based on research' (86%). However, educators were not as confident in their research use skills, with, for example, over one-third of all educators (35%, $n = 1,725$) indicating that they lacked confidence to 'analyse and interpret research for their own context'. As such, they wanted school leaders and system actors to intervene and provide them with skill development. One teacher during the co-design process emphasised this need when they stated: "Research skills need to be taught. You don't just know how to [use] research, you need to be told explicitly what to do".

As discussed in Chapter 4, Survey 3 educators reported specific skill development as critical for their improved research use, including getting help to 'identify relevant challenges' (43% ranked in their top 5 needs), 'assess the usability of research' (42%) and 'assess research fit for context' (41%). To address these needs, educators were clear that skill development could come in different forms. There were many professional learning opportunities that school leaders could provide within schools, as discussed in Chapter 5, but there were also varied developmental supports that system actors could make available. For example, Survey 3 educators indicated that the following system supports would have a 'medium' or 'high impact' on their capacities to use research well in practice:

- 'specialised research use professional learning' (81%, 1st most strongly endorsed item);
- dissemination of 'exemplar case studies of schools using research' (75%, 2nd);
- 'academics sharing what research is out there with schools' (69%, 3rd);
- an 'assessment tool to assess research use skills' (67%, equal 4th);
- dissemination of "regular newsletters with 'top tips' of how to use research" (67%, equal 4th); and
- "research use 'how-to' guides" (66%, 5th).

Additionally, co-design process participants highlighted that one of the 'most important things' system actors could do to enable research use in schools was to provide 'infrastructure', including research use-related skills training. They indicated that such training could take various forms including:

- universities providing specific instruction to pre- and in-service teachers, particularly around different research methods and types of research available;
- wider availability of professional learning programmes focused on how to use research well in practice, and potential funding to access these programmes; and
- the provision of and/or funding for coaches and mentors in schools to guide educators' use of research, which may include dedicated research-focused roles.

Overall, while educators faced challenges to using research well in practice, they were clear that system actors could play key roles in helping to address barriers in schools that impeded use and support educators and schools better in their endeavour to improve their research use. However, educators and their research use practices are just one aspect of understanding quality research use as a system. How system actors use research themselves is also important to understand – which brings us on to questions of system practices.

System practices

Throughout this book, we have presented findings from Australian educators that give shape and form to quality research use. As we make sense of quality research use as a system, it is important to explore the contexts in which system actors exist, the extent to which they use research themselves, and how their research use is connected to the ways in which they influence educators' research use in schools (Maxwell et al., 2022; Torres, 2022).

Drawing on Survey 2 responses, we were able to gain early insights into system actors' research use dispositions and practices. While these insights are not extensive, they do give some shape to broader system aspects of enabling quality research use in schools. Overall, our findings suggest that system actors do not have established research use practices, with two insights identified as key: system actors do not consult research often in their work and demonstrate varied dispositions towards research use, and they have varied evidence-sharing practices.

Varied research use dispositions and practices

Overall, system actors' responses suggested that they had varied dispositions towards research use and did not often consult research in their work. When compared with educators, these dispositions were slightly less positive, while their frequency of research consultation was similar. For example, 73% of system actors 'agreed' or 'strongly agreed' that using research 'helped to improve student outcomes' (compared with 81% of educators, $n = 1,725$), while 51% were 'clear about how research could be used to help change practice' (67% of educators). When consulting research types, just over one-third of system actors frequently sourced 'research disseminated from universities' (37%; 37% of educators) or 'university-based advice or guidance' (38%; 30% of educators).

System actors' responses also suggested that they lacked confidence in their research use capacities, as well as motivation to use research. For example, just over half reported feeling 'confident to analyse and interpret research' (57%; 65% of educators, $n = 1,725$), while less than half felt 'confident to judge the quality of research' (41%; 51% of educators, $n = 1,311$). While system actors' responses suggested that they were quite motivated to 'look for relevant research when confronted with a problem or decision' (61%; 62% of educators, $n = 1,725$), they reported being less action-oriented, with only approximately one-third, for example, 'regularly initiating discussions about research' (38%; 39% of educators).

There were distinct patterns of difference when comparing the research use of system actors by role category. As noted earlier, the Survey 2 system sample comprised system actors working in: higher education institutions; national or state education departments; organisations specialising in service provision to school students; and organisations specialising in service provision to teachers. Looking across these groups, those individuals in higher education roles and those engaged in service provision to teachers had stronger positive beliefs in the value of research use, greater confidence in their research use capacities, were more motivated to use research, and consulted research more frequently in practice, when compared with those individuals in jurisdiction/departmental roles or those engaged in service provision to students.

Across all groups, though, accessing research did not appear to be a routine task for system actors. For example, when asked how often they accessed different types of evidence, just over one-third accessed evidence 'at least weekly' (37%), while less than one-third did so 'fortnightly-monthly' (30%). Those system actors in higher education roles were most likely to access different evidence types frequently (44% accessed 'at least weekly'), while those in departmental/jurisdiction roles were the least likely to do so (21%). Those actors in departmental/jurisdiction roles were also most likely to access different evidence types infrequently (42% accessed 'less than monthly'). Once new evidence was accessed, system actors chose different actions. For example, those in higher education roles or engaged in service provision to students were most likely to 'use it to inform their practice' (60% and 43% respectively), while those in departmental/jurisdiction roles or engaged in service provision to teachers were most likely to 'share it with others' (39% and 41% respectively).

When using high quality evidence to inform their decisions and practices, system actors reported consulting a range of different evidence, including non-research types, such as 'teacher observations' (61%, 1st selected type overall) and 'student data' (56%, 3rd), as well as research-related types, such as 'quantitative studies' (58%, 2nd) and 'qualitative studies' (50%, 4th). Other specific types of university research such as 'meta-analyses/reviews compiled by academics' (37%, 5th), 'empirical research' (35%, 6th), 'randomised controlled trials' (26%, 10th) and 'university-based guidance' (24%, 11th) were seen to be of lesser quality.

Overall, when accessing and using different evidence types, system actors were most influenced by 'high quality or credibility' factors (60%) and how 'practical' the evidence was (58%). They also tended to consult traditional sources such as 'professional journals' (51%, 1st most preferred source) and 'academic journals' (47%, 2nd). By way of comparison, educators were more likely to consult interactive and relational sources, including 'colleagues' (58%, 1st most preferred source), 'professional development programmes' (55%, 2nd), and 'formal professional learning networks' (52%, 3rd).

Varied evidence-sharing practices

Given the nature of their roles, coupled with increasing system-wide expectations for educators to use research in practice, the system actors' own evidence-sharing practices were varied and not as common as might be expected. For example, when asked how often they shared different types of research and evidence, less than one-third of system actors did so 'at least weekly' (31%), with a similar percentage sharing on a 'fortnightly-monthly' basis (37%). Those in jurisdiction/departmental roles and those engaged in service provision to teachers shared evidence slightly more frequently than those in other system roles. System actors reported sharing research because they felt 'it was an important part of being [in education]' (71%, 1st most selected reason) or it was a 'normal personal practice' (55%, 2nd).

There were differences in what evidence was shared by system actors, which may be related to their roles. Those in higher education roles most frequently shared 'teacher observations' (23%, 1st preferred evidence type to share) and 'qualitative studies' (18%, 2nd), while those in departmental/ jurisdiction roles most frequently shared 'student data' (21%, 1st) and 'action research' (14%, 2nd). Those engaged in student service provision most frequently shared 'teacher observations' (37%, 1st) and 'student data' (13%, 2nd), while those engaged in teacher service provision most frequently shared 'teacher observations', 'curriculum documents' and 'literature reviews/meta-analyses by academics' (13%, equal 1st).

Colleagues were the most likely source of research and evidence that was shared (26%, 1st most selected source to share). Colleagues were also most likely to be the recipients (67%, 1st most selected recipients). 'On-sharing' of this research and evidence by the recipient was not perceived to be a common practice, with slightly less than one-quarter of system actors believing that the evidence was shared further (23%). When sharing, system actors did so because the evidence was in a format that was 'easily shared' (38%, 1st most selected reason), or they felt that 'others might find it useful'

(33%, 2nd). They also shared evidence in informal ways, most frequently 'via email' (44%, 1st most selected method), or 'verbally' (32%, 2nd).

In summary, this section has highlighted several practices at the system level that need to be reconciled and resolved in relation to educators' improved use of research. These include system actors' tendencies not to use research often in their own work, their varied dispositions towards using research, and their varied evidence-sharing practices that seem at odds with system-wide expectations for greater and improved research use in education.

Conclusions

This chapter has presented early insights into what quality use of research as a system might mean. It is worth remembering that these insights have been shaped largely by educators' perspectives as users of research. While system actors' responses have been included, these too are from their own perspectives as users and sharers of research and evidence and do not reflect broader views about system interactions or activities that influence research use in schools. So, while this means that our ideas of quality research use as a system are early in their development, we can nonetheless be clear about three key points.

Firstly, our findings indicate that the system dimensions of quality research use are not well developed. System-level influences are not often referenced by educators when sharing their perspectives on using research well, and when they are, they are talked about more as barriers than they are as enablers. These findings suggest that the potential of system actors to enable and support quality use of research within and across schools is yet to be fully realised.

Secondly, through examining the research use practices of educators and different system actors, the system is characterised by infrequent use of research, varied dispositions towards using research, low confidence in individuals' research use capacities, and variable evidence-sharing practices. These system characteristics suggest that there is much work to be done to improve system-wide research use capacities overall. They also suggest that there is scope to better connect the research use-related behaviours and attitudes of system actors themselves with their roles and accountabilities, as well as with their communication to, expectations of and influence on educators' research use in schools. Improved alignment between these factors has the potential to better enable educators' quality use of research in practice (Boaz et al., 2022; Hill, 2022; Maxwell et al., 2022).

Despite these system characteristics, the final point is that there are signs of capacity within the system for positive change. For example, educators are clear about the roles different system actors can play in removing barriers to research use, and how infrastructure can be funded and made available by system actors, both within and beyond schools, to support their improved use of research. Their responses suggest belief in the possibility of change. Additionally, both educators and system actors have some positive beliefs in the value of research use, suggesting there is capacity to increase and improve the use of research across the system. These insights provide critical information about where the productive spaces may be within the system to initiate action. Turning to these now, and drawing on our work with school leaders, we suggest the following as considerations for system action that focus on: knowing and involving system actors in research use; system role modelling of quality research use practices; and supporting the improved use of research at and from a system-level.

In relation to *knowing and involving system actors*, throughout this book, we have shown that quality use of research is a collaborative or shared practice that relies on the knowledge and connection of different individuals to engage with research in deep and meaningful ways. For example, in both Chapters 5 and 6, we emphasised the importance of school leaders being aware of their staff's research use needs, beliefs and capacities, and then connecting and involving them in different research use decisions and processes such that their research use improved. At a systems level, this type of leadership is also important. Torres (2022) suggests that a worthwhile first step for improving our systems thinking about research use within practice is to "carefully and thoroughly map the state of [our] educational research use system in order to identify the factors influencing the use of research" (p. 119). This type of action reflects our idea of knowing and involving and suggests that system leaders could play a productive role in identifying or mapping the relevant actors involved in improving research use in educational practice, raising system awareness of these actors and their accountabilities and activities, and then devising or supporting ways for them to interact.

In relation to *system role modelling*, Chapter 5 highlighted the importance of leaders believing in and using research well themselves, and then role modelling those practices to others. Responses from our educators indicated that when leaders do not use research themselves or are challenged to demonstrate knowledge of certain research and its applicability to different situations and decisions, then not only does this represent 'poor' research use, but it sends messages that research use is not important. Gaining collective buy-in to research use and capacity building to improve such use is difficult when individuals do not see or experience their leaders adopting and demonstrating the same attitudes and behaviours that are expected of them. These same principles apply at a system level. Best and Holmes (2010) emphasise the importance of modelling research use attitudes and behaviours when they observe that, as systems become more complex, leadership needs to be more facilitative, empowering and participatory. Our idea of role modelling then suggests that system actors could productively focus on increasing and improving their own research use and, in so doing, promote this use through their activities and communication such that educators gain consistent messages about using research well in their practice.

Finally, in relation to *supporting the improved use of research*, just as leaders need to provide adequate resources and support at the school level, so too do system actors need to adequately support quality research use at system levels (Boaz et al., 2022). In Chapter 5, we discussed the importance of different research use-related infrastructure being available within schools, as well as the need for leaders to build and sustain an organisational culture that supported quality research use. Taking productive steps towards greater systems support, therefore, may mean that "mechanisms" are initiated and implemented at school (e.g., school processes, provision of scheduled time) *and* system levels (e.g., projects encouraging actors' interactions) (Torres, 2022, p. 108). It may also mean that system leaders take oversight of system-wide research use, including crafting and implementing a system-wide strategy for facilitating the use of research, providing targeted funding for research or systematically commissioning research to address system needs, as well as monitoring and evaluating the impact of educational research across the system (Torres, 2022). Our ideas about supporting quality research use, though, stretch beyond physical resources and social processes. In line with the "wake-up" call made by the recent Global Commission on Evidence to Address Societal Challenges (2022, p. 101), it also involves all system actors supporting the ethos of 'those who can take action to support improved research use, to take action'. In this way, our idea of supporting integrates system-wide leadership and infrastructure with a system-wide culture of and approach to quality research use.

As an example of how these types of considerations can be operationalised by system actors, the vignette below focuses on a school jurisdiction and how they have utilised QURE concepts, resources and interventions to inform their strategic work and individual system practices.

Vignette 11 ("How is it helpful?") – "Quality use of research as a system" informing the strategic work and practices of a school jurisdiction

This vignette features a school jurisdiction and their work regarding research use in educational practice and improvement. Over recent years, the jurisdiction has prioritised a "learning culture" strategy, where teachers and school leaders are encouraged and supported to use research, alongside school data, in their practice. Research use, in this context, is viewed as a key way in which to develop and improve the professional expertise of all staff. The jurisdiction has demonstrated a strong commitment to this strategy through its investments in various research use-related infrastructure and resources (e.g., funded research lead roles in schools), external partnerships with universities, and other professional development initiatives (e.g., staff participation in action research projects).

Since 2020, the QURE Framework and Q Project empirical findings have stimulated a number of developments related to this strategy, particularly with respect to policy guidelines and school supports. For example, jurisdiction leaders recently called out that quality use as a concept had influenced the "naming, for the first time, [of] a number of capabilities associated with research engagement and evidence use in our school improvement materials", and helped them to "decide as a system [...] that it's time to join the dots and find out the capacity building journey of schools who are genuinely interested in evidence use".

The jurisdiction's ideas about quality research use, though, have extended beyond just schools to also encompass their system as a whole. For example, one leader within the Governance and Strategy function recently commented that the "QURE Framework and evidence base that sits behind this [has real potential] to inform the development of our next research strategy and research priorities".

To explore the broader application of QURE concepts, several members of the strategic research team recently participated in the Q Project's professional learning about using research well in practice. Part of their motivation was to understand what was involved in using research well in order to improve their own research use skills and knowledge and be able to role model quality research use to colleagues.

Another motivation was to gain deeper insights about how quality research use concepts could be applied to jurisdiction roles and accountabilities, jurisdiction-supported infrastructure in schools, and connections between jurisdiction functions and schools. Ideas such as improving facilitation of collaborative research use across schools and between system levels, assessment of quality research use capacities, and strengthening of standards around use of research resonated with their strategic priorities.

This vignette provides an example of how the concept of quality use has been relevant and helpful to a school jurisdiction. In particular, it shows how the idea of quality use as a system can influence the research use-related attitudes, skills, motivations and practices of system actors themselves. It also shows how connections can be made between different system actors and levels to facilitate system-wide enablement of improved research use in practice.

This chapter has started to give shape to "quality research use as a system" by considering system influences, supports and practices. It highlights several emerging characteristics of system-wide use of research, where insights about individual and organisational quality research use, as discussed in previous chapters, can be leveraged to facilitate improvements in practices and capacities at and across different system levels. These types of opportunities are discussed in the final chapter where we consider what might come next with understanding and improving quality use of research.

References

Best, A., & Holmes, B. (2010). Systems thinking, knowledge and action: Towards better models and methods. *Evidence & Policy, 6*(2), 145–159. 10.1332/17442 6410X502284

Boaz, A., & Nutley, S. (2019). Using evidence. In A. Boaz, H. Davies, A. Fraser, & S. Nutley (Eds.), *What works now? Evidence-informed policy and practice* (pp. 251–277). Policy Press.

Boaz, A., Oliver, K., & Hopkins, A. N. (2022). Linking research, policy and practice: Learning from other sectors. In OECD (Ed.), *Who cares about using education research in policy and practice? Strengthening research engagement, educational research and innovation* (pp. 125–145). OECD Publishing. 10.1787/70c657bc-en

Cirkony, C., Rickinson, M., Walsh, L., Gleeson, J., Salisbury, M., Cutler, B., & Boulet, M. (2022). *Improving quality use of research evidence in practice: Insights from cross-sector co-design.* Monash University. 10.26180/19380677.v3

Global Commission on Evidence to Address Societal Challenges (2022). *The Evidence Commission report: A wake-up call and path forward for decision-makers, evidence intermediaries, and impact-oriented evidence producers.* McMaster Health Forum. https://www.mcmasterforum.org/networks/evidence-commission

Hill, J. (2022). Who is facilitating research use in education systems? In OECD (Ed.), *Who cares about using education research in policy and practice? Strengthening research engagement, educational research and innovation* (pp. 74–99). OECD Publishing. 10.1787/f872248c-en

Levin, B. (2013). To know is not enough: Research knowledge and its use. *Review of Education, 1*(1), 2–31. 10.1002/rev3.3001

Malin, J. R., Brown, C., Ion, G., van Ackeren, I., Bremm, N., Luzmore, R., Flood, J., & Rind., G. M. (2020). World-wide barriers and enablers to achieving evidence-informed practice in education: What can be learnt from Spain, England, the United States, and Germany? *Humanities and Social Sciences Communications, 7*(1), 1–14. 10.1057/s41599-020-00587-8

Maxwell, B., Sharples, J., & Coldwell, M. (2022). Developing a systems-based approach to research use in education. *Review of Education, 10*(3), e3368. 10.1002/rev3.3368

Nelson, J., & Campbell, C. (2019). Using evidence in education. In A. Boaz, H. Davies, A. Fraser, & S. Nutley (Eds.), *What works now? Evidence-informed policy and practice* (pp. 131–149). Policy Press.

Rickinson, M., Walsh, L., Gleeson, J., Cutler, B., Cirkony, C., & Salisbury, M. (2022) Using research well in educational practice. In OECD (Ed.), *Who cares about using education research in policy and practice? Strengthening research engagement* (pp. 182–199). OECD Publishing. 10.1787/65aac033-en

Torres, J. M. (2022). Facilitating research use: Scary barriers (and super mechanisms). In OECD (Ed.), *Who cares about using education research in policy and practice? Strengthening research engagement, educational research and innovation* (pp. 103–124). OECD Publishing. 10.1787/cd4e8487-en

Conclusion
Quality use of research next steps

Chapter overview

This chapter draws together the key messages of the book and discusses what they reveal about using research well, what they suggest for future improvement efforts and what they highlight as future research needs. It argues that the book:

- opens up the issue of quality use of research as an unfolding picture (where different aspects are revealed by successive chapters), a detailed picture (where specific features are illuminated in detail in different chapters) and a connected picture (where links between aspects are revealed across the chapters);
- provides resources for future improvement in terms of productive uses (examples of quality use ideas being used in practice that could be emulated), productive spaces (factors that are important for fostering quality use that could be nurtured) and productive paradoxes (contradictions that uncover attributes of quality use that could be considered); and
- highlights possibilities for future research in terms of further work on quality use as a capacity, a culture, a practice and a system, and new work on quality use as a journey, quality use as a measure, and quality use across different contexts and sectors.

DOI: 10.4324/9781003353966-8

Introduction

This book was motivated by what we saw as an important gap in the evidence use field – that is, the need to better understand the "quality and qualities of evidence use" (Rickinson et al., 2017, p. 187). As explained in the opening chapter, the idea of quality use of research is about moving from a focus on *whether* we use research to a focus on *how well* we use research. It is about recognising that improved research use requires not only *high-quality research* but also *high-quality use*. But what is high-quality use? How can quality of research use be understood? And what does it mean to use research well in education?

This book and the research project on which it is based represent an attempt to engage with this question of what constitutes high-quality use of research evidence from an educational perspective. Each of the chapters takes up and examines a different aspect of quality use, such as why it matters as an issue (Chapter 1), how it has been conceptualised across sectors (Chapter 2), what it means in education (Chapter 3), what it requires of educators (Chapter 4), what it requires of schools (Chapter 5), what it involves as a practice (Chapter 6) and what it requires of systems (Chapter 7).

Building on these discussions, this final chapter seeks to distil what these different perspectives reveal about using research well in education, how such understandings might inform future research use improvement efforts and what aspects of quality use still need to be better understood through further inquiry. Each of these issues – current understandings, improvement resources and research needs – is summarised in Figure 8.1 and will be discussed in the next three sections.

Current understandings

At the start of the book, we used the image of a slowly opening fan to symbolise the way in which each of the chapters can be seen as contributing to an overall understanding of quality use by exploring it from a distinctive perspective. As shown in Figure 8.1, we can make sense of this overall understanding in three ways – as an *unfolding picture* where different aspects of quality use are revealed by each chapter, as a *detailed picture* where specific features of quality use are illuminated in more detail

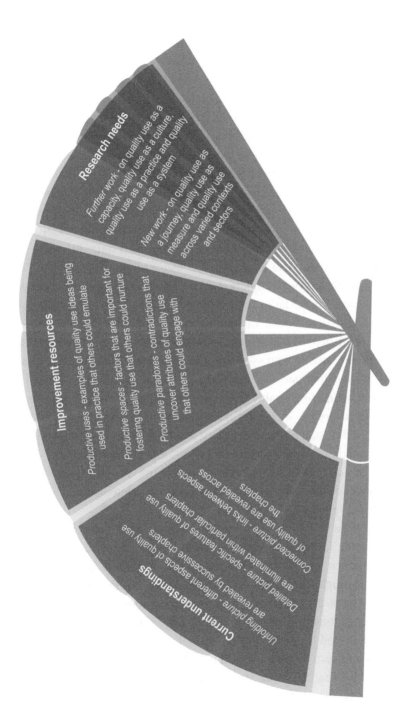

Figure 8.1 Quality use of research – current understandings, improvement resources and research needs

Research needs

Research needs

Further work - on quality use as a capacity; quality use as a culture; quality use as a practice and quality use as a system

New work - on quality use as a journey; quality use as measure and quality use across varied contexts and sectors

Improvement resources

Productive uses - examples of quality use ideas being used in practice that others could emulate

Productive spaces - factors that are important for fostering quality use that others could nurture

Productive paradoxes - contradictions that uncover attributes of quality use that others could engage with

Current understandings

Unfolding picture - different aspects of quality use are revealed by successive chapters

Detailed picture - specific features of quality use are illuminated within particular chapters

Connected picture - links between aspects of quality use are revealed across the chapters

within different chapters, and as a *connected picture* where links between aspects of quality use are revealed across the chapters.

An unfolding picture

As we move through the chapters of the book, different insights about quality use of research come into focus. In Chapter 1 (Quality use as an issue), for example, we learnt about why quality use is an issue that needs to be better understood in the field of education. It became clear that under-standing what it means to use research well within education is important because improving research use is a priority internationally, but the concept of evidence-based practice is contested, the practice of using research is challenging and the question of quality of use has been little discussed.

In Chapter 2 (Quality use as a gap), we learnt about how the issue of quality use has played out in different sectors and what could be gleaned from these sectors for the task of conceptualising quality use of research in education. There was a lack of explicit definitions and descriptions of quality of use in health, social care, policy and education, which made clear how quality use is a cross-sector gap. However, there were a small number of studies that had discussed aspects of quality use in an explicit way. For conceptualising quality use in education, these studies were seen as helpful, for example, in raising questions about the manner in which evidence is used or suggesting vocabulary that might help to capture higher quality use. In addition, there were two themes that cut across sectors – the importance of practitioner expertise in evidence use and the system com-plexity of evidence use improvement – that were also potentially helpful for conceptualising quality use in education.

Drawing on these individual studies and cross-sector themes, we then learnt in Chapter 3 (Quality use as an aspiration) about how quality use of research evidence can be defined and conceptualised in relation to education. Through the Quality Use of Research Evidence (QURE) Framework (Figure 3.1), quality use of research evidence was defined as: "thoughtful engagement with and implementation of appropriate research evidence, supported by a blend of individual and organisational enabling components and system-level influences". By articulating and elaborating quality use of research as an aspiration, we saw how these ideas have the potential to stimulate reflection about current approaches to using research and current approaches to supporting research use by individuals, organisations and systems.

The focus then shifted from the conceptual to the empirical in Chapter 4 (Quality use as a capacity) as we learnt about educators' perspectives on the mindsets, skillsets and relationships that are needed to use research well in practice. It became clear that educators need to feel positive and inquisitive about research, and curious and open-minded about whether and how it can be implemented within their practice. They also need to be able to access, read and appraise research, and be skilled in understanding research 'fit' when adapting and implementing research-informed initiatives. In addition, they need to be able to work with others in various ways within and beyond the school to find, understand and implement research.

In Chapter 5 (Quality use as a culture), the discussion moved from the individual to the organisational level, enabling us to learn about what quality use of research requires in terms of school culture, leadership and infrastructure. Educators' accounts made clear that a supportive school culture is one that encourages collective or collaborative research use and that feels trusting and safe in relation to taking informed risks. A supportive leadership, meanwhile, is one that models quality research use in their own practice and promotes quality research use in the work of others across the school. Finally, a supportive infrastructure is one that provides developmental support through professional learning and material support in terms of time and research access. We saw how these insights into culture, leadership and infrastructure can help leaders to support quality research use at the school level.

Chapter 6 (Quality use as a practice) then examined what is involved in enacting quality use, enabling us to learn in more detail about what using research well looks and feels like as a practice. It shows how educators' accounts depict quality use as an individual practice, a shared practice and an invested practice. These three characteristics highlight the importance of research use being driven by curiosity and professionalism (individual), collaborative and embedded in approach (shared), and purposeful and time and effort-dependent (invested). These characteristics provide a picture where educators and others can better understand the concept of quality use from a practice perspective that illustrates not only the actions and interactions that are involved, but also the intentions and meanings that inform them. Importantly, this practice perspective can inform the context-specific enactment of quality use of research evidence across diverse educational settings.

Finally, in Chapter 7 (Quality use as a system), we learnt about the system dimensions of quality use of research, in terms of system influences, system supports and system practices. It shows that system-level influences do not feature frequently in educators' accounts of using research well in schools and, when they do, are cited more often as barriers than enablers. It also shows that system actors' current practices are characterised by variable levels of research use and variable involvement in evidence sharing. Finally, it highlights key priorities for future improvement around strengthening system actors' involvement in research use, system role modelling of quality use and system-level support for research use.

When we set out the insights of each of the chapters, as we have done above, we can start to see them as contributing to an unfolding understanding of quality use. Yet, the chapters in this book have also generated a detailed picture of quality use by illuminating certain features in more depth.

A detailed picture

One source of this detailed picture has been the way in which different chapters have provided in-depth descriptions or examples of what aspects of quality use look like and involve. In relation to skillsets discussed in Chapter 4, for example, the process of educators assessing the "fit" of research for their context was illustrated in relation to considerations such as "the vision and values that we work within", "what I think is happening in my classroom" and "what is meaningful to us and to our teachers". In relation to culture in Chapter 5, meanwhile, the idea of a "safe" school environment that supports using research well was described in terms of there being "informed risk taking", "critical open discussions" and "time to see the new practices come into fruition". In addition, illustrations of the two core components of appropriate research evidence as well as thoughtful engagement and implementation were highlighted at various points within Chapters 4, 5, 6 and 7.

In some cases, it was in the contrasts between using research well and using research poorly that a more detailed picture became apparent. In relation to quality use as an invested practice in Chapter 6, for example, what is involved in being purposeful was made clearer by descriptions of research use that lacked purpose by being "ad hoc", involving "searching for the sake of searching" and so being "not worthy of attention". Along similar lines in the same chapter, the idea of quality use as a collective practice was brought to life with an example from a school that had moved from a situation where "people were knowledgeable about lots of different evidence-based practices [...] but were not getting traction because we were working independently" to one where "everybody is talking the same language, moving the same way, and there feels this incredible momentum".

Another way in which discussions within the chapters have contributed to a more detailed picture has been through uncovering insights into why and how aspects of quality use matter. The discussion about relationships in Chapter 4, for example, highlighted how collaborations with others can support specific research use processes such as finding research, appraising research, understanding research, and adapting and trialling research. This discussion also made clear that the role of collaboration becomes more important and involved as one moves through the research use process – it is 'light touch' and informal when "chat[ting] with people in [a] Twitter network" to find research, but deeper and more involved when "modelling, coaching and having rich professional dialogue" with others to trial and implement research. The discussion about leadership in Chapter 5 provided another example, in this case about why role modelling by leaders is important to quality use – that is, for getting "staff on board" with the research, linking it "with what is happening in the school", demonstrating "its implementation" in practice, and showing that it is "really valued by the school's leadership".

In relation to quality use as an individual practice, the discussion in Chapter 6 highlighted how being curious is important both in relation to ideas discovered in the research and in relation to one's practice, and how using research well can contribute to professionalism by "using evidence-based practice to achieve better outcomes and have consistency of practice". Similarly, considering quality use as an invested practice underlined several reasons why an investment of educators' time and effort is so important – to be able to "learn more deeply" about the research and "explore things carefully" so that practice changes can be "sustainable and have a long-lasting impact". Then in connection with quality use as a system in Chapter 7, the importance of system-level support is illustrated through examples of how system influences can undermine quality research use through "a lack of connection between different system actors", research dissemination being too "political" and the "wide range of demands" placed on schools and educators.

179

A connected picture

Beyond contributing to an unfolding picture and a detailed picture, the chapters in this book can also be seen as helping to build a connected picture of quality use. This has come through identifying links between different QURE Framework components, between different levels of the system and between different perspectives.

In relation to links between different components of the QURE Framework, there were strong parallels between how a mindset of experimentation was described as an individual enabler in Chapter 4 (such as being open to "experimenting in the classroom by taking risks within evidence-informed practice") and how a culture of trust was described as an organisational enabler in Chapter 5 (such as encouraging "risk taking [and it is] OK to try and fail"). It was also clear that knowledge sharing as a process featured as an aspect of quality use relationships in Chapter 4, a quality use culture in Chapter 5, and quality use as a shared practice in Chapter 6. Another indication of the interconnections between components came within the "looks like in practice" vignettes. Whether it was with the development of research-informed teaching practices in Alex's school (Vignette 4), the creation of a research use culture in Imogen's school (Vignette 6) or the building of a whole-school learning culture in Bianca's school (Vignette 10), the integrated importance of several QURE Framework components was a common theme.

There were also insights into quality research use that highlighted links between different levels within the system. The points made in Chapter 5 about the importance of leaders at the school level role modelling quality use practices, involving other staff in research use processes and providing infrastructural support are reflected by similar arguments in Chapter 7 about what is needed from actors and organisations at the system level. Along similar lines, the investment of personal time at an individual educator level described in Chapter 6 in relation to quality use as an invested practice has strong links to calls for protected time to be made available through support at the level of school infrastructure in Chapter 5 and at the level of system influences in Chapter 7. In addition, the suggestions for research use-related skills development highlighted in Chapter 7 make clear the different levels and types of support that are needed for quality use as a system, including pre-service teacher education, in-service teacher professional learning, coaching and mentoring, leadership development, and capacity building within and across schools.

Importantly, another type of connection flagged across the chapters was between different perspectives on quality use. A clear example of this was the way in which educators' views on using research well, as discussed in Chapters 4, 5 and 6, resonate strongly with ideas identified within the literature in Chapter 3. There were references within educators' survey and interview data to all of the core and enabling components of the QURE Framework – a finding that indicates clear alignment between the views of researchers and the views of practitioners. This point is significant given the dearth of research use models and insights based on the perspectives of research users as opposed to researchers (Gleeson, Rickinson et al., 2023; Oliver et al., 2014).

Future improvement resources

As explained at the outset, this book is intended as a resource for professionals within the education sector and beyond who want to understand what using research evidence well means and involves, and how it can be supported. While the previous section has drawn together and discussed what has been revealed about using research well, the important question now is how these insights might inform future efforts to improve the use of research in schools and systems. As shown earlier in Figure 8.1, we see this book as providing resources for improvement in three areas: *productive uses* to emulate, *productive spaces* to nurture, and *productive paradoxes* to consider.

Productive uses

The ideas related to the quality use of research that are discussed in this book are relatively recent in their development. It will take time for their utility to become clear through wider exposure, engagement and experimentation across different contexts. Notwithstanding this reality, several of the "how is it helpful" vignettes in earlier chapters provide clues to the applicability of the book's ideas in policy and practice settings. As illustrations of actual uses, they can provide pointers for others who are interested in applying quality use ideas and approaches within their work. For example, they suggest that understandings about quality use of research as a gap, an aspiration, a capacity, a culture, a practice, and/or a system can be used productively to:

- **Inform research funding priorities** – Vignette 1 (Chapter 2) provided an example of a philanthropic research funder that responded to the idea of quality use as a gap by signalling quality research use as a priority for future study and cross-disciplinary discussion. Given the importance of "approaches to prioritising challenges to address" (Global Commission on Evidence to Address Societal Challenges, 2022, p. 24), this way of responding to the ideas in this book may be relevant to other research funders and research organisations, and networks that have a role in the development and implementation of research agendas and priorities at different scales.

- **Reflect on evidence use within system organisations** – Vignette 3 (Chapter 3) and Vignette 11 (Chapter 7) both featured system organisations that had used the QURE Framework and related ideas to inform their work as a national ministry and a school jurisdiction respectively. The former had used the framework to review their current evidence use practices and identify areas for improvement, while the latter had used quality use ideas to strengthen their support for research use as part of school improvement. In view of the importance of policy makers not only as evidence users themselves but also as shapers of "decision making by organisational leaders, professionals and citizens" (Global Commission on Evidence to Address Societal Challenges, 2022, p. 24), engagement with the idea of quality use as an aspiration, a practice and a system may well be helpful for other system leaders at regional, national and international levels.

- **Guide improvement efforts within schools** – Vignette 5 (Chapter 4), Vignette 7 (Chapter 5) and Vignette 9 (Chapter 6) all relate to school-based teams applying quality use ideas in their work. In one case (Vignette 5), the focus was on a mixed group of leaders and teachers developing their own research use skillsets and mindsets in order to be able to influence and support others. In another (Vignette 7), an improvement team used the QURE Assessment Tool[1] to identify the need for not only an evidence-informed approach within their work as a team, but also for a school culture that is more supportive of using research well. In the third example (Vignette 9), a group of lead educators used the idea of quality use as a practice to guide their approach to the introduction of a new research-informed pedagogical approach. Taking account of the role of "organisational leaders" as evidence users and enablers (Global Commission on Evidence to

Address Societal Challenges, 2022, p. 34), then, engagement with the QURE Framework and its related ideas and resources may well be generative for middle and senior leaders within schools who want their own work and that of their colleagues to be more research-informed.

Productive spaces

A second way in which the ideas presented in this book might inform future improvement is by highlighting productive spaces in which, and through which, using research well can be nurtured. This idea builds on an argument that we have made elsewhere about the development of evidence-informed practice within complex, contested school systems and the need "to find and work with the productive places that exist within a system" (Gleeson et al., 2022, 124). The thinking here is that insights into what quality use of research looks like can give pointers for others as to where it happens and what can help it to happen. Indeed, drawing on the examples and views shared by educators and system actors through the preceding chapters, there are certain factors that emerge as important in relation to fostering quality use of research. These highlight the significance of creating spaces that foster and leverage:

- **Certain practices** – The need to understand and approach research use as a collective undertaking was a recurring theme across the chapters and one that highlighted the importance of collaborative practices such as "unpacking research as a teaching staff", developing "common knowledge and understanding" about research-informed practices and working towards "talking the same language". Another practice that came through strongly was that of role modelling, both when practising quality use of research explicitly in one's own work (being able to "walk the talk") and demonstrating research-informed practices in action ("what it would look like in the classroom").
- **Certain forums** – There were certain contexts that came up time and again in relation to using research well. Not surprisingly, these included group settings that bring staff together around a common focus, such as team meetings, improvement teams, and forums focused on staff collaborative learning, such as staff reading circles, professional learning communities, and inquiry cycle teams. In different ways, they were all

characterised by professionals working together to build, share and use knowledge.

- **Certain supports** – Two kinds of support came through as key at both the school and system level for promoting quality research use. One was enabling educators to have scheduled time to engage with research ("We must make time, we cannot presume that people will just [engage with research] out of goodwill"), while the other was supporting easy access to research databases, publications and resources ("Schools simply [don't] have the access that we would require to make our teachers understand the importance and relevance of [research]").
- **Certain leadership** – The importance of leaders and leadership came through very clearly in relation to strengthening research use. More specifically, educators' perspectives on using research well made clear the importance of leaders providing a clear vision and purpose for research use, ensuring that research informs decision making, demonstrating research use in one's own practice and working with colleagues to support research use as coaches, mentors, and collaborators.

Productive paradoxes

In addition to highlighting productive uses to follow and spaces to nurture, there is a third way in which the ideas in this book might inform future improvement: by uncovering a set of paradoxes that we see as productive to engage with in order to understand quality use of research. As others have argued (Nutley et al., 2007; Penuel et al., 2015), how one conceptualises the use of research and evidence matters because it can influence how one tries to improve it. With that in mind, we suggest the following quality use paradoxes as helpful to think about in order to develop a more nuanced approach to research use improvement:

- **Quality use as an absence or a presence** – In terms of the current research literature, quality research use can be seen as an absence (in the sense that it has been researched and discussed far less than a related issue like quality of evidence), but can also be seen as a presence (in the sense that there are certain publications that have discussed aspects of quality of use explicitly). Similarly, within contexts of practice, while quality research use can appear very much as an absence (in the sense that there are few, if any, improvement initiatives focused on quality of use), it is also very much a presence within the views of educators (in the sense that educators have strong views on using research well and poorly). This paradox is important because it reminds us that future efforts to strengthen quality research use are not starting from scratch but have conceptual resources and professional capacities to draw and build upon.

- **Quality use as an aspirational practice or a familiar practice.** – In one sense, quality use can be seen as an aspirational practice (in terms of articulating what using research *well* means, involves and requires), but in another sense, it can also be seen as a familiar practice (in terms of involving processes and values that are not at all new to education professionals, such as collaboration and curiosity). This paradox is important because it helps us to see that strengthening quality research use needs to involve not only improving how research is used (e.g., How can we make our use of research more collaborative?), but also identifying existing practices that could support better research use (e.g., Where are we are already collaborating well and how can we use research there?).

- **Quality use as peripheral or integral** – While for some educators, quality research use is seen as something that is peripheral to core business ("not really part of my job"), for others quality use is seen as completely integral ("the bread and butter of my role"). So, while some educators did not see using research well and teaching well as necessarily connected, others saw them as one and the same (such as practising curiosity when using research being the same as encouraging inquiry-based learning when teaching). Similar distinctions can be seen to play out at the school and system levels. This paradox is important because it helps us to see that working towards quality of use needs to recognise and respect the varied starting points of different educators, schools and systems.

- **Quality use as an end or a means** – In one sense, quality use can be seen as an end to aim for, but in another sense, it can be seen as a means to an end. This distinction came up very clearly in educators' views about quality use being a purposeful practice which needed to be focused on "the problem we're trying to solve" as opposed to "searching for the sake of searching". This paradox is important because it reminds us that the really important issue is not how we can improve the use of research in education, but rather how we can improve education using research where it is relevant.

- **Quality use as about research or about practice** – On one level, using research well is very much about research (e.g., being able to find it, make sense of it, decide if and how to use it and so on), but on another level, using research well is very much about practice (e.g., being curious about one's practice, able to identify practice issues that could be improved using research, skilled in integrating practice knowledge with research insights and so on). This paradox is important because it underlines the critical point that using research well is as much about developing practice expertise as it is about developing research expertise.

Future research needs

Notwithstanding the arguments above about how the insights in this book might inform future improvement, it is important to remember that these insights are based on an early exploratory study of quality research use in one specific context. From a research perspective, then, the work presented in this book also highlights future research needs and possibilities (as shown earlier in Figure 8.1).

There are ways in which the perspectives for understanding quality research use that are discussed in this book could be developed further. One area that is ripe for further work is *more in-depth investigation of quality use as a capacity, a culture and a practice*. The insights into these aspects of quality use that are reported in this book are based on survey and interview data, but not observational data or artefact analysis. This situation was unavoidable due to COVID-19 restrictions curtailing data collection in schools at the time of our work, but it now presents an exciting opportunity for follow-up work that is much closer to the context and practice of research use within organisational settings. This type of work is particularly important in light of our earlier arguments about the way studies have tended to overlook *"the practice of evidence use"* (Farley-Ripple et al., 2018, p. 236, emphasis original) and failed to "integrate the fine-grained realities of using evidence with the real-life processes of educational practices" (Rickinson et al., 2017, p. 186).

Another important area for further work is the need *for more comprehensive work on quality use as a system*. As Maxwell et al. (2022, p. 1) noted, "models of research use in education tend to focus on specific elements of education systems". With that shortcoming in mind, it is important to remember that the insights into quality use as a system in this book are based on data collected primarily at the school rather than the system level. To understand the system dimensions of quality use more fully, then, there is an important need for investigations into the quality use perspectives, practices and interactions of more varied system actors. For example, following a recent Organisation for Economic Cooperation and Development (OECD) analysis of organisational-level actors involved in facilitating research use (Hill, 2022), future studies could probe into those working in policy organisations (e.g., government departments), research organisations (e.g., universities), practice-orientated organisations (e.g., professional associations) and intermediary organisations (e.g., brokerage agencies). Another critically important part of the picture is the views and experiences of students, parents and community members. As Tseng (2022a, p. 220) argues, "if we see students and their communities as beneficiaries of education, then their interests should be at the centre of education research", which, of course, includes work aiming to understand research use within education systems.

As well as further developing the current perspectives, there is also potential to develop new ways of understanding quality use of research. One possibility for new work that we see as worth exploring is the idea of *quality use as a journey*. This idea recognises that another limitation of the research reported in this book is that it was not examining quality use over time. While some educators described shifts in their research use practices through time, on the whole, the understandings generated were static rather than dynamic. There is, therefore, real potential for future studies to track the development of quality research use as part of individual growth, organisational improvement and/or system change over time. At the level of schools, for example, how might insights into schools' use of research over time be informed by and integrated with the dynamics of schools' improvement trajectories over time (e.g., Day et al., 2010)? Similarly, at the level of systems, how might understandings about quality use as a system over time be informed by and connected with understandings about system change processes over time (e.g., Maxwell et al., 2022)?

Another related possibility for new work concerns the idea of *quality use as a measure*. The work reported in this book involved developing a way of conceptually framing quality use of research evidence and then empirically investigating its alignment (or otherwise) with the views and experiences of educational practitioners. It did not involve developing and then testing a validated scale to measure educators' quality use of research. This kind of work, though, is critical. As Sheldrick and colleagues (2022, para. 4) have argued, "advancing the field depend[s] on our collective ability to conceptualize and operationally define what quality research evidence use is [...] [in order to] [...] establish the construct validity of our measures". We therefore see the measurement of quality research use as an important potential line for future investigation, particularly given the shortage of reliable measures within the evidence use literature more generally (Dagenais et al., 2012; Gleeson, Cutler et al., 2023; Lawlor et al., 2019).

There is also a critical need for new work on *quality use in more varied contexts and sectors*. While the work that informed this book involved educators and system actors in various roles and organisational contexts, it was still conducted within one national context. There is scope, therefore, for future investigations into using research well in other national contexts and for international comparative studies to examine similarities and differences between countries and jurisdictions. Similarly, while our work was conducted within education, there is a clear need for work on practitioners' perspectives and quality research use within other sectors such as health, social care, policy and beyond.

In conclusion, we hope that this book can be a stimulus for others to become not only curious about what it means for research to be used well, but also committed to enacting and embedding quality use of research within their work. If, as Tseng (2022b, p. 12) argues, "research can play a vital role in pointing policy makers, civil society, and communities toward a stronger, more sustainable, and just world", then it is in all our interests to understand and improve how well research is used.

Note

1   The QURE (Quality Use of Research Evidence) Assessment Tool is an online tool based on the QURE Framework that enables educators, as individuals or as a group, to assess their current research use practices and gain feedback and scaffolded resources for future improvement.

References

Dagenais, C., Lysenko, L., Abrami, P. C., Bernard, R. M., Ramde, J., & Janosz, M. (2012). Use of research-based information by school practitioners and determinants of use: A review of empirical research. *Evidence & Policy*, *8*(3), 285–309. 10.1332/174426412X654031

Day, C., Sammons, P., Hopkins, D., Harris, A., Leithwood, K., Gu, Q., & Brown, E. (2010). *10 strong claims about successful school leadership*. National College for School Leadership.

Farley-Ripple, E., May, H., Karpyn, A., Tilley, K., & McDonough, K. (2018). Rethinking connections between research and practice in education: A conceptual framework. *Educational Researcher*, *47*(4), 235–245. 10.3102/00131 89X18761042

Gleeson, J., Cutler, B., Rickinson, M., Walsh, L., Ehrich, J., Cirkony, C., & Salisbury, M. (2023). School educators' engagement with research: An Australian Rasch validation study. *Educational Assessment, Evaluation and Accountability*, *35*, 281–207. 10.1007/s11092-023-09404-7

Gleeson, J., Rickinson, M., Walsh, L., Cutler, B., Salisbury, M., Hall, G., & Khong, H. (2023). Quality use of research evidence: Practitioner perspectives. *Evidence and Policy*, *19*(3), 423–443. 10.1332/174426421X16778434724277

Gleeson, J., Rickinson, M., Walsh, L., Salisbury, M., & Cirkony, C. (2022). Evidence-informed practice in Australian education. In C. Brown & J. R. Malin (Eds.), *The Emerald handbook of evidence-informed practice in education: Learning from international contexts* (pp. 123–138). Emerald Publishing. 10.1108/978-1-80043-141-620221017

Global Commission on Evidence to Address Societal Challenges (2022). *The Evidence Commission report: A wake-up call and path forward for decision-makers, evidence intermediaries, and impact-oriented evidence producers*. McMaster Health Forum. https://www.mcmasterforum.org/networks/evidence-commission

Hill, J. (2022). Who is facilitating research use in education systems? In OECD (Ed.), *Who cares about using education research in policy and practice? Strengthening research engagement, educational research and innovation* (pp. 74–99). OECD Publishing. 10.1787/f872248c-en

Lawlor, J., Mills, K., Neal, Z., Neal, J. W., Wilson, C., & McAlindon, K. (2019). Approaches to measuring use of research evidence in K–12 settings: A systematic review. *Educational Research Review*, *27*, 218–228. 10.1016/j.edurev.2019.04.002

Maxwell, B., Sharples, J., & Coldwell, M. (2022). Developing a systems-based approach to research use in education. *Review of Education*, *10*(3), e3368. 10.1 002/rev3.3368

Nutley, S., Walter, I., & Davies, H. T. O. (2007). *Using evidence: How research can inform public services*. Policy Press.

Oliver, K., Lorenc, T., & Innvær, S. (2014). New directions in evidence-based policy research: A critical analysis of the literature. *Health Research Policy and Systems*, *12*(34). 10.1186/1478-4505-12-34

Penuel, W. R., Allen, A.-R., Coburn, C. E., & Farrell, C. (2015). Conceptualizing research–practice partnerships as joint work at boundaries. *Journal of Education for Students Placed At Risk, 20*(1–2), 182–197. 10.1080/10824669.2014.988334

Rickinson, M., De Bruin, K., Walsh, L., & Hall, M. (2017). What can evidence-use in practice learn from evidence-use in policy? *Educational Research, 59*(2), 173–189. 10.1080/00131881.2017.1304306

Sheldrick, C., Mackie, T., Supplee, L., Cruden, G., Farley-Ripple, L., Firestone, B. G., Purtle, J., & Wilson-Ahlstrom, A. (2022). *An invitation: Help us to conceptualize what "quality" research evidence use means*. William T. Grant Foundation. https://wtgrantfoundation.org/an-invitation-help-us-to-conceptualize-what-quality-research-evidence-use-means

Tseng, V. (2022a). First things first: What is the purpose of education research? In OECD (Ed.), *Who cares about using education research in policy and practice? Strengthening research engagement, educational research and innovation* (pp. 219–224). OECD Publishing. 10.1787/e83abf22-en

Tseng, V. (2022b). *Research on research use: Building theory, empirical evidence, and a global field*. William T Grant Foundation. https://wtgrantfoundation.org/digest/research-on-research-use-building-theory-empirical-evidence-and-a-global-field

Appendix 1

Q Project Data Collection and Analysis Methods

This appendix describes and explains the methodology of the research that has informed this book. It details the rationale, data collection and analysis procedures of the Q Project's main research activities, namely our: (i) Cross-sector systematic review and narrative synthesis, (ii) Iterative development of quality use framework, (iii) Surveys of Australian educators and system actors, (iv) Interviews with Australian educators, (v) Co-design of improvement interventions and (vi) Stakeholder consultation.

Cross-sector systematic review and narrative synthesis

The early phase of the Q Project involved a cross-sector systematic review and narrative synthesis of relevant publications. The review and synthesis were guided by the question *How has quality use of research evidence been described and conceptualised across sectors?* In line with arguments in the evidence use field about the value of learning from different policy areas and disciplines (Davies et al., 2019), this question was about looking across practice-oriented sectors to understand how this issue of quality use of research evidence had been approached in the health, social care and education literature (with policy emerging as an additional sector during the process).

Informed by the principles of systematic reviewing, the review followed a transparent method with clearly defined and documented searches, inclusion, and quality appraisal processes (Gough et al., 2017). The design included narrative synthesis of the included documents to accommodate the methodological diversity common in systematic reviews of social interventions (Gough et al., 2017; Popay et al., 2006). The process also involved input from specialists in systematic reviewing, information science, evidence use, health, policy and social care.

Search strategy

The search methods aimed to include both research and professional publications, utilising empirical or conceptual approaches, as well as those that focused on research use in the domains of policy and/or practice. We conducted both formal searches of databases (Gough et al., 2017) as well as informal searching to access relevant results (Greenhalgh & Peacock, 2005). Informal searches included internet searches (e.g., Google Scholar, searching evidence use organisation websites), talking to personal contacts (e.g., through relationships with international experts and evidence brokers), as well as checks of the reference lists from the initial set of included papers. The terms for these searches were generated through engagement with the literature as well as consultations with subject librarians and database information scientists at Monash University. This process resulted in two sets of key words that focused on 'evidence and research use', as well as the 'quality of research use' (see Table 9.1).

The searches, conducted from April to July 2019, did not specify date restrictions in order to identify older papers as well as contemporary perspectives. This resulted in 10,813 publications from across four databases relevant to the targeted sectors (ERIC, Medline, Social Services Abstracts, PsycInfo). These results were imported into Covidence (systematic review software) for screening by two reviewers, resulting in 268 publications moving to full-text review. In addition, 175 publications sourced from informal searches, reference checks and recommendations from expert informants were included for a full-text review.

Screening, selection and appraisal

The initial 443 publications were organised by sector and descriptive data were extracted (e.g., aim, methods, findings, etc.) to enable four members of the research team to undertake a series of moderation and quality appraisal processes (Gough et al., 2017). This involved the researchers ranking the relevance of papers to the concept of understanding quality use and papers that were not deemed fit for this purpose were excluded. Given that there

Table 9.1 Key words included in databases and informal searches

Evidence and research use	Quality of research use
Evidence use	Abilit*
Evidence-based decision making	Adapt*
Evidence-based policy	Aptitude
Evidence-based practice	Best practices
Evidence-based teaching	Capabilit*
Evidence-informed decision making	Competence
Evidence-informed policy	Deep
Evidence-informed practice	Shallow
Evidence-informed teaching	Effectiv*
Implementation of research	Expertise*
Research use	Experience*
Research engagement	Quality
Research literacy	Innovativ*
Research utili*	Intelligent
Research implementation	Knowledge level
Use of evidence	Novice
Use of research	Expert
	Professional
	Skill*
	Thoughtful
	Wise

Note: * were truncations used to return variations on a search term (e.g., Abilit* returns Ability, Abilities, etc.)

were very few papers that explicitly focused on quality use, exclusion decisions were based on consideration of whether a paper sufficiently addressed quality use indirectly or implicitly. When differences of opinion arose, they were resolved through consensus. We believed this collaborative approach was suitable given the diverse methods of the papers included (Popay et al., 2006), and the challenges around reaching common agreements about quality (Dixon-Woods et al., 2005). During this process, there were many documents related to policy, resulting in its establishment as an additional sector. Given this, the policy papers that were included were not representative of the sector per se but of the general search strategy.

Narrative synthesis

The appraisal process resulted in a final selection of 112 publications to be included in the narrative synthesis: 30 from health, 29 from social care,

31 from education, and 22 from policy (for the full list of papers, see supplementary information in Rickinson et al., 2021). The papers that were included for each sector were then analysed in detail in order to draft a synthesis document that provided a narrative overview of the papers included for each sector. Each of the narratives aimed to answer the guiding question (i.e., How has quality evidence use been described and conceptualised?) in relation to the chosen sector. They each included a summary of definitions and/or descriptions of evidence use, an overview of frameworks and models of evidence use, and a discussion of issues related to quality of evidence use in that sector. Following the development of the narratives, for the sectors where the research team had less expertise (i.e., the health, social care and policy narratives), these narratives were reviewed by Australian and international researchers in each of the fields. On the whole, they provided positive feedback, with a few making suggestions of other key papers that could be included.

Iterative development of quality use framework

To develop the Quality Use of Research Evidence (QURE) Framework, each of the sector narratives underwent two main stages of analysis. The first stage involved thematic analysis to identify cross-sector insights related to quality use of research evidence across the health, social care and policy narratives. As discussed in Chapter 2, for example, it became clear that all of these sectors emphasised the importance of practitioner expertise in the evidence use process and the complexity of evidence use improvement within systems. These kinds of cross-sector insights were then compared with an early framing of quality use which had been developed prior to the review (Rickinson et al., 2020). This process led to the early framing of quality use being modified and updated in some important ways:

- One of the core components changed from 'thoughtful use' to 'thoughtful engagement and implementation' in order to encompass implementation as well as varied ways of engaging with research.
- The enabling components were re-organised into two levels in order to distinguish between individual-level ('mindsets', 'skillsets', 'relationships') and organisational-level ('leadership', 'culture' and 'infrastructure') enablers.

- A separate 'system-level influences' category was added in order to take account of the systems dimensions of evidence use improvement.

The second stage then involved taking this updated quality use framing and seeking to make it specific and relevant for education. We compared the updated framing with the key ideas that had been synthesised from the education literature in order to be able to develop education-specific elaborations for each of the components. Drawing on the education sector literature, each of the components of the QURE Framework were elaborated in response to the following questions: 'What is it?', 'Why is it important?' and 'What does it involve?'. This process led to the development of the QURE Framework that was discussed in Chapter 3. An important part of this process was sharing evolving ideas and framework iterations with varied project partners and stakeholders locally, nationally and internationally. Feedback received through stakeholder meetings, workshops and conferences informed the further development and refinement of the framework. This collaborative process aimed to ensure that the development of the QURE Framework was reflective of both the research literature and the perspectives of diverse stakeholders within the Australian education system.

Surveys of Australian educators and system actors

The empirical research phase of the Q Project centred on listening to Australian educators' perspectives about how they find, engage with and use research evidence. Specifically, the research phase aimed to explore: i) The types of research and evidence valued by educators, ii) How they engaged with different types of evidence, iii) The barriers and enablers for using research in practice and iv) What 'using research well' meant to them. In service of these aims, three surveys, conducted with separate and valid samples totalling 1,725 educators, were administered between March 2020 and October 2021 (see Table 9.2). Ethics approval was granted from both the Monash University Human Research Ethics Committee and relevant education departments and governing jurisdictions prior to the generation of survey data. The design and implementation of each survey are outlined before giving an overview of the statistical analyses reported in this book.

Table 9.2 Sample details for the three Q Project surveys in schools

	Survey 1		Survey 2		Survey 3	
	n	%[a]	n	%[a]	n	%[a]
Sample total	492		819		414	
State						
New South Wales	149	30	225	27	158	38
Victoria	195	40	228	28	150	36
Queensland	116	24	174	21	83	20
South Australia	32	7	62	8	23	6
Northern Territory	–	–	6	1	–	–
Western Australia	–	–	87	11	–	–
Tasmania	–	–	27	3	–	–
Aus. Capital Territory	–	–	10	1	–	–
Respondent role						
Teacher	281	57	589	72	307	74
Middle leader	60	12	60	7	32	8
Senior leader	99	20	39	5	24	6
Other role	52	11	131	16	51	12
Years of experience[b]						
0 to <5 years	74	15	232	28	77	19
5 to <10 years	76	15	243	30	84	20
10 to <15 years	74	15	144	18	72	17
15+ years	267	54	200	24	181	44
Qualification level[c]						
Undergraduate	273	55	544	66	235	57
Non-research postgraduate	187	38	235	29	151	36
Research-based postgraduate	32	7	11	1	17	4
School type						
Primary (Prep to Year 6)	205	42	459	56	184	44
Combined (P–12)	117	24	107	13	60	14
Secondary (Years 7–12)	156	32	253	31	157	38
Special	14	3	–	–	13	3

Note: [a] Percentages may not add to 100 due to rounding. [b] One Survey 1 participant did not provide their years of experience. [c] 29 Survey 2 participants and 11 Survey 3 participants did not provide their qualification.

Survey 1 – Research and evidence use in Australian schools

Design. The first survey explored educators' perceptions about and use of research in practice and the design was informed by several previous international large-scale surveys of educators' evidence use (e.g., Nelson et al., 2017; Penuel et al., 2016; Poet et al., 2015). The Q Project then engaged WhereTo Research, an external research consultancy, to undertake a four-wave piloting phase with 12 Australian educators to test and refine the survey items. During the second and third waves, key Q Project advisors and stakeholders also provided feedback on the survey development (see Rickinson et al. 2023).

The final survey took approximately 20 minutes to complete and consisted of eight quantitative questions about i) the use of different evidence types in decision making, ii) perceived school support for research use, iii) personal beliefs about research use and iv) the role of research in daily practice (for the survey instrument, see Rickinson et al., 2023). Participants' demographic details, such as school role, years of experience, qualifications, gender and school details (e.g., location, ICSEA, etc.), were also collected.

In addition, Survey 1 contained 4 open-text responses that invited educators to share details about their use of evidence in relation to a school initiative over the past 12 months, as well as their views about what is involved in 'using research well' as well as 'using research poorly'. As these open-text responses were analysed similarly to the interviews, the details about both of these analyses are presented in the 'Qualitative analysis of interviews and survey' section later in this appendix.

Sample. Due to the impact of COVID-19 on research activities in schools during 2020, two samples of participants completed the survey. First, nominated educators from the 78 schools that signed up to be Q Project partner schools were emailed personalised links to the survey through Qualtrics. From the 182 invitations, 125 surveys were completed (69% response rate). Second, the Q Project engaged the Online Research Unit (ORU), an external research agency, to administer the survey to a panel of educators. While identifying information about the ORU educators was not shared with the Q Project team, the respondents were invited to nominate the name of their school to allow for school demographic information (e.g., Index of Community Socio-Educational Advantage (ICSEA), location, etc.) to be sourced from the federal government's MySchool website. ORU provided the Q Project with a total of 367 responses making an overall total of 492 educators participating in Survey 1 (see Table 9.2). The Q Project partner and ORU samples were combined in IBM SPSS Statistics (Version 27.0) for analysis, as outlined later in this appendix.

Survey 2 – Australian practitioners' attitudes and behaviours towards sharing research in education

Design. The second survey investigated practitioners' attitudes towards and behaviours regarding sharing research. Members of the Q Project team worked with key project stakeholders and independent researchers at WhereTo Research to design a quantitative survey of educators' and education system actors' evidence dissemination practices. This involved WhereTo Research conducting six cognitive interviews with Australian educators and system stakeholders to test and refine the survey items. The final survey took approximately 16 minutes to complete and consisted of 20 core questions that were presented to all respondents, with an additional 33 follow-on questions being presented based on a participant's responses to the core questions (for the survey instrument, see Rickinson et al., 2023). It consisted of questions pertaining to practitioners' i) use of information sources for professional development, ii) perspectives about useful and high-quality evidence types and sources, iii) experiences of receiving evidence directly from others, iv) experiences of sharing evidence directly with others, and v) beliefs, attitudes and perceptions about research. Participants' demographic details, such as role, years of experience, qualifications, gender and workplace details (e.g., sector, school type, etc.), were also collected.

Sample. A total survey sample of 1,007 participants was recruited from WhereTo Research's existing database in June 2021. Of the 1,007 responses, 977 were considered valid (i.e., complete and coherent responses). In contrast to Surveys 1 and 3, the panel for this survey consisted of both educators working in schools ($n = 819$, see Table 9.2), as well as system actors who worked in the broader education sector whose role had an influence on teaching practice ($n = 158$, see Table 9.3).

Although the school and system samples were analysed separately, they were analysed using the same general procedures, as outlined later in this appendix. The research team decided to prioritise the analysis of the school population due to time pressures related to sharing the findings from the school sample alongside Q Project's other school-focused activities. Given the complexity of the demographic make-up of the system sample, respondents were grouped into 'categories' based on the information they provided about their role to allow for role-based analyses similar to the school sample (see Table 9.3). These categories were those working in

Table 9.3 System sample details for Q Project Survey 2

	Survey 2 - Systems	
	n	%[a]
Systems sample total	158	
State		
New South Wales	52	33
Victoria	50	32
Queensland	31	20
South Australia	11	7
Western Australia	9	6
Tasmania	2	1
Aus. Capital Territory	2	1
Northern Territory	1	1
System role[b]		
Higher education	45	28
Education departments	33	21
Student-facing providers	40	25
Teacher-facing providers	36	23

Note: [a] Percentages may not add to 100 due to rounding. [b] Four participants did not disclose information about their role.

higher education (e.g., academic researchers, lecturers, etc.), those working in education departments (e.g., administrators, policy makers, communications advisors, etc.), those working for student-facing service providers (e.g., out-of-school care, academic tutors, etc.) and those working for teacher-facing service providers (e.g., trainers, PD facilitators, etc.).

Survey 3 – Barriers and enablers of quality research use in educational practice

Design. The third survey studied educators' perceptions about the barriers of and enablers to their use of research in practice. In consultation with key project stakeholders, members of the Q Project team designed a quantitative survey that aimed to deepen the insights generated from Surveys 1 and 2, as well as quantitatively interrogate the findings that were identified through Q Project's qualitative work (outlined later in this appendix). WhereTo Research was then engaged to test and refine the survey items through a four-wave piloting phase with 12 Australian educators (as was undertaken for Survey 1).

The final survey took approximately 20 minutes to complete and con-sisted of 20 core quantitative questions presented to all respondents, with an additional 5 follow-on sections depending on participants' responses to the core questions (for the survey instrument, see Rickinson et al., 2023). It consisted of questions about educators' i) use of research, including when and where they do so, ii) attitudes and beliefs about using research, iii) research use practices in their school and iv) perceptions of certain resources and supports for improving their research use. Participants' demographic details, such as role, years of experience, qualifications, gender and workplace details (e.g., sector, school type, etc.), were also collected.

Sample. A sample of 414 participants was recruited from ORU in August 2021 (see Table 9.2). Although the identities of ORU educators were not shared with the Q Project team, ORU ensured that participants had not previously completed Survey 1.

Quantitative analysis of surveys

The data were first imported into IBM SPSS Statistics (Version 27.0) and all negatively-worded Likert scale questions were reverse-coded. Respondents' years of experience in the profession – collected as a continuous variable – were collapsed into four categories (i.e., 0 to <5, 5 to <10, 10 to <15, 15+ years) to allow for similar analyses to other demographic variables (e.g., role, qualification, etc.). All three surveys made use of the same question types (i.e., multiple choice questions, Likert-rating scale questions and ranking-style questions), so although they were analysed separately, similar analysis techniques were used.

The percentages for multiple choice questions, such as "What are the main reasons you use certain evidence over others? [Please select all that apply]", were based on the number of respondents who selected an item divided by the number of respondents who were presented with the question in which the item was housed. The percentages for 5-point Likert-rating scale questions were generated based on the summed number of responses for the top two points divided by the number of respondents who were presented with the item. For instance, when edu-cators were asked, "How often did [they] consult the following informa-tion sources to help inform [their] decisions?", the percentages represent the summed number of 'often' and 'always' responses (which was considered 'regular use') for each of the items included in this question. Similarly, for questions about the provision of specific research use supports, such as, "How would you rate your school's provision of the following resources for research use?", percentages represent the number of educators who indicated 'good' and 'very good' (which was considered 'good') for each of the presented items. The percentages for ranking-style questions were generated based on the summed number of instances an item was ranked in one of the top five positions divided by the number of respondents who were presented with the question. For example, when educators were asked, "If you wanted to improve how you use research, what skills would you most need help with? (Rank at least one item)", percentages represent the number of times an item was ranked either 1st, 2nd, 3rd, 4th or 5th.

Fisher's exact tests and Chi-square tests (Field, 2017) were undertaken to test for statistically significant relationships (i.e., $p < .05$) between i) recoded items and demographic variables (e.g., comparing response patterns between teachers and leaders) and ii) between pairs of recoded survey items (e.g., comparing response patterns between educators who do/do not use research regularly). This analysis process was selected for ease of presentation for readers who are unfamiliar with complex statistical analyses.

Interviews with Australian educators

Following Survey 1, follow-up interviews were conducted with Australian educators to develop deeper insights into their views about using research well. This research phase focused on i) educators' understandings of what makes for appropriate research, ii) the situations where they use research and why, iii) their perspectives about what quality use 'looks like' in a school setting and iv) their experiences of the barriers and enablers to research use in schools. Ethics approval was granted from both the Monash University Human Research Ethics Committee and relevant education departments and governing jurisdictions prior to undertaking interviews. The following sections outline the interview sample, interview style and conduct, as well as the analysis of the interviews and qualitative survey data.

Sample

Following their completion of Survey 1, educators from Q Project partner schools were emailed with an invitation to participate in a 45-minute follow-up interview. The invitations contained an outline of the aims of the interview, example questions, an explanatory statement about how the interviews would be conducted and analysed (i.e., interviews would be audio-recorded and transcribed, data would be de-identified for reporting, etc.) and a link to book an interview time. Consent was implied if an educator booked an interview and this was double-checked at the beginning of the interview prior to beginning the recording. From the 125 invitations sent, 29 educators from 27 schools volunteered to participate in an interview, with educators from the same school completing the interview together (see Table 9.4).

Table 9.4 Details about Q Project interviewees

	Interviewees	
	n	%[a]
Total interviewees	29	
State		
New South Wales	5	17
Victoria	13	45
Queensland	9	31
South Australia	2	7
Role		
Teacher	2	7
Middle leader	7	24
Senior leader	20	69
Experience[b]		
0 to <5 years	1	3
5 to <10 years	2	7
10 to <15 years	2	7
15+ years	23	79
Qualification level[b]		
Undergraduate	12	41
Non-research postgraduate	11	38
Research-based postgraduate	5	17

Note: [a] Percentages may not add to 100 due to rounding. [b] One participant did not provide their years of experience or qualification level.

Interview conduct

The interviews were semi-structured in nature, with a focus on open-ended questioning and follow-up of educators' responses (Bryman, 2016). Q Project team members, in collaboration with BehaviourWorks Australia (BWA), designed a general interview schedule containing broad, open-ended questions and prompts that encouraged educators to reflect on their perspectives of using research in school-based examples (for the interview protocol, see Rickinson et al., 2023). For example, common interview questions included, "What do you understand 'research evidence' to be?", "Can you describe for me the types of situations where you use research evidence?" and "On a scale of 1–10, with 10 being high, how well is research evidence being used in your school?". The interviews were conducted online by BWA and Q Project team members (either individually or in pairs) from August to November 2020. Each interview was audio-recorded and transcribed in full, with transcriptions reviewed by the relevant interviewer(s) for comprehension.

Qualitative analysis

The qualitative data from the interviews and the open-response survey questions were analysed thematically to reflexively generate themes, defined as patterns of shared meaning across a dataset that are generated by researchers' interpretative efforts (Braun & Clarke, 2006, 2019). Three authors engaged in multiple readings of the survey and interview data, making notes of initial ideas and discussing patterns that they noticed. During these discussions, it became clear that we were identifying common patterns informed by our own understanding of the research use literature, and in particular the QURE Framework. From this, we made the pragmatic decision to generate an initial codebook that would enable multiple authors to collaboratively code the data across the interviews and surveys (Braun et al., 2019). More specifically, this allowed us to code deductively to components of the QURE Framework (e.g., leadership, skillsets, etc.), while also inductively generating analytic codes and themes (Braun & Clarke, 2019). This codebook was not used to 'fix' the coding process (Braun et al., 2019). Rather, as we moved recursively through the stages of thematic analysis, the codebook developed and changed. For this reason, despite using a codebook as a practical tool, within the three broad 'schools' of thematic analysis, we situated our philosophical approach more closely with reflexive thematic analysis compared with coding reliability approaches (Braun et al., 2019).

The qualitative data from the open-response survey questions were analysed first. Following the initial discussions to develop the guiding codebook, one researcher coded the data using NVivo (Version 12) software. During this coding phase, the broader research team met and re-immersed themselves in the data and developing codebook, aiming to clarify interpretations and develop more nuanced and detailed readings of the data (Braun & Clarke, 2019). The research team then considered how the codes could be sorted into potential themes, with the primary researcher going back and re-coding the data based on these discussions. Following several iterations of this process, the final codebook consisted of overarching domain codes (e.g., deductive QURE components), sub-domain codes (e.g., QURE components as enablers or barriers), descriptive themes (e.g., inductive coding from analytic codes) and bottom-level analytic codes (for the final codebook, see Rickinson et al., 2023).

A second researcher reviewed the analysis to ensure that they agreed on the structure of the domain codes and themes and that these were relevant to both the individual codes and across the dataset (Braun & Clarke, 2006). For example, in the sub-domain code of "Skillsets as an enabler of using research well", we generated the theme of "Using research skills to access, appraise and implement research". This included analytic codes such as "Understanding the research and use", which included this illustrative survey response: "Understand the research, consider possible applications of the research, apply it or draw on it purposefully". It was not uncommon for responses to be connected with more than one code. For example, the same survey response was also coded to the analytic code of "Considered approaches to using research" which formed the theme of "Thoughtfulness as a way of working with research", which was included within the sub-domain code of "Thoughtful engagement as an enabler of using research well".

A similar process was then conducted for coding the interview data, where the research team immersed themselves in the interview dataset and used the initial codebook as a tool for collaborative analysis (Braun & Clarke, 2019). The primary difference in the process was that two researchers primarily undertook the coding and re-coding of data. These two researchers worked closely during the coding phases, regularly discussing what they were noticing and the inductive codes that they were generating, before discussing and refining their work with the broader research team. Following the recursive phases of coding, re-coding and theme generation, the two primary researchers reviewed the structure of the sub-domain codes and themes to ensure that they were relevant to the individual codes and dataset and then shared this with the wider team (for the final codebook, see Rickinson et al., 2023). As another illustration of this process, the response, "It starts with the executive or [...] instructional leaders demonstrating lessons for them, showing them what it would look like in the classroom, and then supporting along the way and slowly taking away support", was coded as "Role modelling research use behaviours" which was included in the theme of "Leaders facilitating understanding" within the sub-domain code of "Leadership as an enabler of using research well". Additionally, this same interview response was also coded as "Actively working together to generate buy-in/momentum" within the broader theme of "Quality research use as a collective practice" under the sub-domain code of "Practices of quality research use".

Co-design of improvement interventions

Following the conceptual (systematic review and framework development) and empirical (surveys and interviews) data collection and analysis processes undertaken in the first two to three years of the Q Project, the focus then shifted to developing ways to support research use improvement in schools. In 2021, the Q Project and BehaviourWorks Australia hosted two series of co-design workshops with teachers, school leaders and other education system actors to develop improvement interventions. Co-design is an approach which involves participants exploring, developing and testing responses to shared challenges (Blomkamp, 2018). The co-design workshops were conducted online for around three hours and involved large and small group interactions, as well as pre- and post-workshop surveys. The first series of workshops focused on developing a research use professional learning programme, while the second series focused on identifying system-wide enablers to support research use in schools (see Cirkony et al., 2022).

Sample

Recruitment of co-design participants drew from Q Project partner schools, as well as system actors and advisors known to the project. The recruitment process involved completion of an expression of interest that gathered relevant information about potential participants to assist in the selection of diverse groups. Most participants included teachers and school leaders with a range of experience and from diverse settings (e.g., school types, locations, etc.). Other participants were from system-level organisations (e.g., professional learning administrators from state-based government education departments, professional learning providers, evidence providers, research brokers, etc.). In total, there were 49 participants from both schools ($n = 28$) and the education system ($n = 21$).

Co-design workshops

For each workshop, participants were provided with readings about the Q Project and educators' research use, to engage with prior to the workshop. Each workshop was organised into three phases. During the 'Digest' phase, participants discussed the readings in small groups, then shared their ideas with the larger group. During the 'Direct' phase, facilitators led whole group discussions around the development focus areas (e.g., PL, accessing research, etc.). During the 'Design' phase, participants were provided with a series of prompts for each focus area and worked in small mixed groups to address these in Google Drive documents. Each workshop also included pre- and post-surveys with closed and open-ended questions regarding the workshop experience, enablers for research use, and priority learning outcomes for a potential professional learning programme.

Data collection and analysis

Whole group discussions were recorded with both video and audio, and the documents generated by participants in Google Drive were collected for analysis. The full data set comprised recordings of all whole group interactions, along with the Google Drive documents generated by each of the groups for each workshop. The recordings were transcribed and edited for analysis. Transcriptions and documents were analysed using the 'document analysis' method, combining content and thematic analysis to organise the data according to the prompts and identify the patterns across the documents (Bowen, 2009). Each summary document was then shared with all participants along with other education stakeholders for their feedback. Participants' open-text survey responses were also analysed thematically (Bowen, 2009).

Stakeholder consultation

Stakeholder consultation was an important feature of all the research processes undertaken within the Q Project. The design and conduct of the cross-sector systematic review and narrative synthesis, for example, was informed by advice and feedback from experts in systematic reviewing, information scientists and evidence use academics and practitioners from all four sectors. During the development of the framework, our evolving ideas about quality evidence use were shared with project partners and stakeholders via meetings, workshops and conferences. Other stakeholders (including researchers, policy makers, evidence brokers and educators) were invited to consider and provide feedback on successive versions of the framework.

For the empirical data collection, all of the surveys were piloted with several groups of educators to test and refine survey items and later versions were shared with researchers, policy makers and research brokers for feedback. Similarly, interview questions were checked and piloted with educators and other stakeholders. Furthermore, the co-design process brought together practitioners, policy makers, research brokers, researchers and other system actors to collaboratively identify ways to improve research use within and across schools and school systems.

References

Blomkamp, E. (2018). The promise of co-design for public policy. *Australian Journal of Public Administration, 77*(4), 729–743. 10.1111/1467-8500.12310

Bowen, G. A. (2009). Document analysis as a qualitative research method. *Qualitative Research Journal, 9*(2), 27–40. 10.3316/QRJ0902027

Braun, V., & Clarke, V. (2006). Using thematic analysis in psychology. *Qualitative Research in Psychology, 3*(2), 77–101. 10.1191/1478088706qp063oa

Braun, V., & Clarke, V. (2019). Reflecting on reflexive thematic analysis. *Qualitative Research in Sport, Exercise and Health, 11*(4), 589–597. 10.1080/2159676X.2019. 1628806

Braun, V., Clarke, V., Hayfield, N., & Terry, G. (2019). Thematic analysis. In P. Liamputtong (Ed.), *Handbook of research methods in health social sciences* (pp. 843–860). 10.1007/978-981-10-5251-4_103

Bryman, A. (2016). *Social research methods* (5th ed.). Oxford University Press.

Cirkony, C., Rickinson, M., Walsh, L., Gleeson, J., Salisbury, M., Cutler, B., & Boulet, M. (2022). *Improving quality use of research evidence in practice: Insights from cross-sector co-design.* Monash University. 10.26180/19380677.v3

Davies, H., Boaz, A., Nutley, S., & Fraser, A. (2019). Conclusions: Lessons from the past, prospects for the future. In A. Boaz, H. Davies, A. Fraser, & S. Nutley (Eds.), *What works now? Evidence-informed policy and practice revisited* (pp. 359–382). Policy Press.

Dixon-Woods, M., Agarwal, S., Jones, D., Young, B., & Sutton, A. (2005). Synthesising qualitative and quantitative evidence: A review of possible methods. *Journal of Health Services Research and Policy, 10*(1), 45–53. 10.1177/135581 960501000110

Field, A. (2017). *Discovering statistics using IBM SPSS statistics* (5th ed.). Sage Publications.

Gough, D., Oliver, S., & Thomas, J. (Eds.). (2017). *An introduction to systematic reviews* (2nd ed.). Sage Publications.

Greenhalgh, T., & Peacock, R. (2005). Effectiveness and efficiency of search methods in systematic reviews of complex evidence: Audit of primary sources. *BMJ, 331,* Article 1064. 10.1136/bmj.38636.593461.68

Nelson, J., Mehta, P., Sharples, J., & Davey, C. (2017). *Measuring teachers' research engagement: Findings from a pilot study.* Education Endowment Foundation. https://educationendowmentfoundation.org.uk/public/files/Evaluation/Research_ Use/NFER_Research_Use_pilot_report_-_March_2017_for_publication.pdf

Penuel, W. R., Briggs, D. C., Davidson, K. L., Herlihy, C., Sherer, D., Hill, H. C., Farrell, C. C., & Allen, A-R. (2016). *Findings from a national survey of research use among school and district leaders.* National Center for Research in Policy and Practice. https://files.eric.ed.gov/fulltext/ED599966.pdf

Poet, H., Mehta, P., & Nelson, J. (2015). *Research use in schools: Survey, analysis and guidance for evaluators* [Unpublished report]. National Foundation for Educational Research.

Popay, P., Roberts, H., Sowden, A., Petticrew, M., Arai, L., Rodgers, M., & Britten, N. (2006). *Guidance on the conduct of narrative synthesis in systematic reviews.* Institute of Health Research. https://www.lancaster.ac.uk/media/lancaster-university/content-assets/documents/fhm/dhr/chir/NSsynthesisguidanceVersion1-April2006.pdf

Rickinson, M., Cirkony, C., Walsh, L., Gleeson, J., Salisbury, M., & Boaz, A. (2021). Insights from a cross-sector review on how to conceptualise the quality of use of research evidence. *Humanities and Social Sciences Communications, 8*, Article 141. 10.1057/s41599-021-00821-x

Rickinson, M., Sharples, J. & Lovell, O. (2020). Towards a better understanding of quality of evidence use. In S. Gorard (Ed.), *Getting evidence into education: Evaluating the routes to policy and practice* (pp. 218–133). Routledge.

Rickinson, M., Walsh, L., Gleeson, J., & Cutler, B. (2023). *The Q Project: Improving the use of research evidence in Australian schools*. Open Science Framework. 10.17605/OSF.IO/V27FX

Index

Page numbers in *italics* indicate figures; page numbers in **bold** indicate tables